Democracy beyond the State?

Governance in Europe
Gary Marks, Series Editor

Democracy beyond the State?

The European Dilemma and the Emerging Global Order

edited by
Michael Th. Greven
and
Louis W. Pauly

ROWMAN & LITTLEFIELD PUBLISHERS, INC.
Lanham • Boulder • New York • Oxford

ROWMAN & LITTLEFIELD PUBLISHERS, INC.

Published in the United States of America
by Rowman & Littlefield Publishers, Inc.
4720 Boston Way, Lanham, Maryland 20706
http://www.rowmanlittlefield.com

12 Hid's Copse Road
Cumnor Hill, Oxford OX2 9JJ, England

British Library Cataloging-in-Publication Data

Democracy beyond the state? : the European dilemma and the emerging global
order /
edited by Michael Th. Greven and Louis W. Pauly.
    p.   cm.—(Governance in Europe)
    Includes bibliographical references and index.
    ISBN 0-8476-9900-5 (alk. paper)—ISBN 0-8476-9901-3 (paper : alk. paper)
    1. Democracy—European Union countries.   I. Greven, Michael Th., 1947–
II. Pauly, Louis W.   III. Series.
JN40.D454   2000
321.8'094—dc21   99-057386

Printed in the United States of America

♾ ™ The paper used in this publication meets the minimum requirements of
American National Standard for Information Sciences—Permanence of Paper for
Printed Library Materials, ANSI Z39.48-1992.

Contents

Acknowledgments

This book grew out of a conversation in the autumn of 1997 between two colleagues at the Centre for International Studies of the University of Toronto. Those colleagues became friends, and then the book's editors.

In the spring of 1998, the contributors to the book came to Toronto and joined the conversation. Spurred by their common interest in contemporary challenges to democratic governance, they brought with them original papers on the subject. Assisting significantly in shaping the terms of the debate that ensued in Toronto were papers on related themes by Wilfried von Bredow (Philipps-Universität, Marburg), Benjamin J. Cohen (University of California, Santa Barbara), and Eric Helleiner (Trent University). Valuable commentary came from Ronnie Beiner, Joseph Carens, Liesbet Hooghe, Larry Leduc, and Melissa Williams, all of the University of Toronto, and from Gary Marks of the University of North Carolina (Chapel Hill). Following the Toronto meeting, the authors redrafted their papers. The final version of Offe's paper was expertly translated by Claude Desmarais. Gillian Manning then copyedited all of the second drafts. Three anonymous referees provided detailed and extremely constructive criticism of those drafts.

Louis Pauly led the process of turning revised chapters into a book. Mary Lynne Bratti and Tina Lagopoulos helped us organize the project from beginning to end. Tina and Joanne Kearney typed the manuscript. Virgil Duff, Siobhan McMenemy, Danielle Goldfarb, Susan McEachern, Karen Johnson, Peter Russell, and Gary Marx played crucial roles in the final production.

We are very grateful for financial assistance from the German Academic Exchange Service/Deutscher Akademischer Austausch Dienst (DAAD), from the Joint Initiative on German and European Studies of the University of Toronto (originally led by Larry Leduc and later by Scott Eddie), from the Social Sciences and Humanities Research Council of Canada, and from the supporters of the Centre for International Studies. The book is dedicated to our students, who will meet the challenges we identify.

1

Introduction
Democracy and Globalization in Theory and Practice

Louis W. Pauly

Oxymorons abound in the discourse of political economy. Chinese leaders currently characterize their system as a "socialist market economy." Without irony, their counterparts in the United States commonly refer to their own form of "democratic capitalism." In contemporary Europe, the combination of terms such as "social democracy" and "liberal market economy" disturbs few outside the rarefied milieu of the academy. In truth, democracy and capitalism have always been in tension, and the social solidarity required to prevent that tension from reaching the breaking point has always had to be created, nurtured, and re-created on the ground, in the rough and tumble of politics. Contradiction, compromise, and often inconclusive contests over the ultimate prize of unquestioned political authority define the terrain.

This book explores that terrain. Its authors are scholars steeped in the history of actual democracies, in the theory behind them, and in the study of modern economies. Think of them as scouts, whose role it is to map the ground before us, to assess movements in its contours, to explore fault lines, and to bring a critical understanding to bear on an important journey.

At the heart of the book lies a deepening dilemma for the citizens of advanced industrial democracies and for their leaders. The sense of legitimacy that underpins their political systems, and that undergirds both the actual exercise of political authority and the willing deference of those subject to it, rests on the common belief that government is responsible to a given people, accountable to that people, and obliged to serve the best interests of that people. The actual form of government in place across

1

most of the developed world goes by the name of representative democracy, wherein the people rule themselves by delegating authority to their
leaders and then by holding those leaders accountable through periodic
elections characterized by universal suffrage. In principle, such a system
ultimately depends on being able to define "the people" comprising a
given society (*demos*) and on treating each individual capable of self-
governance as the legal and political equal of all others in that society.

Since the dawn of the industrial age, however, democratic governments
have presided over economic systems that function on the basis of an unequal distribution of resources and claims on future resources. To a certain degree, the success of market economies in generating prosperity has
fruitfully reinforced the development of representative democracy. But as
modern capitalism has deepened, as corporate and financial power has
become more salient, as regulation has become more technical, and as
economic rewards have become more tightly correlated with specialized
skills, even political equality has become more and more unatttainable.
The "dean" of contemporary studies of democracy, Robert Dahl, puts the
core of the issue succinctly:

> When authoritarian governments in less modernized countries undertake to
> develop a dynamic market economy, they are likely to sow the seeds of their
> own ultimate destruction. But once society and politics are transformed by
> market-capitalism and democratic institutions are in place, the outlook
> fundamentally changes. Now the inequalities in resources that market-
> capitalism churns out produce serious political inequalities among citizens.[1]

Further complicating the problem is the fact that this economic system
in its latest phase seems necessarily to erode the political boundaries sep-
arating the citizens of different democratic states. In now-common parlance, the borders around the nation, defining a discrete set of citizens
who happen also to be the dominant consumers and producers in a discrete economy, begin to blur. As this happens, the democratic roots moor-
ing a discrete state in that nation begin to come loose. In extremis, rule of,
by, and for the people becomes a sham, and a legitimation crisis threatens. The effort of actual governments to continue governing opens up
"democratic deficits," which may be masked for a time by economic prosperity. In less forgiving times, however, citizens seek those responsible
for their problems, and find no one accountable to them and no one obligated to serve them. They have, in practice, become subjects in an undem-
ocratic political order.

The authors of this book are motivated by the desire to understand the
nature of this possibility in the contemporary history of democratic systems of governance. Their collective hope is that understanding can help

mitigate it. They are led, therefore, to look most closely at the empirical case where the dilemma is now most obvious and where its threat is most widely perceived: the case of the European Union (EU). States and citizens within the Union are now far along in a vast experiment involving an attempt to use the dynamism of market-capitalism to secure fundamental social and political objectives. Those states began that experiment as democracies, but a key question for the imminent future is whether their citizens will find themselves still in democratic systems if the experiment leads to the undisputed creation of a regional transnational polity.

A similar question faces the citizens of democratic states outside Europe as they make analogous attempts to reap the economic gains promised by the worldwide spread of a decentralized form of capitalism, a form now conventionally evinced by the word "globalization." The authors of this book therefore set out consciously to place the European case into a broader theoretical and empirical context. In particular, they have compared the contemporary European dilemma with an incipient democratic dilemma in North America.

RESURGENT ECONOMIC LIBERALISM AND ITS POLITICAL IMPLICATIONS

The global trajectory of capitalism is not really new. The last time the world experienced rapidly accelerating economic integration, however, there existed few states that were self-consciously organized around democratic principles. In not one of those states, moreover, were formal decision-making norms tied firmly to principles of solidarity, equity, fairness, and social justice—principles that would later come to be associated with the modern democratic welfare state.

As discussed more fully in the chapters that follow, most democratic states surviving into the modern era did not come by their particular systems of collective decision making easily. Democracy usually had to be fought for, and it had to win out over competing systems for organizing political authority. Most democracies were grounded in a sense of nation, what Anderson famously termed an "imagined community."[2] And most nations had to be forged—by states themselves—in cauldrons of social conflict. The growth and development of industrial capitalism occurred simultaneously and simultaneously began to reshape the state at its very core.

In the years before World War I, trade flows, capital flows, information flows, and human migration across national borders grew by leaps and bounds. "Globalization," as the phenomenon is commonly now called, was a clear trend—in economics, in communications, in travel, and in culture. Alas, this liberal moment ended during the turbulent early decades of the twentieth century. World War I, the Great Depression of the 1930s, and World War II were hardly unrelated events. Out of the ashes of the political structures associated with those events arose the national welfare states of the post–World War II period. Also coming out of the war years was a renewed commitment to recovering the prosperity promised by the earlier experiment with economic globalization.

The relationship between these two partly contradictory and partly complementary trends has been much studied in recent decades. From Polanyi to Ruggie, Dahl to Sandel, Habermas to Held, many scholars have assessed the tenuous equilibrium in the modern era between the forces of international economic liberalism and the endurance of nationally distinctive structures of governance.[3] They have also highlighted the delicate connection between the legitimacy of structures meaningfully described as representative democracies and the policies emanating from them to regulate markets, to temper concentrations of private power, to finance social safety nets, and to protect the natural environment.

From the 1950s to the 1970s, a relatively stable equilibrium emerged between formally democratic polities and a renewed international economy. It rested on five pillars: responsible national governments, viable national policies providing citizens with varying degrees of insurance against economic catastrophe, increasingly open markets, a modicum of systemic leadership provided by one state or by a small group of leading states, and international and regional institutions helping to manage the collective-action problems posed by deepening economic interdependence.

Since the mid-1970s, however, it has appeared to many observers that those pillars have been breaking down. Ever more open and competitive markets—for goods and services, for financial capital, for long-term investment, and for skilled people—have put new pressure on national welfare states and drawn attention to the weaknesses of the transnational governing institutions thus far established. Indeed, as national governments arguably become inefficient regulators of markets that cross their borders, questions regarding the requirements of social welfare and social justice are increasingly being addressed not only to national governments claiming a lack of tools to deal with them, but also ever more frequently to international institutions lacking any clear mandate to build new tools.

While the vast majority of the world struggles to catch up, leading countries are now engaged in the restructuring of their social welfare programs and in the search for global governing mechanisms capable of re-stabilizing capitalism without compromising its ability to deliver prosperity. As happened earlier in the twentieth century, such an impetus meets resistance from the principal beneficiaries of global capitalism, who claim faith in the idea of self-regulating markets. This ideology of universal economic liberalism and the associated political impetus toward stability and efficient management on a global scale together fundamentally challenge the democratic norms and practices through which the power actually to govern has been legitimated in those same leading countries throughout the past century. The chapters below focus directly on that challenge.

OVERVIEW

At the dawn of the twenty-first century, when brutal civil wars, environmental disasters, and wrenching social change continued to afflict many developing countries, advanced industrial societies were prosperous and at peace with one another. In one guise or another, much of the substance of their internal politics dealt with the exigencies and implications of their relative economic success during the last decades of the twentieth century. To varying degrees, that success entailed integrating their domestic economies with one another. The managed economic interdependence of the post–World War II period wove a web of economic, social, and cultural interrelationships that by the end of the century seemed to signify the inception of a truly global economic system. Even if that global destiny remained hypothetical, it was certainly clear that regional or continental economic systems—all of quite different character—had begun to supplement and even to supplant the local and national systems of the past.[4]

What does the resurgence of global capitalism mean for local political structures, especially the structures of formal democracy? Does responsible government have a future? If it is true that democratic practice at the national level is becoming dysfunctional, can it be reinvigorated at a transnational level? Beyond further stimulating economic liberalism—ever freer markets and attendant social choices emphasizing efficiency over distributive justice—could the heritage of past economic policy choices still be meaningfully understood, debated, and reconciled by individual citizens and their elected representatives? To whom do those citizens now owe their most fundamental loyalties? To the extent that actual democratic norms and practices have varied along national and regional lines, is it possible to envisage deep political convergence as economic and cultural integration continues apace?

Nowhere were such questions being more directly addressed at the opening of a new century than in Europe, where several generations of leaders in advanced democratic systems had deliberately exploited the tools of economic liberalization for political and social ends. As their economies approached the long-standing objective of a seamless market from the Baltic to the Mediterranean and the Atlantic to the still-unclear borders of Mitteleuropa, their governing systems began to confront severe stresses. Indeed, insofar as those systems had combined both formal democratic decision-making practices with redistributive policies, economic logic and political reality seemed to many observers to embody a deep contradiction. In North America, similar tensions were coming into clearer view in the wake of negotiated arrangements to advance the cause of more open markets for trade and investment—first between Canada and the United States, and then among Canada, the United States, and Mexico. The European case lies at the center of this book, and the North American case is briefly compared to it.

The book brings together a distinguished group of political theorists and empirically minded comparativists. Some of the following chapters focus directly on problems of democratic theory, whereas others bring theory and practice together as they explore the implications of globalizing capitalism. As the extensive bibliography attests, much good research on the central empirical cases is now coming out of the United States. Since other and generally less centralized federal systems have long had to deal with tensions similar to the one emphasized in this book, our view was that an international contribution to the debate on globalization and democracy could be made by bringing together scholars based in Canada and Germany. In both countries, students of democratic politics are immersed in political environments where the historic task of internal political integration has long been complicated by the pressures of regional economic integration. They have a common experience to share with one another and with a wider world now beginning to grapple with analogous problems.

Stephen Newman opens our conversation with a wide-ranging thematic introduction. He points out that globalizing capitalism is neither new nor simply an economic phenomenon. Indeed, its cultural impact and its ideological core are what most clearly confront democratic systems of government in the contemporary period. Cautioning against the tendency to romanticize democracy, he introduces the issue treated extensively later in the book; of the necessity of redefining a *demos*, a people-in-community capable of self-governance in principle. Without such a redefinition, the extension of democratic political systems beyond the nation-state would seem impossible.

Following a review of the characteristic form of democracy practiced in the United States, Newman initiates a dialogue with pioneers of the concept of "global democracy"—the ideas of one of the most recent and articulate, David Held, are much discussed later in the volume. At base, however, theorists like Held hold out the hope that some semblance of today's far-from-ideal liberal democratic systems of government could one day begin to approach a cosmopolitan scale if the central values—expressed in terms of rights and obligations—could be vested in a corpus of transnational public law. Public law in actual democracies has heretofore been grounded in some notion of a bounded political community. Newman perceives, however, not even a nascent transnational sense of *demos* beyond what might be just emerging on a regional basis in Europe. Newman's own commentary on decision making in capitalist structures, moreover, suggests deepening habits of thought working at cross-purposes to the construction of a truly global political community. As both liberal and radical commentators have argued for some time, the premium now assigned to a self-interested decisional calculus and an efficiency-maximizing organizational culture is hardly conducive to the improvement of either representative or participatory forms of democracy.

Newman nevertheless creates the space for a more optimistic consideration of practicable adaptations in actual democratic structures of governance. Such adaptations are made necessary by the still-apparent unwillingness of citizens-as-consumers to pay the price of reversing the developmental trajectory of global capitalism. They also flow from an underlying sense articulated by some writers that, for all its dangers and difficulties, the combination of democracy and capitalism has, perhaps ironically, softened antagonisms that have threatened both in the not-too-distant past.

Michael Th. Greven brings just such themes into focus with an inquiry into the democratic possibilities of the European Union. In doing so, he initiates a controversy picked up by Offe, Zürn, and Grande in the following three chapters. Greven sees in Europe an emerging system of regional government-in-practice. The process by which this evolution has occurred, however, he finds extremely troubling from the vantage point of democratic theory. The actual practice of problem solving within the European Union erodes the standard of democracy achieved within its member-states over many centuries and with much pain. That standard is defined by a normative body of rights that, according to Greven, ought not to be abandoned unthinkingly as the logic of economic integration spills over from one area of life to another.

Going back to the key issue raised by Newman, Greven contends quite forcefully that there has never existed a European "people." In no sense has there even been in theory a political community capable of claiming the right to constitute political power at the European level or of having that right claimed in its name. Adopting a strict contractarian approach to democracy, he sees right up until the present day no collectivity able to vest sovereign authority beyond the nation. He is, of course, fully aware of the momentous and usually bloody struggles that resulted in what

Bendix summarized as the historic transfer of such authority from "kings to people."[5] He also acknowledges that in the course of those struggles within Europe, the builders of states often also had to construct bounded and distinct nations capable of asserting their right to self-governance. Indeed, the establishment of the rule of law and the construction of national political communities were two sides of the same historical coin.[6]

Nevertheless, having completed that bidirectional process and created representative and social democracies, neither national political communities nor their states have, in Greven's view, even begun to craft a true European constitution. There simply exists no constituting power competent to do so. And without a constitution, there can be no accountable parliament, no effective constraint on executive power, and no definitively binding judicial power. According to Greven, this central constructional defect in the mainly intergovernmental project of the European Union expresses itself today in the absence of pan-European political parties, in the highly limited and idiosyncratic nature of elections for the European Parliament, and in the operations of EU institutions of governance that are ultimately responsible to no one. As a result, the effective priority is increasingly being given by default to the liberties of the Common Market over the potentially countervailing rights of citizens to more than just economic opportunity.

Greven depicts postwar European democracies as extending rights not just to participate in politics but also to basic social benefits, including the right to a decent standard of living. The extension of full citizenship conceived in this manner, then, becomes a vehicle for effectively empowering individuals or groups in a given society who were disadvantaged in the past—including, most prominently, women and immigrants. Citizenship so defined, however, depends fundamentally upon a willingness to share real resources, in effect to engage in redistributive politics. That willingness, in turn, depends upon a sense of togetherness, a "we-feeling." In the EU today, argues Greven, such a sense is altogether lacking.

Finally, Greven expresses the opinion that modern democracy ultimately rests on the ability to communicate. Without a common language of politics, he believes, the EU will have enormous difficulty in developing into a democracy in its own right. As a functioning polity, its legitimacy therefore must necessarily remain derivative of the legitimacy of its constituent nation-states. However, the more significant that polity becomes—the more effective power it actually comes to exert over the lives of Europeans—the more pronounced does its "democratic deficit" become. Extending that logic beyond Europe, Greven, like Newman, asks what the term "global democracy," even in principle, could possibly mean.

Claus Offe picks up the thread at this point in a penetrating comparison of the internal policy-making processes of the contemporary EU, with their analogs in nation-states self-consciously organized as republican democracies. He explores the efficiency of EU governance and probes the possibilities for shifting its underlying rationale to encompass broader social, cultural, and moral concerns. This exploration leads him to a troubling conclusion about the innately oppositional tendencies inherent in any process that seeks to combine the functional logic of economic integration with a particularistic logic of moral and social obligation. In the end, he fears that promoting the former while paying only lip-service to the necessity of a broadly based form of political legitimation promises not to overcome ancient fissiparous tendencies in Europe but rather to exacerbate them.

According to Offe, the duties of citizens in a democracy necessarily imply the abridgement of narrowly defined individual freedoms. The possibility of that abridgement depends upon two basic and mutual beliefs on the part of citizens: Each believes in the integrity of the other, and each believes that compliance is important even if it brings no immediate personal benefit. Like Greven, Offe emphasizes the sense of trust, or solidarity, at the root of functioning democracies, and most especially at the root of democracies that have evolved from a liberal phase, keyed on formal procedures of self-government, to a social phase. The very idea of a collectivity of persons capable of performing the duties that attend to the rights of citizenship in a social democracy seems necessarily to depend upon a sense of boundedness. Without boundaries around a political community, the rights and obligations of citizens become abstract and, in practice, unenforceable.

In this light, Offe sees the project of economic integration among the states of the EU as mainly contractual and limited. He considers alternative visions for Europe, and concludes that the currently operative and only feasible one is guided almost exclusively by the negative dynamic of breaking down barriers. A positive dynamic aimed at creating a community is missing. As a result, every solution to a specific problem of collective action across the member-states of the EU inevitably violates one or both of the key reference values in a social democracy: the protection of welfare systems and the securing of democratic legitimation. In short, the historical bearers of democratic legitimacy cannot transfer it to another level of governance, even as every move toward pan-European economic integration constrains their effective governing power. The consequence of this fundamental dilemma is not simply a democratic deficit in Europe but also a mounting social welfare deficit at the national level.

Acknowledging the profound challenges diagnosed by Greven and Offe, Michael Zürn attempts to reframe the central issue. He sees the de-nationalization of European societies in the modern era as the underlying

contemporary condition, a condition shared with all other advanced industrial societies. He takes seriously the cultural and social break noted
by Newman that is associated with the evolution of the global economy.
For Zürn, however, consequent institution building inside Europe is a secondary phenomenon. The inexorable development of transnational social
space dominates. In such a context, the fundamental challenge for democratic theory and practice is to reconsider and redesign decisional mechanisms that can combine majoritarian procedures with well-adapted structures for continuous negotiation among citizens and interest groups.
European democracy may be in a muddle, but it could do worse than to
adopt a pragmatic approach to muddling through the complex problems
attending the emergence of a truly transnational society.

Although Zürn pins much of his hope for the future—both within Europe and in general—on the idea of mixed constitutions, he presents a
typology that suggests significant room for local variation in feasible
structures of interest aggregation and policy deliberation, the two basic
components in any system of continuous political negotiation and compromise. With Ulrich Beck, he concludes that the notion of democratic
deficits is easy to overstate. On the ground in the real world of contemporary democracies, he argues, considerable resources remain for the preservation and renovation of core democratic values. We may be in the early
stages of the emergence of a truly global *demos*, one that could provide
solid footing for global democracy. In the meantime, pragmatic adjust-
ments in the forms of territorial representation, the promotion of carefully
considered referenda, and the enhancement of the representative nature
of policy networks ("associative democracy," as Zürn calls it) could ame-
liorate the mounting legitimacy crisis diagnosed by Greven and Offe.

Edgar Grande picks up the same argument. He makes an optimistic
case for the extension of democracy into the new world of heightening
economic and social integration. He does so by presenting a model of
what he calls "post-national democracy" against the backdrop of the
emergence of legitimation problems in an expanding and deepening European Union. He conceives the model to be much less demanding than
Held's cosmopolitan democratic system but more complex than either direct or representative forms of democracy.

Convinced that a key part of the problem of conceiving solutions for
Europe is the idealization of majoritarian models of decision making,
Grande reviews nonmajoritarian and nonparliamentary alternatives. This
leads to the recovery of insights from earlier research on consociational
and corporatist decision-making processes, both of which give pride of
place to consensual techniques in profoundly divided societies. In this
way, he seeks to address the flaws in the contemporary political architec-

ture of Europe: the transfer of decision-making competency to the supra-national level and the retention of ultimate authority at the national.

Grande sees the net result of these flaws as transferring real political power within the Union to the executive branches of member-states and to their delegates in Brussels. Here is the concrete challenge facing the proponents of a constitution capable of grounding a multilevel polity. Here is the clear and pressing reason for adapting the mores of consociational systems. And here, finally, is the rationale for building a set of institutional checks and balances akin to those at the heart of the American constitution.

Stephen Clarkson brings the active search for workable democratic forms of governance back from Europe to North America. His focus is not simply on the United States, for he specifically considers the quality of democratic governance both inside each of Canada, the United States, and Mexico, as well as across them in the new world promised by the North American Free Trade Agreement (NAFTA). In contrast to the European case, Clarkson sees underlying legitimation problems just beginning to be recognized in North America's three democracies. Two of those democracies are "advanced," and one is now moving from an authoritarian phase to a phase in which political power is truly contested.

Taking the negotiation and implementation of NAFTA as his starting point, Clarkson depicts the gradual emergence in practical terms of a continental governing arrangement. Effectively if implicitly constitutionalizing a new political order, it is an arrangement that increasingly delivers "decisions" unfiltered by adequate or broadly accountable institutions. In a suggestive attempt to assess such deficiencies only now beginning to manifest themselves, he compares and contrasts national and regional decision-making practices in an integrating North America with those of the European Union. Against this backdrop, he compares the relative quality of democratic forms of decision making actually in place within the United States, Canada, and Mexico.

Clarkson's audit of democratic deficits and surpluses in North America suggests that continental economic integration entails a diversity of effects. No unilinear causal chain is evident. Europe's democratic deficit, according to Clarkson, appears not necessarily to be a harbinger of the future for all democratic systems of government. Conversely, its own true dimensions may themselves be overstated, as aggregate consequences mask diverse local effects.

Clarkson concludes, for example, that a regional economic process that may arguably be improving the quality of Mexico's democracy may have the opposite effect in Canada; this recalls the point made by Dahl cited earlier. In parallel with EU structures that help smaller members offset the dominance of larger ones, the formal political institutionalization of an emergent continental system could assist both Mexico and Canada as they struggle to preserve whatever claims they might respectively now retain to the right of self-government. In a region that now seems most heavily influenced by the power of corporations—corporations over-whelmingly based in the United States and conforming to American laws and policies—fairly structured continental institutions could serve as a counterweight. The question of how the United States could be per-suaded to agree to such a formal restructuring remains an increasingly important one. By raising the related question of what corporate power actually now portends for the quality of democracy in the United States itself, Clarkson brings the book full circle to the systemic political chal-lenge of global capitalism introduced by Newman. I return to that chal-lenge in the concluding chapter of the book.

NOTES

1. Robert Dahl, *On Democracy* (New Haven: Yale University Press, 1998), 178.

2. Benedict Anderson, *Imagined Communities: Reflections on the Origin and Spread of Nationalism*, 2d ed. (London: Verso, 1991).

3. Karl Polanyi, *The Great Transformation* (New York: Farrar and Rinehart, 1944); Jürgen Habermas, *Legitimationsprobleme im Spätkapitalismus* (Frankfurt: Suhrkamp Verlag, 1973), published in English as *Legitimation Crisis* (London: Heinemann, 1976); Robert Dahl, *Democracy and Its Critics* (New Haven: Yale University Press, 1989); John Gerard Ruggie, *Constructing the World Polity* (London: Routledge, 1998); Michael Sandel, *Democracy's Discontents* (Cambridge: Harvard University Press, 1996); and David Held, *Democracy and the Global Order* (Stanford: Stanford University Press, 1995).

4. Comparative research on this theme is currently expanding at a rapid pace. Accessible recent overviews may be found in Peter Katzenstein and Takashi Shi-raishi, eds., *Network Power* (Ithaca, N.Y.: Cornell University Press, 1997); Edward Mansfield and Helen Milner, eds., *The Political Economy of Regionalism* (New York: Columbia University Press, 1997); Etel Solingen, *Regional Orders at Century's Dawn* (Princeton: Princeton University Press, 1998); and Walter Mattli, *The Logic of Re-gional Integration* (Cambridge: Cambridge University Press, 1999).

5. Reinhard Bendix, *Kings or People* (Berkeley: University of California Press, 1978).

6. One of our anonymous reviewers helpfully drew this complex relationship out in the following terms:

Historically in European polities the relationship between the "people" and the rule of law was complex and bidirectional. That is to say, the existence of the "people" was both an outcome and a condition of the rule of law exer-cised in a given territory. As late as 1870, most of the "French" who fought at Sedan could not readily understand each other. Their conception of being French was mediated by their common citizenship. Being "British" was as much an outcome of common citizenship and membership of the British polity as it was a prior requisite for the development of that polity. That is why being "British" is so deeply threatened by devolution. Suddenly, people raise the (old) possibility of an English identity! But there is the problem that there is, as yet, no "English" state.

I return to this theme in the concluding chapter.

2

Globalization and Democracy

Stephen Newman

"Globalization," as Susan Strange noted in one of her last books, is one of those "vague and woolly words, freely bandied about in the literature, but whose precise meaning is seldom if ever clearly defined."[1] No doubt the ambiguity of the term reflects the complexity of the phenomenon. Globalization has been invoked to describe trends toward cultural convergence as well as the internationalization of production and the integration of world markets for goods, services, finance, and credit. In reality, these several trends are simply different facets of the same process. The logic of modern capitalism entails the creation of a global marketplace subsuming the national and regional economies of previous eras.[2]

But this process should not be understood in narrowly economic terms. Globalizing capitalism is a *cultural* as well as an *economic* phenomenon that attempts to reshape world culture and world economy. Wherever one goes in the global marketplace, one is surrounded by familiar brand names. We are entering the age of the universal consumer in which everyone covets the same designer clothes, eats the same fast food, drinks the same soft drinks, listens to the same music, watches the same videos, and goes to the same movies. The trend is often identified with the United States and its dominant culture. If globalization is "a polite euphemism for the continuing Americanization of consumer tastes and cultural practices," it is only because the United States is the capitalist nation par excellence.[3] A long-term reconstruction of American culture is now being played out on a global scale.[4] We are witnessing not so much American cultural imperialism as the cultural logic of capitalist expansion.

Globalizing capitalism is also a *political* phenomenon with its own ideology. The triumph of free markets implies the eclipse of interventionist state strategies worldwide. On this score, the assault on Big Government launched by Ronald Reagan in the United States and Margaret Thatcher

15

in Britain in the 1980s merely served as a sign of the times. Globalization may in fact hasten the permanent retreat of the state and the emergence of a complex, interdependent world economy beyond the effective jurisdiction of any single nation. It's one thing if a government chooses not to intervene in the national economy as a matter of public policy; it's another thing altogether when a government is no longer able to exercise control over the economy. At that point, the ability of the state to secure the public good is severely compromised. Whether we are now reaching that point is a question underlying all of the chapters in this book. The authors' primary target, however, is the implication of broadening economic and social transformation for the principal form of contemporary politics within the leading states of Europe and North America. At the core of their diverse viewpoints on the possibilities and prospects for the emergence of new political identities is the fundamental tension between globalization and democracy.

All successful modern democracies have had market-capitalist economies, and in the aftermath of the Cold War there are those who argue that the global triumph of capitalism can only promote the cause of democracy around the world.[5] In this view, free markets are a prelude to free elections. But this happy optimism, favored by American presidents and conservative pundits, is unfounded. It errs by equating economic liberalization with political liberalization, as though the freedom to buy and sell were identical with freedom from arbitrary arrest or the right to political representation. Although capitalism and democracy have followed the same historical trajectory in the West, there is no logically necessary relationship between them. The compatibility of economic freedom and political unfreedom received implicit recognition from the seventeenth-century English political philosopher Thomas Hobbes, who advised the nascent bourgeoisie of his time to accept an absolute sovereign as the guarantor of private contracts. While there are few absolute sovereigns in the modern world, there is no shortage of quasi-Leviathans superintending market economies in Asia and Latin America, and little reason to believe that these countries must inevitably move toward political democracy.[6] To the contrary, insofar as there exists a cosy relationship between the political and economic elites in these societies, it would appear that no one in a position of power has any strong incentive to press for democratization. Some western observers have even suggested that authoritarian capitalism is the most effective path to prosperity for developing countries with no prior experience of either democracy or free markets.[7]

It would be easier to believe that globalization will foster democracy if globalizing capitalism were itself inherently democratic. If that were true, we could take for granted the creation of a genuinely participatory public culture wherever the capitalist firm put down roots. Alas, it is simply not the case.[8] For one thing, the internal organization of business firms is rarely if ever democratic. Typically, employees are not "equal citizens" but members of a hierarchy.[9] And while the modern corporation is certainly a collective undertaking, it cannot be said to embody a common project. In whatever form it takes, the capitalist enterprise is private property; thus, in contrast with political democracy, it is not membership in the enterprise but ownership that is the source of control.[10] Capitalism is no more democratic in its external relations with consumers, despite often-repeated claims about "consumer sovereignty." In a free market, entrepreneurs will always strive to satisfy consumer preferences; thus, in some sense, consumers are said to exercise the ultimate control over what is produced.[11] Demand rules supply. But this logic ignores the role of advertising in creating demand. It also overlooks the inconvenient fact that no matter how often consumers vote with their pocketbooks, they remain outside the loop of capitalist decision making. Undoubtedly, capitalism is wonderfully efficient at satisfying (and stimulating) the wants of consumers, but it makes nonsense of the concept of sovereignty to describe consumers as truly sovereign over markets. Nor does sensitivity to consumer demand translate into democratic accountability. *Private enterprise does not exist to serve a public purpose.* As Adam Smith famously observed, the social utility of the market economy is an unintended consequence of the profit motive. The business of business, in short, is not democracy.[12]

The ideology of globalization, by conflating capitalism and democracy, tends to collapse the distinction between economics and politics. In itself, this bodes ill for democracy, because the economy and the state form separate "spheres" of social life.[13] Although they interact in ways crucial to society as a whole, they operate under different rules. Thus, as citizens of democratic states and participants in capitalist economies, we do not normally think it unjust that the highest bidder should gain control of a company, or that owners of firms should decide what those firms will produce. Albeit with a differing emphasis across European and North American states, our shared understanding is that ownership gives control and that private wealth is the legitimate arbiter of most economic transactions. But we are offended and consider it grossly unjust when an elected official accepts a bribe in exchange for political favors. Informing our sense of injustice is the normative belief that in a democratic politics, wealth ought not to confer advantage—one ought not to be able to buy law or public policy in the same way that one can buy a loaf of bread. What we want to hear from persons desirous of changing law or policy are good reasons that speak to the shared concerns of citizens at large. That we are frequently disappointed, that politicians do in fact take bribes, and that private wealth exercises an inordinate influence over political outcomes merely points out the importance of policing the borders between the spheres. If we fail in that task, political democracy will disappear. Insofar as capitalism promotes a view of society that begins and ends in the marketplace, it threatens to obscure the political sphere entirely. This is precisely the dilemma the states of the European Union face squarely today, as Offe and Greven emphasize in their chapters.

Indeed, for all the complaints one hears these days about the evils of state interference in free markets, one might conclude that capitalism has no real need of government of any sort.[14] Of course, nothing could be further from the truth. The ideology of globalization obscures but can never overcome the hard fact that modern capitalism, at a minimum, requires a supportive legal regime, so that property rights are protected and contracts enforced. But while capitalism has always needed the protection and encouragement of the state, it has had a markedly ambivalent relationship with democracy for the simple reason that the democratic state affords access to power to societal interests antagonistic to capital. While by no means hostile to market capitalism, the modern democratic state typically has legislated standards for health and safety in the workplace, consumer protection, environmental quality, employment equity, and other domains that limit the discretion of private entrepreneurs and impose additional costs on them. The democratic state has also strengthened the hand of labor by recognizing a right to collective bargaining. It was modern democracy, moreover, that gave birth to the redistributive welfare state of the post–World War II era, a state with somewhat more limited effect in the United States and Canada than in much of Western Europe.[15]

To invoke a familiar metaphor, the rough and tumble of democratic politics resembles a sporting contest. Unless the players are nearly equal in size and strength, the contest will not be fair. Capital has long enjoyed the competitive advantage that wealth bestows in a game where players can literally buy access to policymakers. In principle, globalization enhances the political advantages of capital by increasing its potential mobility; faced with high taxes, stringent workplace and environmental regulations, or high wage demands, transnational corporations can more readily move—or threaten to move—production to another country, where government and labor are more accommodating. As a result, labor standards may come under new pressure, and nations that attempt to maintain social and environmental standards may face a stiff economic penalty. With their economies held hostage by the imperatives of globalization, even the advanced industrial democracies may find themselves unable to prevent a socially disastrous "race to the bottom."[16] In Europe today, preventing just such an outcome provides a key incentive to push the cause of a political integration in lockstep with economic integration.

As Offe and Greven note, however, efficient regulation is not synonymous with democratic accountability.

Aside from the occasional flare-up of economic nationalism in political campaigns, there has been surprisingly little opposition to globalization in the advanced industrial democracies. This lack of opposition testifies perhaps to the entrenched structural power of business interests, but it also points to the inherent strength of capitalism as an ideology. Capitalism fosters a consumer culture that elevates the satisfaction of private wants above consideration of the public good or the performance of public duties. This saps a democratic political culture of its vitality. Simply put, possessive individualists make poor citizens. They lack what Michael Sandel refers to as the requisite "civic virtue," or public-spiritedness, that true democracy demands.[17] The eclipse of civic virtue, in turn, makes it easier for globalizing capitalism to usurp certain functions of the democratic state through privatization. Privatization erases the border between the public and private spheres. As Benjamin Barber writes:

> There is today a disastrous confusion between the moderate and mostly well-founded claim that flexibly regulated markets remain the most efficient instruments of economic productivity and wealth accumulation, and the zany, overblown claim that naked, wholly unregulated markets are the sole means by which we can produce and fairly distribute everything human beings care about, from durable goods to spiritual values, from capital investment to social justice, from profitability to sustainable environments, from private wealth to the essential commonweal.[18]

Perhaps, as some argue, democracy is a transitory historical phenomenon, one now coming to the end of its relatively brief run on the world's stage. From this rather gloomy perspective, democracy in the West appears anachronistic; a government of and by the people designed for a nation of small property holders is ill-equipped to deal with the power of multinational corporations and the border-defying forces of globalization. More and more, real power does indeed seem to reside with corporate managers not responsible to the public at large, and with faceless public technocrats only nominally responsible to the people's elected representatives and wholly unaccountable to the voters themselves. In fact, if not in name, a true pessimist might conclude, the advanced democracies are tending toward some form of oligarchy. Meanwhile, developing nations with no history of democratic self-governance, no attachment to European notions of political liberty and individual rights, seem unlikely candidates for democratization after the western model.[19]

Such dour assessments of democracy's prospects get close enough to the truth to be unsettling, but there are good reasons to resist the pessimist's conclusions. For one, there remains a striking variation, even among advanced western democracies, in the relative power of bureaucrats and elected politicians. Moreover, changes continue to occur in the balance of such power; observers of British governance commonly point out, for example, that both Margaret Thatcher and Tony Blair managed to centralize authority at 10 Downing Street, thereby reducing the traditional power of the civil service. Consider also the situation on democracy's frontier. Yes, modern democracy is the product of a specific set of historical circumstances; however, this does not necessarily mean either that the concept of democracy is viable only within western culture or that the practice of democracy (in the West and elsewhere) is incapable of adaptation to keep pace with social, economic, and technological changes. The democratic idea is one of the West's most successful exports. There is hardly a nation-state in the world today that does not declare itself to be a democracy; and even where this claim is patently false, it appears to be the case that there almost always exists a longing for genuine democracy among a significant portion of the populace. (One only need think of the Chinese students in Tiananmen Square.) Even peoples for whom European traditions are alien may be assumed to aspire to democracy for the same basic reasons as did the peoples of Europe and North America: those who have experienced authoritarian rule want to be free, and they intuitively understand that the best safeguard of liberty is popular self-government.

While fledgling democracies in divided societies are terribly vulnerable, the democratic state is in principle a mechanism for securing peace and order.[20] Nations plagued by severe racial, ethnic, and religious conflicts are always difficult to govern. It is not at all clear, however, that authoritarian regimes have any great advantage in this regard. Repression may create the illusion of order, but should the state loosen its grip even for an instant, a divided society is likely to dissolve into chaos. Surely, this is one of the lessons taught by the collapse of the Soviet empire. If multiracial, multiethnic, multireligious societies are to avoid partition, their only hope for civil peace lies in democracy. Only the liberal democratic state has managed to foster a political culture of civility and tolerance within a pluralistic society.[21] It must, of course, be conceded that no actually existing democracy has perfected this culture; racism and prejudice are to be found everywhere. Nonetheless, democratic norms favor inclusiveness and mutual respect, while democratic practice can encourage mutual accommodation among rival groups. This, indeed, is the lesson Grande draws below from the experience of certain European states, a lesson that may be recovered even for the European Union as a whole.

We may concede to the pessimist, nevertheless, that it remains an open question as to whether such democratic experience can be recovered and applied more broadly in the face of globalization, even in the West. The shift of effective power away from elected representatives to government bureaucrats and corporate technocrats is worrisome in this respect, as is the apathetic response of the public. With our taste for politics dulled by the never-ending pursuit of material wealth and our desire for personal autonomy satisfied through the virtual freedom afforded by new technologies, it is conceivable that even the beneficiaries of a new global economic order will complacently allow political democracy to fade out of existence.

To be sure, we must resist the temptation to romanticize the modern democratic state. A sprawling, populous country like the United States or Canada cannot be run like a town meeting, nor can all citizens be known to one another, let alone feel a strong sense of personal attachment. Even so, the formal institutions of democratic governance (notably parties, elections, and representative assemblies) create both vertical and horizontal linkages, establishing connections between the people and their governors, and among the people themselves, as joint participants in the political process. A well-organized democracy holds the political leadership accountable to the governed and provides various institutional mechanisms to enforce accountability. Through the state's regulatory and police powers, democracy also has the capacity to rein in private power and hold it accountable. At the same time, democratic citizenship creates a shared political identity, which transcends, however imperfectly, particular identities (such as class, culture, ethnicity, gender, race, region, religion). While conflict and competition remain an enduring feature of democratic politics, in a healthy democracy their scope and intensity are limited by the norms of citizenship and by a shared faith in the democratic process itself.

Students of democracy have long recognized the importance of small-scale, participatory self-government to the cultivation of a democratic ethos. Civic space must allow for a degree of intimacy. It is a place where neighbors converse about matters of common interest and organize themselves to achieve their common goals. Participants in local voluntary associations experience politics as active citizens. Their decisions count for something, and their actions directly influence the affairs of their community. In nineteenth-century America, when the federal government played a modest role in domestic affairs and the state governments lacked any extensive administrative capability, these sorts of local voluntary associations were very important to the public life of the nation.

Both the modern state and the marketplace, however, encroach on civic space. The modern state tends to appropriate local authority, reserving to itself decisions that might be left to regional or municipal levels of government or placed in the hands of citizens' groups. As my colleagues in the book note with regard to contemporary Europe, decisions taken by distant politicians or still more distant bureaucrats can render citizens passive, ultimately transforming them into clients. (The extent to which such tendencies are, in fact, resisted lies at the heart of renewed theoretical and empirical analysis of federal or confederal models of governance or in the parlance of prominent analysts of the European Union, "multilevel governance."[22] I return to this issue below.) The marketplace, for its part, presents itself as an alternative to civic space, recasting citizens as consumers of services designed and delivered by private entrepreneurs. (The Disney Corporation recently took this trend to its logical extreme and built a private town in Florida. Celebration, as the town is called, is wholly owned and operated by Disney, eliminating any need of or opportunity for residents to participate in its governance.) The globalization of the marketplace tightens the squeeze on civic space in at least two ways. First, as argued above, it extends the reach of capitalism at the expense of democratic politics. Second, by eroding the state's autonomy, it weakens the capacity of the state to regulate or insulate the domestic economy.[23]

In order to strengthen existing democracies, ways must be found to preserve (or, where necessary, re-create) the small-scale civic spaces where the lessons of citizenship are learned. In countries like the United States, which has a strong tradition of local government and where voluntary associations still thrive, a renewal of such spaces is conceivable, given the requisite political will. Elsewhere, it might require the devolution of at least some degree of meaningful political authority. Among the member states of the European Union, this is precisely the sort of rebalancing conjured by debates surrounding the term "subsidiarity." Though by no means an easy assignment, the creation of civic spaces would not require Rousseau's omniscient Legislator. Models may exist in the country's own history, or they might be adapted from the experience of other nations.[24] The single greatest difficulty with any such scheme is that, however much power they are given, local governments and voluntary associations will be hard-pressed to withstand the forces of economic integration and concentration. Pressures that compel the modern state to surrender a portion of its sovereignty could more easily crush smaller centers of resistance. For that reason, shoring up local democracy is only the beginning. Democracy must also be strengthened at the national level and, perhaps, beyond. A national government that is more responsive to its citizens is far less likely to become the willing tool of transnational interests.[25]

Unfortunately, democratic practice too often falls short of the ideal even in the most successful western democracies, a point Clarkson expands upon below. Consider the example of the United States. Congressional districts have grown so large as to render the very idea of representation problematic, and the fact that these are single member constituency districts with a first-past-the-post electoral system only makes things worse. Which persons or groups in these sprawling districts have an effective claim on their "representatives" when members of Congress owe their seats to a plurality of voters?[26] The decline of American political parties as instruments of mass mobilization and their reincarnation as handmaidens to hugely expensive, televised electoral campaigns close off yet another avenue of democratic representation. As broadly but not yet deeply acknowledged, there is a desperate need for campaign finance reform to curb the extraordinary influence of wealthy contributors in American elections. When it comes to legislation, moreover, the U.S. Congress all too frequently ignores Locke's warning against delegating the lawmaking power by handing broad discretionary authority over policy to unelected bureaucrats. This sidesteps political accountability. It also threatens the rule of law, since in practice adherence to bureaucratic regulations tends to be negotiable in a way that the obligation to obey the law is not.[27] Again, my colleagues return to analogous problems currently confronting Europe.

These several impediments to democracy in America are not insuperable. Elections could be publicly funded, or at the very least a strict ceiling could be imposed on campaign contributions. The House of Representatives, which has been frozen at its present size since the mid-1940s, could be enlarged. More ambitiously, the United States could switch to multi-member districts and a system of proportional representation in an attempt to ensure that even the voices of marginalized groups are heard in the legislature. Mass parties no longer educate voters or act as their surrogate in public debate; however, new technologies like the Internet could be utilized to provide ordinary citizens with access to a vast library of public information and to create virtual town meetings where citizens could speak for themselves. Congress, in exercising its legislative function, could be required to provide executive branch agencies with firm guidelines that would limit bureaucratic discretion, and to use sunset laws to force the periodic review of policies and programs.

Admittedly, none of these reforms is a magic bullet that will cure the ills of American democracy. The lesson of the American case is that circumstances change; democrats must be attentive to the changes and willing to experiment with new institutional modes and practices if they wish to preserve democracy itself. Pragmatism also dictates that local conditions demand solutions tailored to that particular place, respectful of its people's history and traditions. No one set of institutions or practices will be right for every democracy. Still, democracies can certainly borrow ideas from one another—cultural differences need not be absolute barriers to understanding.[28] One of the positive aspects of globalization is the spread of new technologies that make it easier to learn about what goes on in other places. Whether the goal is to reform an existing democracy or to bring about a transition to democracy in nations without a democratic tradition, democrats must proceed in a spirit of pragmatic experimentation.

This spirit of pragmatic experimentation characterizes a number of recent attempts to theorize global democracy beyond the nation-state. New technologies of communication may make it possible to construct civil society—conceived as a network of locally based civic organizations—on a global scale (but only if the means of communication are publicly accessible and democratically controlled).[29] In this manner, a kind of unity-in-diversity might be achieved without trivializing cultural differences or deprecating the group identities so important to the construction of the individual's personal identity. There is a need, however, for some form of global organization to facilitate cooperation among these groups. A loosely joined global confederation, for example, could over time become more closely connected, approaching if not ever achieving something like a multicultural, democratic, world state.[30]

The idea of a global confederation has been around for a long time. At least since Kant's day, cosmopolitan dreams have foundered on the rock of nationalism. Contemporary concerns with the implications of globalization have brought them back. The stubborn persistence of parochial identities, even in an age of globalization, nevertheless suggests that whatever existential needs such identities satisfy may be deeply rooted in the human psyche. In any event, there are good reasons for democrats to respect the importance persons freely attach to belonging to this or that group. It might be that membership in a particular group is what makes people's freedom valuable to them by enabling a particular way of life. Moreover, from a purely practical point of view, so long as national feeling endures, the nation will likely continue to have first claim on the loyalty of its citizens. Only a scheme of global democracy that respects these moral and political facts will have any chance of success.

In this regard, it is worth noting the peculiar difficulties posed by liberal democracy as it has been known in the West. Stronger versions of democracy, inclining more toward Rousseau than Locke, place few if any limits on the majority.[31] This runs contrary to the democratic experience in the West, which has for the most part been a record of *liberal* democracy. Liberal democracy is counter-majoritarian insofar as it places the individual's interest in autonomy above the will of the majority, creating through fundamental law a sphere of personal liberty that is (normally) beyond the reach of the state. It is sometimes objected that liberal democracy reflects a particular class interest or, more broadly, a cultural perspective unique to the western democracies. Thus, in order to avoid forms of oppression associated with class domination or cultural imperialism, we should be willing to give more weight to the freely formed preferences of the majority. Strong democracy might better suit the collectivist or communitarian orientation of many nonwestern cultures and may be more conducive than liberal individualism to the promotion of civic virtue.

There is no denying that even on a purely procedural level, considered as a framework for politics rather than a comprehensive way of life, liberal democracy poses a challenge to collectivist and communitarian visions of the good society. Nonetheless, liberal democracy may still be the best alternative even for persons committed to collectivist or communitarian conceptions of the public good. The liberal commitment to personal autonomy assures that in a pluralistic society where diverse persons are committed to rival and possibly incommensurate conceptions of the good life, most will be able to pursue their notion of the good as they see fit (either singly or in collaboration with others). They must, of course, accept certain limits on their actions. Simply put, they cannot act in ways that abridge the autonomy of others. The consequences of this constraint may be profound for some persons and groups. It can mean that they will have to share space with people whose beliefs and practices are an affront to everything they hold sacred or cherish most dearly. It can also limit their ability to police the behavior of their children and bring them up within the traditions of their own spiritual or cultural community. Likewise, it limits what the group can do to sanction deviant behavior by its adult members, perhaps weakening the integrity of the group and compromising its survival. Small wonder that collectivists and communitarians are suspicious of liberal claims of neutrality. Liberal democracy *is* neutral, but only in the sense of allowing rival and incommensurate conceptions of the good to coexist peacefully within the same state. The terms and conditions set by the liberal democratic framework, however, are decidedly *not* neutral.

It could be argued for this very reason that we would be wrong to insist on liberal democracy as *the* model for democracy around the globe. After all, we could hardly expect liberal democracy to hold great appeal for nonwestern peoples whose normative traditions do not place a high value on individual autonomy. Where, say, family comes first, persons are less likely to desire (or recognize) a moral "right" to self-fulfillment that comes at the expense of one's filial obligations, much less the sorts of legal rights intended to privilege the autonomous self. As Daniel A. Bell and Kanishka Jayasuriya write, "a liberal democratic political system, informed and justified by the ideals of equality and freedom, as well as by a recognition and accommodation of the 'fact of pluralism', is a culturally distinct, historically contingent artefact, not readily transferable to East and Southeast Asian societies with different traditions, needs, and conceptions of human flourishing."[32] Much the same could be said with respect to other parts of the developing world. Insofar as globalizing capitalism tends to remake these cultures in its own image, globalization might well be accused of promoting liberalization at the expense of democracy (conceived of as collective self-determination) by undermining a people's capacity to protect its traditional way of life.

David Held, in a supremely ambitious attempt to theorize global democracy referred to throughout this book, implicitly rejects this line of argument by defending the centrality of freedom and equality to democratic thought. He contends that "the idea of democracy derives its power and significance . . . from the idea of self-determination; that is, from the notion that members of a political community—citizens—should be able to choose freely the conditions of their own association, and that their choices should constitute the ultimate legitimation of the form and direction of their polity."[33] If one class of persons is not allowed to participate because of race or sex or religion or some other ascriptive characteristic, then the polity is not fully democratic—even if it allows all other persons full participation. Likewise, if the political community does not do its utmost to enable citizens to develop the capacities required for full and equal participation in public life, it cannot be described as fully democratic. Held's argument does not stipulate radical individualism as a necessary condition for democracy—citizens might freely choose to subordinate their own ambitions to the well-being of their families or of the harmony of the group—but he does insist that it be their choice and not a decision forced upon them by others.

Held would guarantee autonomy through the medium of what he calls "democratic public law." At its core lies a set of rights, or "entitlement capacities for members of a democratic society." Democratic public law provides "the 'grand' or meta-framework which can legitimately circumscribe and delimit politics, economics, and social interaction."

> It specifies the conditions necessary for members of a political community to be free and equal in a process of self-determination. It provides, thereby, criteria by which one can judge whether or not a given political system or set of arrangements is democratic. By inscribing a set of democratic rights into a constitution, a political community commits itself both to safeguarding individuals in certain ways and to protecting the community as a democratic association; for these rights are the rules and procedures which cannot, without inconsistency and contradiction, be eliminated: they are the self-binding conditions of democracy.[34]

Held describes seven categories of rights corresponding to seven "sites of power" where a lack of resources or unequal resources can deprive persons of the degree of autonomy required by democratic citizens. The sites of power are the human body, institutions of social welfare, cultural institutions and practices (including religion), civic associations, the economy, coercive relations/organized violence, and legal and regulatory institutions. The corresponding rights pertain to health and physical well-being, access to community services necessary for the development of one's abilities and talents, freedom of thought and faith, freedom of association, access to the necessities of life and freedom from financial vulnerability, peace and security, and due process and equal treatment before the law. Held asserts that the imperative to secure these rights creates an agenda for democratic politics everywhere; however, he concedes that their implementation will vary according to the "traditions, values, and levels of development of particular societies."[35] Thus, different societies would be free to deliver, say, medical or social services in different ways; however, in order to be considered *democratic*, they would all have to make a good faith effort to secure the health and well-being of their citizens.

Democratic public law is given bite by vesting enforcement in supranational institutions. Believing that the nation-state is no longer competent to protect the democratic rights of its citizens, Held would have democratic public law entrenched within the constitutions of parliaments and assemblies formed at the national, regional, and global levels. He envisions a number of regional associations along the lines of the European Union, only having greater authority, and "an independent assembly of democratic peoples, directly elected by them and accountable to them" at the global level, perhaps sitting as a second chamber alongside the UN General Assembly.[36] At the same time, he would extend the competence of international courts "so that groups and individuals have an effective means of suing political authorities for the enactment and enforcement of key rights and obligations, both within and beyond political associations."[37] This is a controversial provision, subject to the same sorts of criticisms directed against "juridical democracy" in the United States, where an unelected judiciary has the authority to invalidate legislation duly passed by a representative assembly. Given the extensive nature of the rights Held believes are required by the principle of autonomy, it can be anticipated that there will be a strong temptation for some persons to make an end-run around the democratic political process by going to court. For example, Held considers the right to control one's own fertility to be an example of the general right to health that democracy must protect. What would happen if a woman residing in a community where the majority opposed abortion were to contest her community's restrictive laws in an international court? What standard of right would the court be bound to uphold? Who would adjudicate the dispute if the local community refused to yield its prerogative to decide on the content of the contested right? Under conventional notions of sovereignty, lower authorities must yield to higher ones, but Held's "cosmopolitan democracy" lacks a conventional sovereign. Instead, sovereignty is dispersed throughout the system, with decision-making authority located in multiple associations (some smaller than the nation-state, some larger).

This could be a recipe for chaos, though it need not be. A gradualist approach might allow the scope of Held's democratic rights to be more or less extensive from one locale to the next, so long as their content was collectively determined through the democratic process and subject to periodic reconsideration in the same manner. The general categories of right, however, would be specified by the democratic public law and would not be subject to majoritarian democracy. Thus, to stay with the previous example, given the opposition to abortion in certain communities, we would not expect abortion services to be available everywhere, even though all political associations would be expected to accord individual women the right to decide for themselves whether to bear children.[38] This scheme does not assume that people's democratic rights will become more homogeneous over time; cosmopolitan democracy does not require a cosmopolitan world culture sharing uniform beliefs, values, and norms. In this sense, Held's theory remains a framework for (liberal) democracy, not a singular prescription for the good life.

As Offe and Greven contend below, theories of cosmopolitan democracy have not and possibly cannot overcome a stubborn political fact: there is as yet no transnational *demos* to support transnational democracies in practice. Divided by language, race, ethnicity, religion, and culture, the diverse peoples of the world seem ill-prepared to function as a democratic public under the jurisdiction of a common or overlapping set of political institutions. National communities separated by language, culture, and perceptions of (national) self-interest can hardly be expected to behave with the degree of civility and mutual tolerance shown by rival interest groups within pluralistic societies like Canada or the United States. Indeed, the absence of a *demos* plagues even the most favorable case for political integration, the European Union. Despite monetary and economic union in western Europe, the idea of a United States of Europe still strikes most observers as an impossible dream. Genuine political union on either a regional or world scale seems to require the same shared sense of membership that sustains existing political communities at the level of the nation-state. Schemes for expanding democracy beyond national borders continue to founder for lack of a democratic subject capable of willing the common good.[39] Zürn and Grande return to this dilemma in their own chapters.

Presumably, it is the absence of a world *demos* that itself suggests the idea of a confederacy of democratic nations rather than a unified world state or various multilevel, multijurisdictional schemes of transnational governance. It may also account for the recurrent enthusiasm of theorists for political decentralization and the emphasis each places on strengthening local democracy. While it is true that a democratic world culture does not yet exist *and might never exist* (for the triumph of democracy is by no means inevitable), it is also the case that a convergence of political norms around democratic values is not unthinkable. The creation of democracy beyond national borders, like the building of democracy *within* the nation-state, must be seen as a long-term historical process.

Insofar as globalization brings the peoples of the world into closer contact with one another and causes them to recognize their mutual interdependence, it might actually contribute to the formation of a global public. One does not need to be a starry-eyed idealist, for example, to draw just such a conclusion from the post–World War II experience in Europe. Nonetheless, democrats are justified in regarding such examples skeptically. Interdependence verging on deep integration can threaten democracy, not on account of some wicked design, but because the core process at work—globalizing capitalism—can hollow out political sovereignty and ride roughshod over democratic institutions. With regard to the relative empowerment of corporations, Clarkson returns to this theme in his chapter below. The essential possibility remains that a globalizing process may, in the end, not be perceived as progressive or broadly empowering. In some states, at least, it might well provoke a hostile public reaction.[40] Nevertheless, we cannot be sure that the outcome of a popular revolt would always favor democracy. That is why democracy needs champions.

In his defense of the democratic idea, David Held cheerfully admits that his own theory of cosmopolitan democracy is utopian—it describes the world as it might be, if we can find the political will to make it so. Though scorned by self-described "realists," utopian thinking is not necessarily a political handicap. Any theory of democracy we might come up with must be utopian in some respect, because nowhere on earth has the promise of democracy been fully realized. The democratic idea itself is perhaps best thought of as a utopian aspiration, a hope for the future and a standard by which to assess our progress. We need such aspirations if we are to resist the notion, made plausible by the seeming inevitability of globalization, that democracy, self-determination, and the common good are ideas whose time is past. Such aspirations, indeed, are evident in the central debate joined in the following chapters of this book.

NOTES

1. Susan Strange, *The Retreat of the State: The Diffusion of Power in the World Economy* (Cambridge: Cambridge University Press, 1996), xii.

2. My conception of globalization owes a debt to Theodore J. Lowi's "Think Globally, Lose Locally," *Boston Review* (April/May 1998): 4–10.

3. Strange, *The Retreat of the State*, xiii.

4. Benjamin Barber, *Jihad vs. McWorld: How Capitalism and Tribalism Are Reshaping the World* (New York: Ballantine, 1996).

5. Robert Dahl, *On Democracy* (New Haven, Conn.: Yale University Press, 1998), 166–172. The relationship between capitalism and democracy described by Dahl is historical and contingent, though he is inclined to treat it here as though the western experience will likely be reproduced throughout the world. My concern is with the rather more naïve view, common at the end of the Cold War, which obscures the tension between capitalism and democracy. Dahl briefly discusses that tension at pp. 173–179. See also his article "Why Free Markets Are Not Enough," *Journal of Democracy* 3, no. 3 (July 1992): 82.

6. For a discussion of the affinity between capitalism and authoritarianism in Asia, see Daniel A. Bell et al., *Towards Illiberal Democracy in Pacific Asia* (Oxford: St. Martin's, 1995). But see Dahl's argument on the democratizing forces unleashed by capitalism in *On Democracy*, 170.

7. See, for example, Robert D. Kaplan, "Was Democracy Just a Moment?" *Atlantic Monthly* 280, no. 6 (December 1997): 55–80. Such views build on a conviction central to much of the social science literature concerned with democratization—i.e., that the success of democracy is tied to rising economic fortunes. Surveying the emergence of new democratic states in the period 1974–1990, Samuel Huntington writes: "The conclusion seems clear. Poverty is a principal and probably the principal obstacle to democratic development. The future of democracy depends on the future of economic development. Obstacles to economic development are obstacles to the expansion of democracy." See Huntington, *The Third Wave: Democratization in the Late Twentieth Century* (Norman: University of Oklahoma Press, 1991), 311.

8. Of course, political democracy does not require that businesses or other private organizations themselves be democratically organized. My concern here is with the transmission of democratic norms and the creation of a democratic public culture where none has existed previously. Clearly, there is a tension between the participatory ethos of democracy and the hierarchy of the firm that renders the latter ill-suited to the role of schoolhouse of democratic politics.

9. To the contrary, in *The Twilight of Sovereignty: How the Information Revolution Is Changing Our World* (New York: Charles Scribner's Sons, 1992), Walter Wriston (former chairman and CEO of Citicorp and Citibank, N.A.) argues that the computer revolution is leveling business hierarchies by doing away with middle management. However, as William Greider observes, the new work system, which gives the CEO and his team direct command of the shop floor, "also creates a steeper pyramid between [workers] and the commanding heights." See Greider, *One World, Ready or Not: The Manic Logic of Global Capitalism* (New York: Simon

and Schuster, 1997), 29. In his now-classic study, *Politics and Markets* (New York: Basic Books, 1977), Charles Lindblom observes that bureaucratic hierarchies are characteristic of all systems of industrial production (11).

10. See Robert A. Dahl, *Democracy and Its Critics* (New Haven, Conn.: Yale University Press, 1989), 327.

11. For example, Friedrich Hayek, *The Road to Serfdom* (Chicago: University of Chicago Press, 1944), 93–94. See also Murray Rothbard, *Man, Economy and State* (Los Angeles: Nash Publishing, 1962), 560–566.

12. On this theme, William Greider remarks:

One of the striking qualities of post–Cold War globalization is how easily business and government in the capitalist democracies have abandoned the values they putatively espoused for forty years during the struggle against communism—individual liberties and political legitimacy based on free elections. Concern for human rights, including freedom of assembly for workers wishing to speak for themselves, has been pushed aside by commercial opportunities. Multinationals plunge confidently into new markets, from Vietnam to China, where the governments routinely control and abuse their own citizens. In Singapore, some leading tribunes of the free press—the *Wall Street Journal, Newsweek, The Economist*—have published meek apologies to the ruling politicians who were offended by certain news items, rather than lose access to Singapore's burgeoning market. (*One World, Ready or Not*, 37)

13. The notion of politics and economics occupying different "spheres" of social life is adapted from Michael Walzer, *Spheres of Justice: A Defense of Pluralism and Equality* (New York: Basic Books, 1983). See especially chapters 4 and 12.

14. See Lindblom, *Politics and Markets*, 173: "One of the great misconceptions of conventional economic theory is that businessmen are induced to perform their functions by purchases of their goods and services, as though the vast productive tasks performed in market-oriented systems could be motivated solely by exchange relations between buyers and sellers. On so slender a foundation no great production system can be established. What is required in addition is a set of governmentally provided inducements in the form of market and political benefits." A seriously intended, if less than credible argument for the abolition of the state is advanced by such theoreticians of the Libertarian movement in the United States as Murray Rothbard and David Friedman (son of the neo-classical economist Milton Friedman). See Rothbard, *For a New Liberty: The Libertarian Manifesto*, rev. ed. (New York: Collier, 1978); and Friedman, *The Machinery of Freedom* (New York: Harper & Row, 1973).

15. For a discussion of the relationship between capitalism and democracy in theory and practice, see Robert A. Dahl, "Why All Democratic Countries Have Mixed Economies," in *NOMOS XXXV: Democratic Community*, ed. J. W. Chapman and I. Shapiro (New York: New York University Press, 1993), 259–282. Also Dahl, *On Democracy*, chapters 13 and 14.

16. Much contemporary work by comparative political scientists is devoted to this problem, and existing research has illuminated both upward and downward tendencies. See, for example, David Vogel, *Trading Up: Consumer and Environmental Regulation in the Global Economy* (Cambridge: Harvard University Press, 1995);

and Wolfgang Streeck, "Neo-Voluntarism: A New European Social Policy Regime," in *Governance in the European Union,* ed. Gary Marks, Fritz W. Scharpf, Phillipe C. Schmitter, and Wolfgang Streeck, (London: Sage, 1996).

17. Michael Sandel, *Democracy's Discontent: America in Search of a Public Philosophy* (Cambridge: Harvard University Press, 1996).

18. Barber, *Jihad vs. McWorld,* 239.

19. A strong statement of the pessimist's view can be found in Kaplan's "Was Democracy Just a Moment?" For another popular treatment of the subject after the same fashion, see Patrick E. Kennon, *The Twilight of Democracy* (New York: Doubleday, 1995). The scholarly literature tends to be more circumspect; nonetheless, an element of pessimism is to be found here as well. On the cultural barriers to democratization outside the West, see, for example, Michael Ignatieff, *Blood and Belonging: Journeys into the New Nationalism* (New York: Farrar, Straus, and Giroux, 1994); and especially Samuel Huntington, *The Clash of Civilizations and the Remaking of World Order* (New York: Simon and Schuster, 1996). On the antidemocratic effects of globalization, see Stephen Gill, "Globalization, Democratization, and the Politics of Indifference," in *Globalization: Critical Reflections,* ed. James H. Mittelman (Boulder, Colo.: Lynne Rienner, 1997), 205–228. On the corporate challenge to democracy, see, for example, David Korten, *When Corporations Rule the World* (West Hartford, Conn.: Kumarian Press, 1995).

20. See Stephen Holmes, *Passions and Constraint: On the Theory of Liberal Democracy* (Chicago: University of Chicago Press, 1995), 18–23.

21. Daniel A. Bell, drawing on the work of Will Kymlicka, argues to the contrary that "plurality and mutual respect do not . . . require democracy, so long as a relatively benign paternalistic government allows ethnic and religious groups to pursue their own cultural activities in peace." *Towards Illiberal Democracy in Pacific Asia,* 171. Bell's real-world example is Singapore, where minority religious groups are allowed to preach to their own flocks but not to Muslims. This variety of "tolerance," however, cannot be described as a civic virtue. It is not the citizens who must be tolerant, but the state. Domestic peace depends not upon the mutual respect of citizens for one another but on the coercive apparatus of the state and the political will of rulers to use force in order to preserve the cultural autonomy of rival groups.

22. Gary Marks et al., eds., *Governance in the European Union* (London; Thousand Oaks, Calif.: Sage, 1996).

23. See Leo Panitch, "Rethinking the Role of the State," in Mittelman, *Globalization: Critical Reflections,* 83–116.

24. Stephen Gill points to "the new forms of local political organization and multi-lateralism that have begun to emerge among the poor and marginalized (*e.g.,* the indigenous peoples of North and South America and parts of Asia)" in response to globalization. See Gill, "Globalization, Democratization and Indifference," in James H. Mittelman, *Globalization: Critical Reflections,* 222. See Jeff Haynes's recent study of grassroots "action groups" in the Third World and their contribution to the strengthening of civil society in *Democracy and Civil Society in the Third World: Politics and New Political Movements* (Cambridge, Mass.: Polity Press, 1997).

25. In *Preparing for the Twenty-First Century* (New York: Random House, 1993), Paul Kennedy argues that despite globalization, the nation-state remains the primary locus of loyalty for most people, adding that "even if the autonomy and functions of the modern state have been eroded by transnational trends, no adequate substitute has emerged to replace it as the key unit in responding to global change" (134).

26. For a timely discussion of proposals to reform the American Congress, see the collection of articles gathered under the title "This Old House: Remodel or Rebuild?" *PS: Political Science and Politics* 31, no. 1 (March 1998): 5–31.

27. Theodore J. Lowi, *The End of Liberalism*, 2d ed. (New York: W. W. Norton, 1979), 50–61.

28. Samuel Huntington argues in *The Clash of Civilizations* that in the aftermath of the Cold War, insuperable "civilizational" differences will determine the lines of international conflict. While not without insight, his argument tends to exaggerate the extent to which cultures are impermeable. He observes in Chapter 4 that globalization as often as not places new technologies in the service of traditionalist (antiwestern) forces in the Third World. He fails to note, however, the degree to which these new technologies (and the global economy to which they are connected) at the same time can have a transformative effect on even the most parochial orientations.

29. This is the position of Benjamin Barber in *Jihad vs. McWorld*. In this context, it will also be necessary to ensure equality of access. A recent survey reported in the *New York Times* reveals that American blacks are far less likely than whites of the same socioeconomic status to own a personal computer or have access to one. Not surprisingly, therefore, black Americans are also far less likely to make use of the Internet.

30. In a similar vein, Michael Sandel argues that "the most promising alternative to the sovereign state is not a one-world community based on the solidarity of humankind, but a multiplicity of communities and political bodies—some more, some less extensive than nations—among which sovereignty is diffused. . . . Different forms of political association would govern different spheres of life and different aspects of our identities." Sandel, *Democracy's Discontent*, 345.

31. Benjamin Barber, *Strong Democracy: Participatory Politics for a New Age* (Berkeley: University of California Press, 1984), 309.

32. Bell et al., *Towards Illiberal Democracy in Pacific Asia*, 9. See also Bell's solo contribution to this volume, "Democracy in Confucian Societies: The Challenge of Justification," 17–40.

33. David Held, *Democracy and the Global Order* (Stanford, Calif.: Stanford University Press, 1995), 145.

34. Ibid., 200.

35. Ibid., 211.

36. Ibid., 273.

37. Ibid., 205.

38. Again, this does not presume radical individualism. A woman need not make her choice in isolation. It may be presumed, depending on the traditions of her culture, that her decision will be more or less influenced by the wishes of her

husband and family, the expectations of her religious or national community, and so on. These influences provide the context within which her choice is made. In some communities, such influences may prove extremely difficult to resist; however, there is a world of difference between the woman who feels compelled to bear a child in order to satisfy the demands of her religious faith and the woman who is raped by her husband. The former is acting on a conception of the good that she herself accepts. The latter is a victim of her husband's aggression, which deprives her of all control over her own fertility.

39. See Dahl, *Democracy and Its Critics*, 320.

40. Immanuel Wallerstein writes that globalization is polarizing societies throughout the world on a class basis. "This is the worst of all situations for those interested in the political stability of the existing world system. On the one hand, the populations in the South, who will still be worst off and the most desperate, may be ready to contemplate more serious antisystemic disruption. On the other hand, the bottom strata in the countries of the North will no longer enjoy some of the amenities which they had been invited to share in the post-1945 period, and even more importantly will no longer believe that it is certain that their children will enjoy a higher standard of living than they." See *The Age of Transition: Trajectory of the World System, 1945–2025* (London: Zed Books, 1996), 234.

3

Can the European Union Finally Become a Democracy?

Michael Th. Greven

In the late 1990s, every discussion about the future of the European Union (EU) seemed to focus on the establishment of economic and monetary union (EMU). It was implicitly, and often even explicitly, assumed in associated debates that the fulfillment of the Maastricht Treaty criteria and the establishment of EMU would be a major step toward the Union's political integration as well. However, the implications of further integration in the post-EMU period were not often discussed in detail. When they were, the discussion tended to focus narrowly on the policies and institutional prerequisites for a future common monetary policy and its likely impact on labor markets and national welfare systems. My contribution in this chapter is related but different. I look at the future of the emerging European system of government. With the establishment of EMU, this system will gain additional dimensions and extend its influence over people's lives. Unfortunately, I believe it will also diminish the standard of democracy hitherto achieved in most of the national political systems concerned.

The standard of democracy in an emerging system of government beyond the nation-state is my major concern in this chapter.[1] In criticizing the relatively lower standard of democracy exhibited on the transnational level as compared with the nation-state, I am neither arguing that the nation-state is the "natural" or "best" form of government, nor defending any "nationalistic" approach to political problem solving in an era of "globalization" and transnational integration. I am simply suggesting that current EU policies, limited as they are in their intellectual and normative scope to rational or effective problem-solving aspects of the problem of integration, will contribute to the erosion of institutions, normative standards and public support for existing national democracies. How inadequately these democracies may have measured up to the normative principles of democracy is another story, one taken up especially in chapters of this book by Newman and Clarkson. My argument here is that the model of "western democracy" operative in most EU member states has established a normative standard of rights, benefits, and possibilities for citizen participation that ought not to be carelessly abandoned in the building of transnational institutions of government. In this sense, the case of the EU illuminates better than any other the normative dilemmas outlined by Newman that today confront all democracies.

National governments now face increasing pressure in a number of policy domains to move the locus of their problem-solving efforts from the level of intergovernmental cooperation to that of transnational regimes, or even new institutions of transnational government such as the EU.[2] These developments raise important questions about the future of democracy:

- Can these new forms of governance be as democratic as their national predecessors?
- In Europe, are existing forms and institutions of democratic participation adequate to meet this new situation at the national and transnational levels, or have the politics of the emergent "European" level of government diminished national standards and practices of democracy? If the latter, is this an unavoidable consequence of the growing disembedding of democratic forms of government from their national environments, or is it simply the result of the policy style and method of integration that currently prevails in the process of European unification?
- In the final analysis, can the European Union become a democracy?

Although this chapter focuses only on some limited aspects of the problem of transnational democracy, I will answer the final question with a conditional "no." If the policy style and focus of the prevailing politics of European integration are not substantially changed, the resulting European regime of government will not and cannot become a democracy, either in any traditional understanding of the word or in any innovative way. Whether the changes required to develop democracy on a transnational level are already thinkable, their practicability is quite another problem. By discussing some of the obstacles to transnational democracy inherent in the present politics of European integration, I hope to shed some light on what such changes might entail.

THE EUROPEAN UNION AND THE DEMOCRATIC DEFICIT

The so-called democratic deficit of the EU is a well-established topic in social science research on European integration.[3] This research has been informed by a variety of analytical and normative perspectives and has produced a wealth of evidence that, among other things, suggests:

1. There exists no European people that, as a prepolitical "given," could play the (virtual) role of a European *pouvoir constituant* and sovereign; instead, there exists a multitude of peoples, each with a respective national identity and sense of belonging (*Wir-Gefühl*).[4] It is true that in many paradigmatic cases of state creation, such as the French and British cases, no single collectivity, no "people," preceded the top-down institutional strategies of powerful elites. The point here, however, is that neither the capacities nor the intentionality now exist for the implementation of similar strategies in the European Union.
2. There exists no European constitution or even a "Bill of Rights," usually seen as a prerequisite to a democratic regime; the system of treaties that legally constitutes the EU is not a functional or even a normative equivalent.
3. The European Parliament is not part of a valid parliamentary regime because it lacks certain rights and effective control over the Commission (not to mention the European Council).[5]
4. There are still no true European parties; rather, there are merely intraparliamentary coalitions and strategic alliances on the one hand, and more or less ineffective and symbolic associations of national parties on the other. This remains true despite the fact that interparty interaction with national party leaders and the inception of formal party programs have recently intensified.[6]
5. European elections are more precisely "national by-elections," because electoral campaigns in the various member states almost invariably focus on national issues and a national agenda.[7]
6. Neither the Commission, the Council, nor the various councils of ministers, all of whom effectively share governing power within the emergent European system of government, are democratic institutions in the sense of traditional democratic governments in nation-states.[8]
7. The legal system of the EU has a strong bias toward processing the so-called four liberties constituting the Common Market (free movement of goods, services, people and capital), but is ineffective in providing citizens with rights and legal support against the impact of European government.

Much analysis of the democratic deficit of the EU is based on the assumption—often openly declared as a value statement—that the set of
principles, institutions, and rules that have evolved over the short history
of "western democracy" is an appropriate benchmark against which to
measure the democratic quality of transnational governments and regimes. This assumption has led some theorists to call for the creation of
similar institutions for the EU—namely, a constitution, a real European
parliament, and a government responsible (only) to the parliament. Theorists of this persuasion have effectively been searching for a kind of democratic European Federal State, similar in type to the (often unstated)
"ideal" of the United States of America. Working from the same assumption, other observers have concluded that certain democratic institutions
cannot easily be transferred from the national context to transnational
and especially transcultural systems.[9] In reaching this conclusion, they
have found themselves in the not always comfortable company of anti-
European nationalists and other reactionaries.

It is only recently that the assumption itself has come under scrutiny,
and this is what I shall focus on here. I will proceed by looking beyond
the institutional settings of historical democracies as criteria for democratic conditions of political life—deconstructing them, so to speak—and
considering the idea that the familiar institutions of modern democracy
are only one possible "crystallization" of more abstract principles.[10] Political scientists often forget—and the rhetoric and logic of constitutions and
political declarations turn this negligence into a virtue—that the institutions of "modern democracies" are the contingent result of an historically
very recent process of institution building, which entailed binding together and mixing occasionally opposing concepts from the medieval,
Greek, and Roman traditions. Only in the early nineteenth century did
the concept of "representative democracy" become the overall conceptual
framework for this unprecedented fabric of democratic principles and institutional arrangements.[11]

There is no such thing as the western democracy that could serve as
a blueprint for further institution-building,[12] particularly in light of the
dramatic changes that have taken place in our environment over the last
twenty years—changes that continue to occur at such a speed and of such
a magnitude that they make even the immediate future difficult to fore-
see. Space limitations make it impossible to list all the dimensions of these
transformations. However, I would note that they could affect behavior
from the micropolitical level, where they influence the psychological and
social constitution of "individuals," to the macropolitical level, where
they shape the reproduction of communities and societies as a whole.

Indeed, the very concept of "society," which forms the underlying sociological assumption of most political science, has become problematic

of late, because it has become increasingly evident that, even in abstract versions of system theory, the "boundary question" (the way in which a distinction is drawn between a system—for example, the encompassing system "society"—and its surroundings) has never been properly solved analytically. Rather, it has been answered with what has been called a "naturalistic (mis)conclusion," whereby the historical boundaries of nation-states are implicitly taken as the "boundaries" of "social systems" on an analytical or theoretical level.[13] However, if a system is in fact constituted—be it in the Parsonian tradition as a "system of action," or in the more recent tradition of Niklas Luhmann as a "system of communications"—and is distinguished from its surroundings or other systems not by a territorial boundary but through an operationally defined and empirically testable difference in the appearance of its elements and operations "inside" and "outside" its boundaries, then it becomes evident that the naturalistic (mis)conclusion no longer provides an adequate answer to the boundary question. "Actions," interactions, or "communications" of various kinds of systems—especially in the field of economic and social transactions—are no longer restricted by the national borders of a given international system to an extent that could justify this understanding of boundaries. Furthermore, networks and systems of action and communications have emerged—for example some international financial markets—that have virtually no territorial base at all.

There have also been exceptions to this overall tendency toward cross-boundary networking, and they are of particular relevance to our question. For example, one might still speak in an empirical and practical sense of nationally formed boundaries of "systems" in certain areas of law, political participation and political legitimacy.[14] This is by no means accidental, as I demonstrate in this chapter by briefly discussing several fundamental aspects of the constitution of political communities in general, and democratic communities in particular. I argue that some aspects of "politics" are necessarily based on membership—on a logic of inclusion and exclusion. I also argue that democratic politics, especially in the "modern" sense, necessarily rests on a very special and conditioned concept of political space ("civic space" in Newman's chapter), which, although based on territory, is not identical with it in analytical or practical terms. Indeed, the future of democracy beyond the nation-state may well depend on precisely this decoupling of political space and territory.

THE CONSTITUTION OF DEMOCRATIC COMMUNITIES: MEMBERSHIP

Politics, at least in the sense that we understand and use the concept today, is not a natural part of the human race in the sense of Aristotle's *zoon politicon*, but an historical achievement.[15] Indeed, at its inception, the Aristotelian concept itself reflected the recent invention of politics as the art and capacity of intentionally establishing communities according to a set of principles, rules and institutions, which are artifacts and known as such.[16] This technique of "constructing" political regimes was not an abstract playground for philosophers during the history of Athenian democracy, but a practical and political prerequisite for the establishment of various Athenian "colonies" from Asia Minor to Sicily.

Politics begins when the rules of common life become reflexive and contingent—when people begin to realize that their practical communal life is not governed by "nature," the "ancestors," "God," or any other suprahuman powers, but rather by habits, customs, rules, and laws they have produced themselves. Since Solon's venerated legislative settlement of conflicts between landowners and dependent peasants, this realization has steadily grown to become the fundamental self-perception influencing first Greek culture and ultimately western culture in general and its political constitution in particular.[17] As a result, this period of human development has, with the conscious misapplication of a concept developed much later, been called the "first enlightenment"—occurring almost 2,000 years before the second became possible and necessary.

Every polity has to establish a community of members to which its authority is effectively and, in the non-normative Weberian sense of the word, legitimately extended. Membership roles and markers have to be developed and put into practice to distinguish those who belong to the polity from those who effectively do not. Usually, this membership will inhabit a certain territory, with political and legal authority ending at its borders. However, the boundaries of membership and territory are analytically different and, in practice, do not always coincide.

For example, there are always persons living within the territory of one polity who are not members, but foreigners or visitors. Think of the *metökes* in the ancient polis, who have been compared with the *ausländer* in present-day Germany and non-naturalized immigrants in similar countries.[18] These outsiders are typically subject only to certain aspects of local authority, and they usually enjoy fewer rights but sometimes are assigned more duties. Most important, at least in principle, they can leave and return to their country of origin. Thus, living somewhere else does not automatically mean deprivation of one's former membership status.[19] Conversely, even individuals permanently residing outside the territory to which their polity exclusively and effectively extends its authority may still be subject to some of its legal rules and requirements. Present-day examples include the right and duty to vote of even second- or third-generation expatriate Italians, or the duty of young Turkish men, regardless of the country in which they were born and raised, to fulfill their military service for Turkey after having reached the age of eighteen.

Moreover, the territorial boundaries of a polity are not always clear, as in the case of the Holy Roman Empire of German Nations. Nor have territorial boundaries historically been a prerequisite for the recognition of a political unit—think of the case of the French or Polish governments-in-exile during World War II. Then there are territorially restricted polities like the German and Israeli ones, which extend their membership, virtually at least, to all persons of German and Jewish descent, respectively, regardless of where they live; they will immediately recognize a person's citizenship status if it is claimed. Analytically, then, the territorial boundaries of a polity must be distinguished from those that establish membership. The polity is, in a fundamental sense, established by the latter. Territorial boundaries are established by the effective capacity of a polity to enact and enforce its authority. Membership constitutes a common polity not necessarily bound to a certain territory. We will have to keep this in mind when we evaluate the prospects for democracy in the EU.

In addition to the aforementioned problems of constitution that all polities confront, democratic polities face a further difficulty. In accordance with certain historically developed and politically established normative principles, democratic polities have transmuted some of the more general aspects of the membership principle—aspects that are part of any political regime—into a more specific concept of citizenship.[20] Even taking into account the great variety and complexity of western democracies, some principles of citizenship seem undisputed:

1. A democratic polity is constituted out of and by its citizens only, who together form its artificial "body politic" and are the last and only source of sovereignty.[21]
2. By definition, these citizens accept each other as "equal" in their capacity as citizens—in other words, in their political rights and duties—and following from this, they accept each other as "equal" under the rule of law. It is especially important to understand that, inasmuch as this "equality" is the result of the practical application of a political principle, it is abstract and artificial. It is true only in the field of political rights and duties, and does not necessarily extend to the economic and social realm.[22]
3. The very idea of democratic "citizenship" is based on the concept of the "individual" as the basic unit of the "body politic"; it is the individual who holds fundamental rights, and it is the individual's "voice" that counts in elections and the deliberative formation of the "public will" (Rousseau's *volonté de tous*), again, as "equal."[23]
4. A responsible and responsive government of representatives of the

citizens is limited in time and is constituted by "offices." These de-
serve respect, but their members remain citizens, hence "equal" and
equally under the rule of law.
5. Despite its relatively recent emergence, "citizenship" is a complex
   historical concept. Following from T. H. Marshall's classic account,
   we currently distinguish three levels, which interact to establish an
   individual's "citizenship": the fundamental liberties, the right to
   participate in the political process, and finally (and most recently)
   some basic social benefits for those who are either temporarily or
   permanently incapable of sustaining a minimum standard of
   living.[24]

It is clear from the above that membership and citizenship in a democratic polity ought to be almost identical. So far, however, this has not
been the historical and empirical reality of modern democracies. Thus,
just as it is analytically necessary to distinguish between membership and
territory, it is also necessary, even in democratic polities, to distinguish
between membership and citizenship. Furthermore, there is empirical evidence that this decoupling is of great practical relevance.

Until very recently, the decoupling of membership and citizenship was
most evident in the case of women. The phrase "It is evident that all men
are created equal," so familiar and ubiquitous in the history of western
democracy, has never meant that membership in a democratic society automatically conferred citizenship (especially voting rights). Even today,
we do not question the fact that young people are members of a polity,
but not citizens. Thus, a young person is expected to pay taxes[25] and even
defend his or her political community in war[26] without being granted citizen status, including the right to vote or to be elected to certain offices.
Still, we accept this as "natural," just as some of our forefathers thought
it natural that blacks, women, and persons with an inadequate income
should not be granted the status of citizens in a democracy.

The growing complexity of modern citizen status has affected its practical applicability. Some communities seem to find it easier to grant, and
afterwards guarantee and reinforce, "liberties" to new members—be they
women or different ethnic groups and immigrants—than to allow these
members effective political participation, or even self-government. Cultural perceptions and an unwillingness to share power seem to be the
major forces behind this status quo orientation of many social groups and
political elites.

From an analytical point of view, it is important to see that these first
two dimensions of citizenship—the fundamental liberties and the right to
participate in the political process—can be distributed without restriction,

either separately or coupled, because they are not a scarce resource. The liberties and right to participation in principle are endlessly divisible "goods"; there are no logical obstacles to their becoming universally and effectively accepted. The same is not true of the third and most recent dimension of modern citizen status—namely, social benefits for those in need. These benefits, which are the product of political decisions and which are implemented through various forms of welfare and social security policies, establish a public "good," which in principle and in practice is a scarce resource. The capacity of a political community to distribute "goods" of this type can and must be logically construed as a "zero-sum game." As popular wisdom holds, you can only spend a dollar once. No voter forfeits his rights by granting voting rights to others (however much the distribution of power in the form of voting rights decreases the influence of each vote); he is, however, deprived of a share of society's resources when these resources are distributed to others in the form of public benefits.

Many of the problems western democracies have encountered with their welfare systems arise from a particular political consensus about citizenship—that decoupling the third dimension from the other two would not be legitimate and would constitute a relapse into a premodern form of "uncivilized" capitalism. Thus, most of the discussion today about recent cutbacks in welfare benefits is aimed at "down-loading" costs to local communities and private organizations.[27]

If, however, an uncoupled "Marshallian" citizen status is a limited resource that cannot be granted beyond a political community's capacity to redistribute collective "goods" and welfare benefits, studies of national welfare systems show that this capacity has no absolute margin. Rather, it can adjust—as international and intertemporal comparisons demonstrate—to quite different standards of public welfare supports. Many factors seem to have an impact on the willingness of a political community to maintain a high standard of welfare redistribution and its capacity to do so. With respect to the latter, almost everything depends on the ability of the political regime to collect—through taxes, duties and other resources—the necessary amount of money.[28] But with respect to the former, the willingness of the electorate and of political representatives to support generous redistributive measures seems to depend crucially upon the range of inequality and the sense of "togetherness" (*Wir-Gefühl*). Inasmuch as the EU currently lacks a sufficient sense of togetherness embedded in a common political culture and widens the range of inequality enormously in comparison with individual member states, it seems likely that both of these factors will play a key role in the future process of integration.

THE CONSTITUTION OF DEMOCRATIC COMMUNITIES: COMMUNICATION AND POLITICAL SPACE

The second fundamental aspect of the constitution of any polity is related to the fact that every polity is based on a distinct realm of communication and meaning through which it establishes its unique political space. This political space may differ from the territory in geographical terms. Indeed, it is to some extent virtual and even metaphorical (as in identifying oneself with political symbols as represented by institutions, flags, anthems, or persons). However, it also requires practically grounded fundaments in face-to-face communication. The terms "western democracy" and "the West" (used frequently throughout this book) are examples of concepts that refer to a virtual space. They lack a clear territorial base, but their use denotes a historical political space[29] that, while vaguely specified, is still distinct from "the other."[30] Although not always clearly defined in this manner, these terms are understood to imply clear differences, as did the older distinction between Orient and Occident.[31]

Then, there are those processes and acts of communication by which a polity is de facto constituted and continued. All political and social interactions can be seen as "communication"; without this communicative aspect of interaction, social and political life, particularly in the sense already described, cannot develop and continue.[32] This seems almost trivial. But political science has not paid much attention to the various factors that shape this "trivial" prerequisite of politics. Both the will and decree of an absolute ruler or dictator and the content of constitutional rights and parliamentary laws in representative democracies must somehow be communicated throughout the polity. The differences between the face-to-face communication of ancient times, that of "town criers" running through the streets of medieval city states, and modern mass communication with its sophisticated use of TV, the Internet, and satellites, may be quite marked. Even so, every polity has to secure a steady flow of at least some information within its various sectors just to maintain basic functions. In particular, the public sphere—as distinct from the *arcanae imperii*—has always been essential in establishing a polity's identity.

The truism that any polity rests upon communication changes into a fundamental ontological and normative principle in the case of democratic polities, for it is their claim, with some historical basis, to be rooted in the communication of citizens.[33] Both the Federalist Papers and the minutes of the French Assemblée Nationale of 1789 describe the founding of "western democracies," a process in which public deliberation contributed to a revolutionary creation of polities and institutional and legal order. That this kind of communication took place in public and was reflected in the public sphere was essential to the creation of the United States of America and the modern French Grande Nation. The French debates between the Girondistes and the Jacobeans, in particular, were heard and discussed all over Europe. As far away as Koenigsberg on the eastern Baltic coast, a Prussian professor of philosophy recognized the revolutionary principles of that discourse and incorporated them into a philosophical system for a modern republic based on the assumption that only the unrestricted use of men's capacity to reason and deliberate could establish a world order of "free republics," thereby creating the "eternal peace" for which mankind longed.[34]

Public deliberation is the unrestricted exchange of opinions that takes place in certain political institutions (for example, parliaments and councils) or in public meetings and demonstrations through the programs and platforms of associations, organizations, and parties. This exchange may be expressed in writing or in other ways and is delivered through the media or face-to-face. It is a permanent process and constitutes the democratic regime that, by no accident, has been called "government by opinion."

Regardless of the various institutional manifestations of this political regime, at the heart of its normative principles is the belief that the exchange of opinions among free and politically equal citizens or their representatives is the only legitimate basis for the generation of laws and the exercise of political power. The use of other means of influence—money, pressure, or even violence—can undermine and ultimately replace any democratic polity's rhetorical fabric. It cannot, however, replace the public exchange of arguments and opinions as the source of legitimacy once this has been established. Democracy, more than any other form of polity, is a communicative order, and the adequate support and loyalty of its citizens, notwithstanding their dissent on various matters at any point in time, are the only precondition of its existence.[35] If this support is withdrawn, as it was in Germany at the end of the 1920s, then true democracy ceases to exist.

THE EUROPEAN UNION AS AN INDEPENDENT SOURCE OF GOVERNANCE

I want to use the preceding discussion of the two fundamental conditions for the creation of a democratic polity as a basis for evaluating the institutional and political realities of the contemporary EU to demonstrate that, though the Single European Act and the Maastricht Treaty have made the EU a powerful and effective polity sui generis, they have not made it a democratic one. Furthermore, I show why, if integration proceeds on its present trend, it is not probable that the new polity will become democratic.

I start with the assumption that the EU already exists as a polity in its own right beyond the member states that created it, though I shall have more to say later about what kind of polity it is.[36] The EU can be categorized as an independent source of governance because it effectively and legitimately establishes political aims and policy programs and reinforces their implementation through its own competencies, resources, and instruments. The policies relating to the establishment and subsequent processing and regulation of the European Common Market (ECM) for goods and services are a particularly good example of this, as are those in related fields, for example research and development, food production and supply, and most recently, electrical energy.

As Fritz Scharpf has ably demonstrated, the legislative and legal actions of the EU (especially the Commission and its instruments) during the introduction of the ECM have led to a continuing process of "negative integration," whereby national standards and market restrictions are being erased or reduced to the lowest common denominator.[37] This is especially evident in the "labor market," where the introduction of European market rules has severely weakened national welfare programs by exposing them to the "free" competition of labor from markets where such programs are nonexistent. The erosion of national welfare standards in the wake of the ECM is inevitable, however, because the EU has never had either the mandate or the resources to create effective substitutes at the regional level.[38] Indeed, from the EU's perspective, all programs of this sort, whether in the area of job security or health care, are nothing more than illegal obstacles to the growth of a free market in Europe.

Insofar as it lacks a strong ideological foundation, the ECM is consistent with the neoliberal economics currently fashionable in international economies. The sole, but very important, exception to this is the common market for agricultural goods, which alone consumes over 40 percent of the total budget of the EU. With its policy mix of protectionism and subventionism, it is almost the opposite of a liberal market policy, and its existence attests to the fact that the dismantling of regulative policies and the growing power of markets are the product of political decisions alone, not historical logic or necessity.

But if the ECM project poses a threat to national welfare policies in the member states, it also furnishes incontrovertible evidence that the EU has for some time been an increasingly relevant, independent, and effective source of governance within a polycentric, multilevel political regime.[39] This regime must be considered a multilevel system, because today each member state operates on at least three levels of government (four levels, for the Austrian and German federations).[40] It must be described as "polycentric" because the EU's centralist institutions and competencies exist alongside national governments and local authorities, which continue to enjoy their own legacies, authorities, and policy capacities.

As for the EU's independence, it is sometimes argued that the national governments remain more powerful than their counterparts in Brussels. This is difficult to ascertain, since to date there has not been a sufficiently fundamental power conflict between the EU and the member states. Such a conflict is indeed unlikely to arise between the EU and each of the national governments simultaneously; at most, there might be a confrontation between the EU and a "weak coalition" of member governments. Under present circumstances, moreover, a victory of national sovereignty in those fields in which the EU has effectively and legally established its governing authority (such as all questions concerning the European Common Market) is no longer certain.

According to Max Weber's famous definition of a modern state, a "monopoly over the legitimate use of violence" is a necessary element of sovereignty. Certainly, the EU does not possess military or police forces of its own to enforce its authority in the face of national resistance; even fines levied by the European Court for failure to comply with EU policies must be paid voluntarily. However, by classifying the EU as an independent and effective level of governance, I do not presume its "sovereignty." Rather, I question whether sovereignty in the Weberian sense is any longer a necessary and realistic requirement of governance. For example, a great many states today, especially smaller ones, are no longer sovereign in any practical sense. Beyond the purely formal sense of the term, modern-day federal states provide instructive precursors of the new reality, with federal governments frequently having fewer resources and instruments of enforcement than their member units.[41] The most remarkable case might be that of the Swiss federal government, which, in conflicts with important cantons, cannot rely on superior instruments of enforcement. Or, consider the case of Canada. Can anyone seriously imagine the federal government in Ottawa embarking on an armed crusade against Quebec?

What these federal systems demonstrate is that sovereignty is not a precondition for effective governance; rather, today's federations can accommodate sophisticated systems of distribution and sharing of legal competence and power resources. Often, the federal government has to rely on the support of subfederal units of government and administration for the implementation of internal policies and the performance of basic functions, such as collecting taxes. But this does not mean that the federal government is unable to govern. In opposition to Carl Schmitt, I submit that the evaluation of a political regime's capacity to govern should not focus on the extreme cases of constitutional conflict, states of emergency, or civil war, but instead on the routine business of day-to-day governing.[42] In the EU, as in other federations, a situation might arise in which internal authority becomes precarious and the usual procedures of conflict resolution and negotiation are no longer adequate. Such rare situations, however, should not be made the exclusive basis for judging the political capacities of a federation.

What about the fact that none of the European treaties provides for the eventuality of a member state choosing to quit the EU? This indicates only that no legal grounds exist for secession. As any historian or political scientist would acknowledge, it does not mean that secession or even the breakup of the federation cannot occur. The same is true of the EU's opting-out procedures—for example, Britain's long-standing refusal to accept the EU's Social Charter, which it reversed only recently, or the May 1998 decision by Britain, Sweden, and Denmark to stay out of the first round of EMU. While the use of such measures does indicate that national governments question the EU's authority in certain areas, it does not argue against the EU functioning as a government in all other respects. On the contrary, the practice of opting out and thereby allowing for different speeds and intensities of integration within the EU has proved to be a good means of reinforcing integration in the medium and long terms. The Schengen Treaty, which at the behest of some member states is increasingly becoming the basis for a common European security and immigration policy, provides an excellent example.

So, it seems clear that the EU has successfully established itself as a government on the European level, relatively independent like any national government, but acting above and beyond the national member states. What is less clear, however, is of which polity it is a government, and whether this polity, in light of the above discussion of traditional polities, has a definite membership and occupies a specific political space.

THE EUROPEAN UNION: POLITY, MEMBERSHIP, AND POLITICAL SPACE

The EU has been established through international treaties, whose signatories have been national governments using traditional legal and political competencies to enter international contracts, competencies resting on the principle of majority rule. In most cases, the national parliaments of the member states have ratified these treaties; national plebiscites have also sometimes been part of the ratification process. In Germany, the Constitutional Court has ruled that any action the German government takes as part of the process of European integration and any impact European policies have on German citizens must meet the normative standards and requirements of the German Basic Law. The Court has also established a parallel legal reservation with respect to the rulings of the European Court. Thus, while it has not yet declared any aspect of European politics or law as illegal, it has definitely established its right to do so.

The emergence of the EU and its respective transnational level of governance must therefore be seen as an intergovernmental affair, with "government" construed broadly enough to include executive agencies, legislators, and courts at national and EU levels. Furthermore, we must add that "membership" in this emergent new political unit is defined by political elites and bureaucrats at the EU national levels.[43] Despite the fact that each possesses a legitimate general political mandate and a general political authorization for political action, none has a special European mandate or even a specific national mandate for European transnational politics. Although the issue of European integration has figured prominently in national election campaigns, elections to the European parliament, the proper forum for dealing with such matters, do not allow the electorate a democratic voice.

While the EU seems to be perceived—and accordingly treated—as an independent and special polity in its own right by national governing elites,[44] all available evidence suggests that the vast majority of national citizens have quite a different perspective. Apart from a small and politically almost irrelevant minority of European enthusiasts, most citizens still identify themselves as members of their various national polities. They view the European level of government as an international appendage of their own national government, which implicates some of their national interests and "shares," but which is not itself their polity. The fact that a majority of Europeans in regular polls of the "Eurobarometer" has a generally positive reaction to the EU is not relevant in this regard.[45] Polls, in which voters are asked about their general orientation toward the EU, are quite different from elections, in which voters are structurally forced to identify and prioritize issues in order to make coherent use of their single vote. Another reason for the relative disengagement of European citizens is the "abstract" scope of European policies: taxation, welfare benefits, and normative issues like abortion or immigration are still not seen as issues definitively to be dealt with at the European level.[46]

Although the EU recently began to use the term "European citizen" in official documents and treaties—and national governments accordingly have begun issuing "European passports"—none of these documents has any real operational function so far. After all, the principal precondition for holding a European passport is citizenship in one of the EU's member states, and passports are still issued by national governments. While the emergent political institutions and organizations of European government have gained an existence and power sui generis, European "citizen-

ship" is merely derivative of national legacies. It remains mainly symbolic, and evokes a false impression of the new political status of
individuals in the EU, which is not based on reality. It is true, however,
at least at the local level in the so-called European election, that all "European citizens" now have the unrestricted right to vote and to stand for
election. But, again, the national parties that control the process of nomi-
nation make rare use of the possibility of running non-national candidates. The task of evaluating the dimensions of any such transformations
in grassroots politics across the Union awaits deeper empirical research.

Thus, if we wish to categorize the system of European government not
only as a government but also as a polity, we must immediately acknowledge that its body politic is constituted not by citizens but by political
and administrative elites.[47] These elites fall into two groups: the agents of
national governments constituting the various Councils, and the genuine
European bureaucrats and politicians (especially the members of the
Commission, the European Court, and, to a lesser extent, the members of
the so-called European parliament). Members of the former group are in
a somewhat paradoxical position. Although they act on the European
level and may occasionally be forced in this capacity to transgress their
national interest in order to deepen European integration, they are still
perceived as national representatives by their own citizens and those (insofar as they care at all) of other nation-states. The latter group, by contrast—especially the members of the Commission, who constitute the effective executive power on the newly generated European level of
government—is almost unknown to national publics. If it is identified at
all by the national electorates, it tends to be as the subject of bureaucratic
or nationalist denunciation.[48] The European Court, for its part, is virtually
unrecognized outside a small circle of juridical and academic experts, and
the work of the European parliament remains obscure to the vast majority
of citizens. Finally, the citizens themselves exist only as citizens of the
member states and as such are only subject to the EU's rulings—they do
not have any real opportunity to participate in formulating them. To the
extent that the EU is a polity, then, it is a polity without real citizens.

And what of the other constitutive dimension of a polity—a political
space grounded in communication? Communication related to the EU,
and particularly communication concerning its various policies, seems to
be structured in a very complex and fragmented way. European communication in the true sense of the word exists only within specific European
elite networks that are part of the European governing apparatus, or
closely related to it. European political, juridical, and administrative elites
are one example; other examples would be the networks of European research that seem to play an important role in establishing and reinforcing

something like a European "spirit" or even "creed," and the ongoing networking process in various political, cultural, and economic fields.[49]

Many observers refer to this growing Europe-wide system of communication networks—in which a large number of national organizations, associations, and, more recently, social movements and nongovernmental organizations try to coordinate their actions—as the emergent "civil society" of the EU.[50] I reject this characterization, however, because very few citizens are involved on this level. Owing to the lack of a common public space beyond the national level, social movements and voluntary groups are seldom able to use their unique resources and patterns of action and mobilization (such as demonstrations, sit-ins, and acts of civil disobedience), and must rely instead on professional support and expertise to be effective. For example, although unions try to coordinate negotiations, industrial conflicts, and strikes, they have not yet reached, nor are they likely to reach, a capacity for combined and integrated action at the European level. The entire repertoire of informal protest action usually depends on amplification via mass media and requires the resonance of the national public sphere; at present, hardly any public action or demonstration, whether in Brussels or Strasbourg, achieves more than a local response.

From these examples of political action, interaction, and communication, we may conclude that a genuine political space within the EU has been established. Like any political space, it is restricted and exclusive; otherwise, we could not identify it as a specific political space at all. In contrast to most democratic nation-states, however, the political space and the communication that constitute the EU are semipublic, at best. In the governmental sphere, the most important legislative body of the EU, the European Council, as well as the various Councils formed by national ministers to address specific policy areas, typically do not sit, debate, and decide in public. This is a quite understandable consequence of their character as intergovernmental bodies, but while in this respect their action has to be seen as international negotiation, the outcome in many cases establishes European legislation. In truth, although these actors have legitimate national mandates as executives, they do not have any legitimacy as European legislators.

As for the spreading pan-European system of networking and communications, it too contributes to a European political space, but only in an issue-fragmented and semipublic way. In practice, most information is available exclusively to experts; its recognition and appropriation require expertise and facilities, such as access to networks and European agencies or to national ministries in charge of European matters. Here, it would be more appropriate to speak of a fragmented sublevel of European political space, subdivided into numerous policy arenas and not reintegrated into an interconnecting public sphere of European political concern.

Such a European political space, controlling and integrating various European policies as part of a coherent political agenda, does not exist beyond these various levels. Europeans who are not members of the elite, and who lack access to the genuine but restricted European political space described above, can see European politics and the EU only through the lenses of various national publics and mass media. European mass media beyond the national level do not exist.

One of the main reasons for the lack of a fully public European political space—a reason terribly neglected by social and political scientists, as well as by the political and administrative elites—is that all social communication is language based. The political space of every polity depends on its constituent "body politic" fulfilling certain language requirements; at a minimum, communication has to be understood. European political elites solve this problem, more or less successfully, by using a mixture of a lingua franca and translation services (especially for documents). The EU has adopted an official policy by which any language of any member state is also an official language of the EU.[51] As a rule, elites speak English as their lingua franca,[52] and all official EU documents are translated into each of the official languages, which usually takes months and is often finished only after even the experts have lost interest.[53]

While the practice of using English as a lingua franca facilitates elite communication and integration, the difficulty of disseminating information in other languages is a serious impediment to public participation.[54] Those who resist this argument point to multicultural and multilingual societies like Belgium, Canada, and especially Switzerland—the latter having four official languages. In the Swiss case, political communication is based on what has been called "passive foreign language capabilities" among the three largest language groups of the country (excluding the Rhätoromanisch minority, despite its legal recognition). The Swiss educational system seems to guarantee that any native speaker has the capacity at least to understand the other two languages. Canadian language policy is based on the same assumption, though empirical observation raises grave doubts as to whether official claims would hold up under practical tests.[55] But whatever the success of these multilingual polities, they cannot serve as a blueprint for the establishment of a common European political space.[56] Even with substantial educational support, only passive knowledge of one or two languages, including English, would be attainable for most European citizens. Clearly, the introduction of English as the official lingua franca of the EU is the only solution to the language aspect of the problem of creating a common European political space. Given the present political and cultural realities of the EU, the possibility of such a decision being taken must be seen as utopian, particularly in light of the EU's plans to enlarge its membership.

In any case, practical language requirements are only one precondition for a common European political space. A polity must also have a common political culture; it must ascribe the same meaning to the same phenomena, refer to common social practices and symbols, and have common institutions.[57] Despite the fact that European nation-states share, in a very broad sense, a common European historical and cultural heritage, they are also home to a diverse array of cultures in general, and political cultures in particular. This cultural diversity has contributed to enormous institutional variation in legal systems and constitutional politics, in procedures and understandings of western democracy, and in systems of taxation, public health care, schooling and education, welfare, and retirement. There seems little doubt that the EU would have to adopt a multicultural policy of some sort in order to forge the common institutional or cultural links necessary to foster the development of a common European political space. However, in so doing, it would be grappling with a greater number of languages and a wider variety of local and national political cultures and institutions than any federal polity has ever done before. Furthermore, although federal systems can accommodate a great deal of internal variation in their institutions and legal foundations, they also need "something" that holds them together as a polity and that constitutes a common political space. This "something" might have been partly contingent in history, in which case different "somethings" could play that role in the future. What is certain, nevertheless, is that not every aspect mentioned above could be different at the same time. If the federal example seems to hold some promise, European enthusiasts must remember that most of today's federations were not voluntarily created out of a variety of formerly separate polities; they were established long ago and usually by force.

CAN THE EUROPEAN UNION BECOME A DEMOCRACY?

Taking all of the above into account, I would conclude that the current integration process in the EU, with its limited focus on economic matters, will fall short in the project of creating a common European political space beyond the elite level. The functionalist theory of political integration, which has portrayed and accompanied the process of European integration since its inception, was altogether too optimistic about the possible long-term "spin-offs" and "spill-overs" of economic integration into a common market.[58] It was correct only in its assumption that the requirements of creating a common economic market—and subsequently of controlling its functioning—would, over some period of time, give rise to a system of European governance. In this respect, institutions have followed function as theoretically predicted. These institutions have since acquired substantial and independent political power, and a new power center and form of governance has been established. The new form, however, is not as responsible, not as accountable, not as accessible to citizen participation, and not even as visible as its predecessors—the national governments in the EU's member states. Worse, the more power it gets, the more pronounced its democratic deficit becomes.

To reach this conclusion, no very elaborate concept of "participatory" or "deliberative" democracy has been used. The new system of European governance falls short even of the elite model of representative democracy or polyarchy explored in the normative tradition of Schumpeter. It lacks the fundamental prerequisites: namely, a common political space in which competition among political elites and elections for government could take place, a "body politic" of citizens to which it would be responsible, and, finally, a political space and public sphere of its own in which agenda setting and issue prioritization could take place and be recognized by the governed.[59] If we were to raise our normative expectations of democratic politics in keeping with current trends in elite-based representative western democracies, and consider the EU in relation to the models of "participatory democracy," "strong democracy," and "deliberative democracy," our judgment would have to be even harsher.[60]

The prevalence of these latter models in the discourse of western democracies today reflects a growing sense of dissatisfaction with traditional democracy. As political scientists should recognize, the legitimacy of political regimes—and democratic ones, in particular—rests not only on their simple normative acceptance as regimes, but also on the evaluation of their policy outcomes and their openness to citizen participation. What has been called input legitimacy and output legitimacy in comparative research on democratic regimes may vary across political cultures and regimes, but no regime could completely neglect one of the two dimensions of legitimacy and still call itself democratic. Public dissatisfaction may currently encompass both dimensions, but insofar as the models referred to above call for more participation, more responsibility for citizens, and a more "open" process of policy formation, they clearly indicate a crisis on the side of input legitimacy. Such a crisis cannot be resolved merely by increasing satisfaction with policy output. Citizens want to be informed, to be involved, and to have their concerns taken seriously in democratic politics; it is not just better politics "for the people," it is also "by the people."

In the EU today, citizen activists of all stripes seem to favor an antielitist, activist, participatory, often antiestablishment, anti-institutional, antiprofessional, issue-oriented, and problem-solving approach to democratic politics, which emphasizes the importance of voluntary action and participation by citizens. This trend has echoes throughout western democracies and is "beyond left and right."[61] Whether it could be properly interpreted as portending a renaissance of democratic citizenship in the republican tradition, or marks the beginning of what Robert Dahl foresaw as the "third wave" of democratization in the progress of western civilization, remains to be seen.[62] What is clear, however, is that the stronger the trend toward increased citizen involvement, the greater the difference in political quality between national governments and the EU system of governance, and the wider the gap between national political spaces and the restricted European political space.

Representative political regimes can encompass much larger and more complex political spaces than participatory democracies. The latter require more face-to-face communication, and the extent to which virtual communication by means of computer networks and audiovisual techniques could meet this need is still open to dispute. Certainly, these media, almost like spoken languages, establish specific requirements and thus create selective barriers against open and equal participation. More to the point, despite utopian technical visions of "computer democracy" and "globalization," it seems as if increasingly more citizen activists have developed a new awareness of what has always been the historical experience of democracy—specifically, the experience that democratic politics is always locally based. Only certain kinds of political space, therefore—space that is not too abstract or too far extended—are within the realm of practical experience. In other words, there may be a correspondence between human nature and the size and concreteness of a certain political space, which current trends toward expanding networks of communication in general, and political communication in particular, run against. The expansion of regimes of rule and power beyond this measure, whether by means of technical assistance or more abstract systems of representation, would render people mere subjects.

The present political regime of the EU is already in danger of overstretching the national mandates of representative elites acting on the European level. If these elites were to be put under greater pressure in their respective national polities by the demands of citizens for a more democratic political process, their room for maneuvering on the European level would be reduced. This would endanger even the elitist approach to European unification. The EU cannot become a democracy by following the road thus far taken. If it is to continue to develop as a regime of legitimate governance, it urgently requires a new model of democracy that will be acceptable beyond the limits of national political space. A simple expansion of the model of representative democracy is not likely to be adequate to this task of legitimation. Indeed, whether much larger political spaces can be reconstituted democratically is perhaps the most important political question today. We are left to ponder much more than the phrase "democracy and global order" usually implies.[63] Can the emergent global political order in principle be democratic, and what would that mean? The search for answers is becoming more urgent.

NOTES

1. This is meant as a *terminus technicus* of political analysis; see Michael Th. Greven, ed., *Demokratie—eine Kultur des Westens* (Opladen, Germ.: Leske & Budrich, 1998).

2. Taking the EU as an example does not limit the scope and intention of my arguments, which target any form of "translocal" politics.

3. See Michael Th. Greven, "Political Parties between National Identity and Eurofication," in *The Idea of Europe: Problems of National and Transnational Identity*, ed. Brian Nelson, David Roberts, and Walter Veit (New York and Oxford: Berg, 1992).

4. "Wir-Gefühl" in the sense of the political sociology of Max Weber and especially Rudolf Heberle, who turned this notion into the key concept of his political sociology. See Heberle, *Social Movements: An Introduction to Political Sociology* (New York: Appleton-Century-Crofts, 1951).

5. A valid parliamentary regime is usually defined in textbooks as a regime with a government created out of and responsible to the parliament. Despite the fact that the EU parliament has gained some additional rights, especially in agenda setting and codetermination competencies, it has not even aimed at true parliamentarism. On the issue of agenda setting in particular, see George Tsebelis, "The Power of the European Parliament as a Conditional Agenda Setter," *American Political Science Review* 88, no. 1 (1994): 128–142.

6. See Simon Hix and Chris Lord, "Partisanship and Party Formation in European Union Politics," *Comparative Politics* 24 (1997): 167–186.

7. In addition, "European elections" are not even held on the basis of a common electoral law, nor are they held on the same day.

8. To what extent they effectively share governing power is the subject of much dispute among experts on European integration.

9. In an earlier article, I came close to that conclusion; see Michael Th. Greven, "Der politische Raum als Maß des Politischen: Europa als Beispiel," in *Europäische Institutionenpolitik: Mannheimer Jahrbuch für Europäische Sozialforschung*, ed. Thomas König and Edgar Reiger, vol. 2 (Frankfurt am Main and New York: Campus, 1997), 45–64. My chapter here carries the analysis beyond that dead end.

10. Restricting my argument for the purpose of this chapter, I neglect the very likely possibility that the "principles" of democracy are of a historical character as well and, as a result, are open to change. Too many contingencies at once render impossible not only any consistent argument, but also social and political order.

11. Indeed, when Alexander Hamilton used this concept for the first (docu-

mented) time in the history of political thought in the *Federalist Papers*, it was still understood as an oxymoron, if it was understood at all.

12. For a review of recent theoretical literature on "institutions" and the analytical approach of "Neo-Institutionalism," see Michael Th. Greven, "Political Institutions and the Building of Democracy," *European Journal of Political Research* 27, no. 4 (1995): 463–475.

13. Michael Th. Greven, *Systemtheorie und Gesellschaftsanalyse: Kritik der Werte und Erkenntnismöglichkeiten in Gesellschaftsmodellen der kybernetischen Systemtheorie* (Darmstadt und Neuwied: Luchterhand, 1974).

14. Louis W. Pauly has asked exactly this question with reference to the disembedded international finance, "inevitably governing the lives of citizens in an increasingly global economy, [but] the consent of the governed has not been adequately sought." See Pauly, "Capital Mobility, State Autonomy and Political Legitimacy," *Journal of International Affairs* 48, no. 2 (1995): 371. See also his *Who Elected the Bankers?* (Ithaca, N.Y.: Cornell University Press, 1997).

15. A position still held by Hannah Arendt in her famous *The Human Condition* (Chicago: University of Chicago Press, 1958).

16. See Christian Meier, *Die Entstehung des Politischen bei den Griechen* (Frankfurt am Main: Suhrkamp, 1983).

17. This is intended to cut a long story short—namely the influence of Christianity on public thinking and political "theory" after Augustine, bringing the superhuman powers back for another millennium.

18. See Mogens H. Hansen, *The Athenian Democracy in the Age of Demosthenes: Structure, Principles and Ideology* (Oxford and Cambridge: Basil Blackwell, 1991).

19. I exclude here the problem of so-called stateless people—people who have, for various reasons, lost or never gained membership status anywhere—so lucidly and poignantly analyzed by Hannah Arendt in *The Origins of Totalitarianism* (New York: Harcourt, 1951).

20. I refer here to the more abstract level of "principles" and not to the historical process of building a democracy out of "something," a process that in many cases contrasts sharply with the somewhat idealistic self-perception of this type of regime. Think of Hannah Arendt's famous essay *On Revolution* (New York: Viking, 1963), a nice example of permanently confusing both levels.

21. As symbolized in the famous front-page engraving of Thomas Hobbes's *Leviathan*, for instance, which metaphorically suggests the "body politic" constituted by human beings, but which also confirms that this idea is not restricted to the democratic tradition.

22. There is substantial empirical evidence that western democracies tolerate enormous inequality in wealth, income, and the supply of public goods.

23. "One man-one vote"—recently called the "omov-principle" in analytical democratic theory by Claus Offe.

24. See Thomas H. Marshall, *Class, Citizenship and Social Development* (Garden City, N.Y.: Doubleday, 1964).

25. "No taxation without representation . . ."?

26. In the Greek *polis*, the capacity to defend the polity in war was the fundamental requirement for citizenship. Since women, slaves, and *metökes* were not seen as trustworthy warriors, they were not granted this status.

27. The principle that modern citizen status must in⸱ ⸱⸱de the third "Marshall-ian" dimension is seldom questioned, with one telliⁿ⸱ ⸱⸱⸱eption—the treatment of and propaganda against immigrants and refugees. Center-right European governments of the 1980s and 1990s provide a compelling example of this exception. The most straightforward and outspoken claims to decouple social benefits from other rights of membership for immigrants and refugees have all been made by parties and groups on the extreme right in Europe. By focusing attention on the basic scarcity of social benefits (coupled regularly up to now with citizenship), these claims hit at a weak point of western democracies. This might help to explain why there is so much hidden support for such policies in even the more moderate parts of the electorate, and why democratic parties have begun to respond to public pressure by taking action against the formerly well-established consensus.

28. Although I leave aside the question of public debts here, I will mention that incurring debts against the public budget does not avoid the zero-sum character of the game of distributing scarce resources. Rather, it merely hides it temporarily from the public, which enjoys the benefits today, leaving others to "settle the bill" later on.

29. Since my focus in this chapter is the polity, I do not refer explicitly to the obvious fact that most of what is said here would also be true for cultural space. In fact, each is historically not quite separate from the other, though they may differ in extension, and polities that are different in character may share a common cultural space. On the cultural foundations of democracy see Greven, *Demokratie.*

30. See Melvin Richter, "Europe and 'The Other' in Eighteenth-Century Thought," in *Politisches Denken: Jahrbuch 1997,* ed. Karl Graf Ballestrem et al. (Stuttgart/Weimar: J. B. Metzler, 1997), 25–47.

31. Rainer Brandt, "Europa in der Reflexion der Aufklärung," in *Politisches Denken: Jahrbuch 1997,* ed. Karl Graf Ballestrem et al. (Stuttgart/Weimar: J. B. Metzler, 1997), 1–24.

32. "Language—not money or force—provides legitimacy." See John Ralston Saul, *Voltaire's Bastards: The Dictatorship of Reason in the West* (New York: Free Press, 1992). I owe my knowledge of this text and quotation to Pauly, "Capital Mobility, State Autonomy and Political Legitimacy."

33. James S. Fishkin provides a good account of this part of the democratic tradition. See Fishkin, *The Voice of the People: Public Opinion and Democracy* (New Haven: Yale University Press, 1997).

34. Volker Gerhardt offers a remarkable account and analysis of Immanuel Kant's still extremely modern and revolutionary political philosophy—if you overlook its foundation in transcendental idealism. See Gerhardt, *Immanuel Kants Entwurf zum ewigen Frieden* (Darmstadt: Wissenschaftliche Buchgesellschaft, 1995).

35. I must stress that a democratic polity's constitution through "communicative action" does not automatically imply the idealistic premises of a specific philosophy of language, such as that of Jürgen Habermas. For an examination of normatively founded political philosophies such as that of Habermas, see Michael

Th. Greven, "Power and Communication in Habermas and Luhmann: A Critique of Communicative Reductionism," in *Political Discourse: Explorations in Indian and Western Political Thought*, ed. B. Parekh and T. Pantham (New Delhi: Sage, 1987), 179–193.

36. While the older literature frequently used the concept "state" or "super-state," it has recently become common practice to use "polity" and thus avoid closer questions with reference to the EU's specific political character; that the EU is now a genuine polity of its own is no longer seriously contested. See Liesbet Hooghe, ed., *Cohesion Policy and European Integration: Building Multi-Level Governance* (Oxford: Oxford University Press, 1996); Gary Marks et al., eds., *Governance in the European Union* (London: Sage, 1996); and Neil Nugent, *The Government and Politics of the European Union* (London: Macmillan, 1994).

37. See Fritz W. Scharpf, "Negative and Positive Integration in the Political Economy of European Welfare States," in *Governance in the European Union*, ed. Gary Marks et al. (London: Sage, 1996), 15–39.

38. See Stephan Leibfried and Paul Pierson, eds., *European Social Policy: Between Fragmentation and Integration* (Washington, D.C.: Brookings, 1995).

39. See Hooghe, *Cohesion Policy and European Integration*; Markus Jachtenfuchs and Beate Kohler-Koch, eds., *Europäische Integration* (Opladen, Germ.: Leske & Budrich, 1996).

40. I do not address here the question of whether the so-called regions could or should be counted as additional independent levels of government, as it is not relevant to my argument.

41. I suggest this comparison with modern-day federal states just for the sake of comparison, and ignore the implicit assumption that one could describe the EU as a federal *state*.

42. See Carl Schmitt, *Politische Theologie: Vier Kapitel zur Lehre von der Souveränität* (Berlin: Duncker & Humboldt, 1934).

43. Remember that I treat the Councils, the Commission, and its *apparatus* throughout this paper as a government, so my thesis does *not* lay claim merely to the residual character of EU politics, as William Wallace and others have done, but includes the European government. See Wallace, "Walking Backwards Towards Unity," in *Policy-Making in the European Communities*, ed. William Wallace, Helen Wallace, and Christopher Webb (London: Wiley, 1983), 301–323.

44. In addition, more than 100 regional or local governments from the territory of the EU had opened permanent offices in Brussels by the mid-1990s. Functionally and institutionally, these offices bear a strong resemblance to traditional "embassies."

45. Recently, Ulf Hedetoft convincingly criticized the usual interpretation of "Eurobarometer"-based data. See Hedetoft, "National Identities and European Integration 'From Below': Bringing the People Back In," *Journal of European Integration* 28, no. 1 (1993): 1–28. One does not need to assume, however, a zero-sum relationship between national and European identities. See Soledad Garcia, ed., *European Identity and the Search for Legitimacy* (London: Pinter, 1993). But my point here relates to how citizens continue to resolve contested policy questions.

46. Again, we have the interesting exception of the European agricultural pol-

icy—the farmers and their national associations all over Europe constitute something like a *single policy area polity.*

47. See Helen Wallace, "The Institutions of the EU: Experience and Experiments," in *Policy-Making in the European Union,* ed. Helen Wallace and William
Wallace (Oxford: Oxford University Press, 1996), 37–68.

48. For example, and most prominently, the commissioner responsible for the
European agricultural market.

49. I refer both to research on the EU and the various aspects of the process of
European integration, as well as to research within and by European institutions,
programs, and networks, initiated and sponsored by the EU.

50. See Beate Kohler-Koch, "Changing Patterns of Interest Intermediation in
the European Union," *Government and Opposition* 29, no. 2 (1994): 166–180. In the
early 1990s, the number of interest groups regularly present in Brussels was already estimated at more than 3,000; see Sven S. Andersen and Kjell Eliassen, eds.,
Making Policy in Europe: The Europeification of National Policy-Making (London:
Sage, 1993).

51. There arises the problem that, in some member states, more than one official language is established and legally recognized for internal use, as in Spain.
The Belgian case is of particular interest. Because the EU has French-, German-,
and Dutch-speaking members, Belgium has ready access to documents in these
three "national" languages and does not have to confront the problem of asking
the EU to translate all official documents into three additional languages. This
fortuitous circumstance has allowed Belgium to circumvent its internal problem.
The case of Catalan or Corse clearly would pose a more difficult problem.

52. With the exception of the French diplomats . . .

53. Close to 40 percent of the budget for personnel expenses on the level of the
EU *apparatus* is spent on translators and interpreters.

54. This argument is reminiscent of the centuries-old debate about the use of
Latin in Catholic services.

55. Despite the fact that a French-speaking immigration to Quebec also exists,
the steady growth of an overwhelmingly English-speaking, or at least English-
learning, immigration (accounting in Toronto for more than 40 percent, and in
Vancouver for more than 30 percent, of the total population) will rapidly contribute in the future to the domination of English as the sole practically used lingua
franca in Canada outside of certain schools and institutions in Quebec.

56. I also have personal experience of the Indian case, where two lingua franca
coexist and every educated person at least understands three languages; when
this is not the case, then either Hindi or English is the individual's mother tongue.

57. In a well-researched article on the adoption of Beethoven's "Ode to Joy" as
the new European anthem, Caryl Clark recently quoted a wonderful example
from the committee in charge, which indicates the intricacies of language policies
involved; although the music of the "Ode to Joy" was a relatively straightforward
choice, members "expressed doubt about the words [of the German poet Friedrich Schiller], which were in the nature of a universal expression of faith rather
than a specifically European one. Other committee members wondered whether
any words acknowledged as 'European' could ever be translated into another lan-

guage and accepted as such by linguistic groups of the European family." See Clark, "Forging Identity: Beethoven's 'Ode' as European Anthem," *Critical Inquiry* 23 (Summer 1997): 798.

58. See Ernst B. Haas, *The Uniting of Europe* (Stanford, Calif.: Stanford University Press, 1958).

59. This is also the reason why such proposals as the "National (*sic!*) Issues Convention" (James S. Fishkin, *The Voice of the People: Public Opinion and Democracy* [New Haven: Yale University Press, 1997]), useful as they may be within an established polity, could not solve the problem within the EU.

60. There are many other concepts used by political actors in citizen groups, NGOs, and even parts of the more traditional European parties, as well as by scientific observers or political theorists.

61. See Anthony Giddens, *Beyond Left and Right: The Future of Radical Politics* (Cambridge, U.K.: Polity, 1994).

62. See Benjamin Barber, *Strong Democracy: Participatory Democracy for a New Age* (Berkeley: University of Berkeley Press, 1984); and Robert A. Dahl, *Democracy and Its Critics* (New Haven: Yale University Press, 1989).

63. See David Held, *Democracy and the Global Order: From Modern State to Cosmopolitan Governance* (Cambridge, U.K.: Polity, 1995).

4

The Democratic Welfare State in an Integrating Europe

Claus Offe

Everywhere, one reads the same thing: the European Union is a political construct sui generis—no (longer) a confederation, not (yet) a federal state, but a "would-be polity." It is an accurate but not very useful observation. If this definition "by process of elimination" were to have real informative value, it would include a clear accounting of the structural differences that set the EU apart from the more familiar form of political rule, the nation-state. We would then have a tool with which to assess the EU's functional capabilities, and in particular, its ability to organize society's exercise of power over itself that was as legitimate and efficient as that for the nation-state.

Accordingly, the first part of this chapter, like Greven's, will be devoted to a consideration of how the internal relations of the EU contrast with those of a nation-state republic.[1] This is followed in the second part by a review of the practical, political motives that have driven the process of integration thus far, which in turn are shaped by that process. The aim here is an assessment of the EU's political efficiency. The chapter concludes with an examination of the prospects for the development of a mode of European integration that enhances the EU's democratic legitimacy. Special attention is paid to the skeptical assumption that, on the way to "Europe," political resources (understood as society's ability to exercise control over its own quality and development through the means of governance) will be lost rather than gained.

THE INTERNAL RELATIONS OF A NATION-STATE REPUBLIC

Constitutional states differ from authoritarian and absolutist states in that political power in the former is not only exercised through law, but also established and limited, beforehand, by way of a special law—namely, the constitution. Thus, in a constitutional state, the body through which the state exercises its power is not just an empirical fact or a factual system of interactions, but also a formal, judicial fact vested with normative validity. Before the governing agency becomes active and expresses itself in concrete acts, it is already present as a normatively constituted fact, as something that "should be"—as a normative description of the governing body's method of operation, its jurisdiction, and the limitations thereon.

The act of establishing a constitution not only sets the modalities and limits of the (future) use of power but also reflects upon the author of the constitution. The establishment of the constitution must be conceived as an act in which the constituent member, the "people," forms itself and at the same time submits itself to the constitution. "The full sense of the term constitution implies . . . that it can be traced back to an act which the citizenry puts into place, or which is at least attributed to them, and in which they provide themselves with the political ability to take action."[2] In this respect, the act of establishing a constitution implies not only that a legal, ordered, and limited authority of the state exists but also that a political community of the "people" exists. This political community is created when a "people" submits itself to a political order of its own invention, in the process gaining an identity both within itself and toward the outside world.

Thus, in the act of establishing a constitution, the "people" ceases to be a mere ethnic fact—that is, a multitude of persons made distinct through their origin and common culture—and starts to become a *demos*, understood as the subject-object of a deliberately founded governing body. And yet, between *"ethnos"* (as the embodiment of an exclusive linguistic, religious, cultural community of origin) and *"demos"* (as the ethnically neutralized instance of the legitimation of state power), there is also continuity. Working as a catalyst, "the national self-image builds the cultural context in which subjects could become politically active citizens. It is only the sense of belonging to a 'nation' that establishes an interrelation of solidarity between persons who up to that point had been strangers to one another. . . . The nation or the spirit of the people . . . supplies the judicially constituted state with a cultural substratum."[3]

The foundation of a political community by an act of will is not a chance occurrence. Rather, it is the product of dispositions that Max Weber has characterized as "a belief in commonality" (*Gemeinsamkeitsglauben*) or "feelings of belonging to a community" (*Gemeinsamkeitsgefühle*); these dispositions "are nothing definite and can be fed by very different sources."[4] Despite the vagueness with which Weber outlines this empirical anchor of an act of will imposing set duties, it seems clear that in the case of the nation-state, the things believed or felt to be in common would be of a spatial or temporal nature. In other words, the self-recognition of a people as a *demos* has an empirical frame of reference, which encompasses a (usually undivided) territory settled together and a history understood as "concerning all of us." It is a fund of positive and negative traditions and historical protagonists, whose appropriation makes up the factual "particularity" of those who reciprocally recognize each other in normative terms as belonging to the same *demos*. Above all, the self-recognition of a people as a *demos* is grounded in the nation's history, which functions as a reference point for the establishment of a constitution in both positive (as a source of examples and traditions) and negative ways (as is often the case with post-totalitarian constitutions).

The historical-geographical grounding of the societal and governmental contract, which is completed *uno acto* with the establishment of the constitution, not only is a contingent condition for the formation of this contract but also may be a necessary condition for its continued existence. The importance of the historical or temporal aspect is demonstrated by settler societies such as the United States, where citizens' explicit memory of their common descent from far-flung ancestors becomes a basis for strengthening the willingness to practice interethnic tolerance, or by societies like Germany, where moral catastrophes remembered as part of a national history provide the foundation for the concretization of a constitutional consensus based on civil rights.

The geographic or spatial dimension of the determination of a political community centers on the role that well-established (that is, recognized by both sides) borders play in delineating the state's territory. National borders help integrate the people into the state's constitutional political order by minimizing conflicts over the area in which the order of law is valid as it pertains to individuals; that is, they guard against the emergence of a legal grey zone on the periphery, or a political claim to represent external ethnic minorities. Set territorial borders are also a reference point for the formation of a "people," as the crisis in southeastern Europe demonstrates. They serve this function by limiting the authority of the state to its spatially determined "area of validity" and preventing it from taking on a political "obligation to care for the welfare of persons" who may be "our" ethnic "brothers and sisters," but are not by virtue of this also our "cocitizens." Territorial borders are also essential for maintaining public welfare within states. They permit the political community to ensure that scarce resources are conserved for internal use and to stave off the intrusion of unwelcome outside influences. Borders are not barriers, but rather filters or membranes, which can be selectively opened from within—for example, to stimulate exports or control the flow of migration. They are the "decision points" at which the balance of positive and negative influx and outflux can be registered and controlled.[5]

Thus, the separate recognition of a common history and its meaning, and the shared recognition of a territory and its inhabitants, are together the indispensable catalysts for a political community coming into being. Conversely, sharp "historical-political" polarization is just as decisive a barrier on the way to the formation of a political community (or "republic") as is discrimination against internal minorities or care for the welfare of people outside the borders of the political community.

Geography and history are not, however, the end of the story. The political community of a *demos* is also defined by a third dimension—a duly constituted authority of state.[6] This authority manifests itself by imposing duties on citizens within the limits of basic rights and demanding the fulfillment of these duties within the framework of the state's monopoly on the legitimate use of force. In addition to the obligation to obey the law generally, there are most commonly three such civic duties: compulsory school attendance, compulsory military service (or the duty of military personnel to accept risks to life and limb caused by politics), and the obligation to pay taxes. Civic duties entail a loss of freedom for the individual, who must yield this freedom without the certainty of earning any benefit in return. In this respect, civic duties are informed by a principle similar to that of nonaffectation from budgetary law—that is, fulfilling one's duties does not create any right to a corresponding service. Rather, it is an offering "to all," the burden of which, under certain circumstances, is made lighter by the certainty that "all others" are likewise disposed toward fulfilling their duties, or can be forced to do so.

The double restriction civic duties place on freedom of action is illustrated by comparing them with a simple purchase. Purchases are the result of a two-tiered decision, made freely. In the first step, the buyer decides how much money to spend (instead of, say, giving it away or saving it); in the second step, the buyer decides which to obtain for the money spent. With civic duties, both of these freedoms are annulled. For example, schoolgoers (legally represented by their parents) typically have neither the freedom to refuse to attend school nor the right to determine the curriculum. Instead, curricula—like state budgetary expenditures or military defense obligations—are decided upon politically by the institutions and officeholders of the three areas of state authority entrusted with those responsibilities. The individual citizen is thereby integrated into a compulsory association of cultural, defense, national budgetary, and legal communities. Although all citizens ultimately determine the content and purpose of this association through the processes of democratic legitimation and political accountability, they perform this function not as individuals but as constituent members of a political community.

This account of civic duties is not intended to provide fodder for neoliberal attacks on the "vampire state," but rather to introduce two propositions. Vertically, the efficacy of a state's actions requires that citizens fulfill their duties automatically, or at least that the state be able to secure their compliance with minimal use of its resources. That which is expected of the individual citizen is nothing less than the feat of taking part "obediently" in an organization of rule that compels one to be a member of a cultural, economic, and defense community at the cost of some freedom, some possessions, and, in some cases, one's life. Horizontally, the fulfillment of civic duties depends upon every "duty-bound" citizen thinking of the collective author of normative duties (that is, the state, which is established by a democratic political process) and thus of "all other citizens" (who participated in that process) as capable of sufficient reason and goodwill to accept these duties as legitimate and binding.

In order for a citizen to recognize a duty as legitimate and binding and thus to fulfill it "voluntarily," rather than as a calculated avoidance of punishment or in deference to tradition, that person must hold two robust and resilient core beliefs about "everyone else." First, the citizen must have enough faith in the integrity of the other citizens that there is no perceived reason not to perform those civic duties; there is an assumption that all others will fulfill the same duties. Second, a citizen must believe that individual compliance is important even when it does not bring any direct personal benefit but rather redounds to the advantage of others, whose welfare is included in "external" preferences. The first of these beliefs is passive and can be defined as *trust* (or the absence of fear). It can be strengthened through a constitutional and legal order, which, in guaranteeing basic rights, limits the power of the collective to make decisions affecting the individual, but it cannot be established this way. The second is an active belief and is called *solidarity* (or the absence of indifference); it, too, cannot be forced on people formally, but rather merely encouraged through state social services and the redistribution of wealth.[7]

The horizontal phenomena of trust and solidarity are preconditions for the "vertical" phenomenon of the establishment and continued existence of state authority, manifested in effectively ensuring the performance of civic duties. In simple terms, this means that before citizens can recognize the authority of the state, they must first mutually recognize each other as being motivated by trust and solidarity. It is true that the process through which this mutual recognition develops has often been a confrontational and violent one, but until it occurs the authority of the state is uncertain. It is, moreover, precisely when this abstract but resilient trust in "everyone else" as the collective coauthor of the obligating norms is undermined, or when citizens' active interest in each other's well-being is successfully discredited, that liberal notions about curtailing the scope of state authority flourish. Trust in one's fellow citizens provides the cognitive and moral foundations for *democracy*, the risks of which no one would

reasonably accept otherwise.[8] The solidarity citizens feel toward one another, or to which they allow themselves to be obligated through their
representative institutions, is also the moral basis of the *welfare state*. Thus,
both democracy and the welfare state are fundamentally dependent upon
the prior existence of binding motives, which in turn are tied to the form
of political integration found in the nation-state.

The special ability to place citizens under obligation, which arises from
their affiliation with a national political community, is, in itself, nothing
mysterious. Belonging to a "people" is essentially a *status* right. This right
can be conferred upon someone (through naturalization), but it cannot be
obtained contractually (say, through purchase)—just as children do not
become family members through contracts (except in the case of adoption). Because nationality is not contingent upon a contract, it is a remarkably "fixed" status. Unlike companies or even states, nations are a form
of societal organization that can neither be "founded" nor go into liquida-
tion. Their origin loses itself in the mist of the past (which is also the birth-
place of founding myths), and they are perceived to exist "forever."

For those who belong to the special social construct "nation" (to which,
in this respect, only the social group "family" corresponds), the defining
features of membership—affiliation as a status right and the fiction of
permanence—make it relatively easy to engage in risky interactions such
as a demonstration of trust or solidarity. Expressions of trust are made
safer by the common national culture, the improbability of migration, and
the ability to impose sanctions in cases of defection. Demonstrations of
solidarity are less risky because the exchange relation is understood as
temporally unlimited; the duties each citizen performs need not be repaid
directly to that citizen, but rather can be passed down from one generation to the next in a never-ending chain. Following the conceptual model
of the generational contract in social retirement insurance and the principle of what Kenneth Boulding calls "serial reciprocity," no member of a
nation is ever in danger of being the "last" one (and hence the "dumb"
one), who contributes without being able to claim the right to services in
return. Like the family on the microlevel, the nation on the macrolevel
constitutes an unusually favorable structural and interpretive framework
for "assurance games"—those interactions with cooperative solutions
that reproduce themselves and for which functional equivalents are not
easily located above or below that level.

The idea of a totality of persons, integrated through relations of trust
and solidarity and extending beyond family and tribal affiliations, though
not to the extent of being "limitless," appears to be a necessary condition
for democracy. The universe of citizens who achieve their collective self-
recognition, whether by ascription or after such coercive acts as civil war,
has its outer borders in the nation and its "people." The people, not as an

ethnic affiliation by origin and culture, but as a political community, self-constituted in reference to history and territory and made distinct by a willingness to demonstrate trust and solidarity, is an indispensable conceptual building block for political analysis.[9] It is the social substratum of the polity, which produces a legally formalized constitutional order and strengthens that order through its ability to integrate.

MOTIVES FOR SURMOUNTING THE LIMITS OF THE NATION-STATE IN EUROPE, AND CONSEQUENT DILEMMAS

Although the nation-state generates the relations of trust and solidarity upon which democracy and the welfare state depend, it is structurally a suboptimal formation. The nation-state is economically suboptimal because it restricts the mobility of consumer and capital goods at its borders, making it less efficient than a common market, which in theory provides for the unlimited internal exchange of all goods and services under uniform conditions. It is politically suboptimal because it tends to prioritize narrowly defined national interests over transnational interests, even to the point of accepting the collective harm of war. The rational solution would be to transfer political responsibilities from national to transnational governmental authorities, particularly in the areas of foreign affairs, security, law, and monetary policy. However, if this argument appears compelling on the surface, attempts to put it into practice quickly run up against a fundamental fact of social life: it can be perfectly rational for actors to choose noncooperative tactical moves that manifestly violate long-term, global-optimization criteria if these moves maximize their utility under given "local" opportunity and incentive structures. Actors will be particularly inclined to do this when they perceive that other actors, upon whose cooperation global success is dependent, are caught in the same dilemma. Global-rational solutions are impeded even further if there is an uneven distribution in either the cost or the expected profits of cooperation. Clearly, then, what is needed is a rational method of resolving conflicts between local and global efficiencies, or short-term and long-term efficiencies.

Because of the lack of clear normative-analytical standards, political science research on Europe has largely avoided identifying "rational" ways to create regional institutions, and instead has limited itself to offering explanatory reconstructions of dilemmas and the paths actors have followed in attempting to overcome them. These paths are characterized by antithetical idealized concepts such as "negative" versus "positive" integration,[10] or "contract" versus "constitution."[11] National governments are typically seen as responding to the common market program and its neutralization of their economic sovereignty by seeking to preserve their political sovereignty, yielding it only through voluntary and revocable contractual agreements. Without any formalization of the players, themes, and processes, and in the absence of any authorization from a central governmental power, an involuntary process of negotiation begins. This process pushes on at random, arrested or accelerated by changing environmental conditions and shaped by a functionalistic logic of emergent problems, "spill-over" effects, problem solving, and consensus building.[12] The idea that consistently emerges, from both "realist" and "functional" interpretations of transnational processes of integration, is that the interdependencies between relevant governmental and nongovernmental protagonists are noted and cumulatively included in cooperative arrangements. This process, however, is not itself embedded in political institutions, nor is it politically steered.

The conceptual alternatives that dominate the social science debate on Europe are clearly divided and are indicated by the conceptual pairings of intergovernmental voluntarism versus "neofederalism" or "supranationalism." The two alternatives refer to different dynamics of integration. "Intergovernmental voluntarism" describes a functionalist dynamic driven by national and sectoral interests or contractual compromise, wherein progress is made through cooperative tactical moves that cumulatively fulfill emergent functional necessities. Neofederalism and supranationalism both refer to a dynamic that envisages the intentional establishment of a political order for all of Europe, oriented toward the fulfillment of shared values and standards—that is, a federalist state order. This latter perspective can be described as intentionalistic.[13] The difference between "negative" and "positive" integration corresponds to the distinction drawn between intergovernmental voluntarism and supranationalism. Negative integration is understood here as the elimination of tariff and other barriers to trade and capital mobility sanctioned by decision of the European Commission, and, when necessary, the European Court. Positive integration refers to the emergence of a uniform, EU-wide system for the regulation of economic, trade and social relations, and presupposes a corresponding development of political will in the Council of Ministers.

In a system of economically interdependent but politically independent nation-states, there are two principal problems of cooperation, which give rise to mutually exclusive solutions. The first problem occurs when national governments act unilaterally or intergovernmentally in a manner that threatens other players with negative externalities. Behavior of this sort can be eliminated only by reducing the scope of the nation-state's discretionary authority. One way of achieving this would be through a higher-ranking, Euro-federal governing capacity, based on positive integration and the principle of subsidiarity, which had the power to limit the exercise of national sovereignty to "internal affairs"—affairs whose regulation would not create negative externalities. Another approach would be to foster an understanding that a strong, formally composed, European executive is the only entity capable of counteracting the homogenizing forces of the market. In both cases, however, a marked expansion of "positive" integration is clearly required, not just in the areas of foreign, domestic, and judicial policy, but also for labor market and social policies.

This leads to the second problem of cooperation. Consent to a "strong" governmental form arouses the opposite fear among a significant number of member states—namely, that a potent European "governing capacity," based on majority decisions and not hamstrung by voluntary adherence, could render individual member states defenseless against the political agendas of the dominant players. The most typical scenario is one in which the national preference of the majority in individual member states is drowned out as a minority position within Europe. At the core of this fear is a sense of the impending loss of the democratic nation-state's autonomy in shaping its own will.[14] This leads to a rational preference for a negative form of integration, which maximizes the political jurisdiction of the nation-state.

In assessing the relative merits of negative and positive integration, it is important to recognize that the former can be just as damaging to the socioeconomic order as the latter is to national autonomy. In the case of purely negative integration, the threat is to the social welfare system, which nation-states are able to maintain only by virtue of having control over their own labor market, social, monetary, and economic policies. In the case of purely positive integration, it is the nation-state's well-adjusted mechanisms for democratic legitimation that are imperiled; these mechanisms cannot be reproduced at the European level because Europe lacks the inner structures of a "nation" as described above. The choice is thus between the plague of negative externalities caused by voluntarism and the cholera of political determination by European institutions, against whose claim to sovereignty nation-states perceive no democratic remedy. Rather than confront the implications of this choice directly, each national government imagines that it lives in the best of all possible worlds—one in which all other governments are bound by the chains of a European government, but in which it is free to make policy in harmony with national majority preferences.[15]

My thesis is that every provisional solution between the two extremes of full nation-state sovereignty and European supranationalism inevitably violates *both* key reference values in the contemporary period—the protection of the social welfare system and the severing of democratic legitimation. The present approach to European integration thus would appear to represent a descent down the ladder that T. H. Marshall proposed as a model for the process of European political modernization.[16] The three rungs of this ladder are liberal rights, democratic rights, and social welfare rights, achieved cumulatively. The question is whether in Europe today the social welfare and democratic rungs are being passed in reverse, reducing Euro-citizens to the status of mere participants in a neoliberal marketplace.

The degree of integration achieved in Europe since the signing of the Treaty of Amsterdam in June 1997 bears out this thesis. Post-treaty Europe is effectively suspended between the intergovernmental and supranational models. On economic matters, the EU functions as a confederation of states. The member states are engaged in the creation of a unified, transnational realm through a contractual transfer of jurisdictions. This confederation of states joined by treaties, however, is not so much a legally irreversible entity as a practically irreversible one. The parties to the contract perceive no serious option of terminating it, for such a move would trigger built-in economic sanctions of a compelling deterrent value. This makes it difficult to speak unambiguously of intergovernmental *voluntarism*.

On the other hand, there can also be no talk of a perfected European federal state. That would require a constitution establishing a balance of legitimation such that European citizens exercised democratic control directly (and not through their national governments) over the representatives of European sovereignty (the Council, the Commission, and the Court). Instead, the nation-state remains an indispensable intermediary in European politics. Such European civic duties as exist can be executed only indirectly, through nation-state administrations. Actions can be taken on the European stage only on the basis of nation-state empowerment of European authorities. Legal orders ("directives") of the European Commission develop binding effectiveness (if they are not already limited to the status of "recommendations") only after their adoption by national legislative bodies. The European executive does not have the capacity to levy taxes, implement defense measures, enact effective orders of law, or take charge of public education.[17] As for the EU's legislative wing, its two representative bodies, the European Parliament and the Council of Ministers, are hamstrung in their efforts to generate legally binding European civic duties by exceptionally rigid procedural rules. Even the so-called *acquis communitaire*, the massive store of norms of secondary European law, has limited binding effect. Members already opt out of regulations in the interests of a "variable geometry." Although this remains rare, the special provisions that are certain to accompany the EU's expansion eastward are likely to increase the scope for discretion in the future.

In short, Europe today is in a muddle. National governments are the bearers of democratic legitimacy, but the transfer of authority that has accompanied the implementation of the Single Market program has reduced their power to shape the prospects and safeguard the interests of their national populations. More and more, this role is being played by the European Court and the Commission. However, those organs act largely in accordance with the logic of "negative" integration because, without their own base of political legitimacy, they lack the mandate (and the resources, for that matter) to spearhead the development of new political initiatives. The European Council cannot transfer this mandate to the Commission and the Court, because its members, who act on behalf of national electorates and are responsible to these electorates, currently lack the trust or solidarity to furnish "positive" integration programs with a political and fiscal basis. Thus, there is a disjunction between the ability and the mandate to act; the former is already largely in the hands of European institutions, but the latter still resides with national governments. Together, these mirror-image deficits threaten to demolish both the democratic and the social welfare achievements of the modern European nation-state.

There are two alternatives for addressing the democratic deficit in Europe: a transfer of the ability to act (governing capacity) back to the nation-state, or a transfer forward of democratically backed mandates to European representatives of governmental power. The first alternative is often expressed by a call for "subsidiarity"—for the preservation of domains in which the nation-state remains sovereign. The evidence to date, however, suggests that this avenue offers little real hope. No matter how determinedly they endeavor to preserve their autonomy, national governments increasingly find their hand forced by the economic and fiscal imperatives of the Single Market, which seems inexorably to sweep national institutional structures for the development of programs of interest mediation (such as those of Rhenish capitalism) into the vortex of market-driven institutional arbitrage.

The second alternative—the transfer of legitimated mandates and resources for action to supranational authorities—confronts the following question: Can the Council and the Commission acquire a positive identity in the eyes of European citizens and become the object of demands and expectations for a truly European political agenda? The initial outlook on this score is not promising. There has been a sharp rise in the negative politicization of European institutions since the beginning of the 1990s, owing largely to the strains the Single Market has placed on the institutional and regulatory-political *acquis nationale* established in European countries during the postwar period. This *acquis nationale* has consisted not only in the installation of strong liberal democracies but also in the introduction of a wide range of policies of government intervention, which collectively make up the modern democratic welfare state. These policies vary across nations, but generally include measures to promote employment and modernization, social insurance agencies, tariff and political codetermination arrangements, and other market-limiting ("decommodifying") agreements. Praised as a vehicle for fostering cohesion and institutionalizing class conflict during the Cold War period, they are now seen as creating locational disadvantages in the new dynamic created by the Single Market. Their survival is threatened by competitive deregulation, regressive taxation, and a rollback of redistributive measures. European institutions have become "negatively" politicized in this process because they are perceived to have allowed this progressive dismantling of the democratic welfare state to proceed unchecked. In essence, the charge is that they have subjected the structures of the welfare state to an efficiency test without ensuring that equivalent institutional alternatives exist in the event that reregulation is deemed necessary.

As fears mount about, for example, the effects of monetary union on employment, social standards, and monetary stability, European citizens continue to look to their national governments for a response. European institutions are not yet seen as having a valuable role to play in the search for a framework that will ensure equitable relations between states, regions, and social classes. Part of the reason is a lack of vertical efficiency in European politics; European institutions simply do not have the ability—for example, the political and fiscal "governing capacity"—to pursue such ambitious goals. But there is also a more serious horizontal deficiency. Europeans still think of themselves primarily in national terms; they have not yet developed the relations of trust and solidarity on the European level that would be necessary to underpin a stronger European governing capacity. Only when a more abstract and wider frame of reference for a truly European people has been adopted will the cultural and cognitive prerequisites for a positive politicization of European institutions exist.

Today in Europe, a *pouvoir constitué*, limited in its ability to govern and weak in its legitimation, controls the scene without a corresponding *pouvoir constituant*. The only remedy for this situation is the development of a widespread predisposition toward a European internationalism. Ideally, European institutions themselves would help foster this horizontal dimension, but they can do so only as a political and cultural by-product of an increase in the vertical efficiency of European politics. The development of relations of trust and solidarity on the European level is contingent upon good governance, and this means that Europe's first priority must be to establish a legitimate, transparent, and effective European governmental authority that cannot be "negatively" politicized as a form of supranational foreign rule. Five means of supplying the institutional protagonists of the EU with the legitimation and recognition necessary to cultivate a common frame of political reference at the level of the citizens have been identified in the literature.[18]

The most economistic approach to surmounting Europe's democratic deficit sees the legitimation problem as eventually resolving itself. This argument is premised on the technocratic belief that, by placing limits on its own authority, demonstrating knowledgeable competence, and ensuring the impartiality of its executive decisions, the Commission could earn itself sufficient political credit with the European public to make further formal legitimation unnecessary. In light of the increasingly negative politicization of the EU and its agencies, however, it now seems indisputable that this strategy was sufficient, at best, for an initial phase of negative integration during which the work of the Commission could still be presented as a pure coordination game—that is, as a process with utility that was universal and even.[19]

The second approach, which dates back to 1979, calls for transforming the EU into a parliamentary system through direct elections to the European parliament (EP). This proposal is as unworkable today as it was then, for several reasons. The EP's role remains limited relative to that of the Commission, and there are no truly pan-European parties (at most, these are now coordinated elements in their program of national parties), no coordinated system of franchise throughout Europe, and, above all, no European public opinion connected by the media to train a critical eye on the activities of the EP. In its capacity as a legislative assembly, the EP competes as a kind of second chamber not only with the Council but also with the national parliaments. Its potential for political legitimation, as set out by the Treaty on European Union, remains rudimentary (despite its right), restricted in terms of scope and time to participate in decisions of the Commission.[20]

The third path to democratic legitimation focuses on the Council of Ministers. This approach is flawed, however, because the Council's members are the executives of the member states, not the representatives of a European legislature. Although the issues dealt with by the Council can be discussed and voted upon by national parliaments, the cognitive resources of those bodies are inferior to those of the Commission. The Commission simply "knows" more about the conditions necessary for successful transnational coordination and consensus building in the Council, and this gives it principal influence over the Council.[21] A further problem with relying on the Council is that its activities, unlike those of national parliaments, are usually scrutinized only by groups whose interests are directly affected, rather than evaluated in terms of their impact on the broader European public.

The fourth option for strengthening the democratic legitimacy of the EU is the expansion of the practice of qualified majority voting to the Council of Ministers. By canceling the veto rights of individual (or smaller groups of) member states, goes the argument, it will no longer be possible for a minority of states to halt the decision-making process outright or to manipulate it by extortionary means. It is questionable, however, whether this proposal genuinely aims to enhance the legitimacy of the decision-making process, or simply to increase its speed and effectiveness. One obvious concern is that "the citizens of countries whose governments are outvoted have no reason to consider such decisions as having democratic legitimation."[22]

The fifth and final possibility depends on strengthening the mechanisms of territorial representation (elections, parties, parliaments, governments), as well as those of functional representation through interorganizational negotiations or the investiture of existing organs with political representational functions. This latter strategy is predicated upon the existence of a system of *quasi*-corporatism, with organizations representing the interests of employees, employers, financial institutions, agriculture, and so on, and whose protagonists would have the capacity to lobby European institutions and build responsible compromises. The problem is that no such system currently exists on the European level, nor is one likely to be created in the near future. Neither the Economic nor the Social Committee approaches these criteria, and, when they exist, the social partners (especially the unions) are not organizationally or politically equipped to play the same role on the European stage that they have played in the corporative nation-state.[23] Furthermore, those organizations that are in a position to play this role (chiefly the sectoral industrial organizations) generally see Euro-corporatism as inimical to their interests, which they believe are better served by the free functioning of the market.

The constraints on these five reforms to enhance the legitimacy of European institutions reinforces the claim that the EU presently lacks the qualities that would make for a political community expressed in the form of a state. The EU is today neither a unified organ of efficient governance nor one expressing the democratic will. As for the demand voiced by some today that republicanism must manage without the support of the nation-state and learn to stand on its own two feet, it must be countered that the environment conducive to such learning is missing.[24] Vertical and horizontal efficiency can only be improved simultaneously. Strengthening the ability of European institutions to govern is not conceivable without an expansion of their formal democratic basis of legitimation. The EU will become the focus of the democratic will of an informed European public opinion only when it appears as a unified organ of governance, and this will require that national publics yield ground on the issue of subsidiarity and give up their opting-out privileges in favor of greater participation in pan-European politics.

It is my personal contention that steps taken to surmount simultaneously the European governmental and democratic deficits must not be thought of according to the logic of the vegetative process of "ever closer" integration—that is, as the result of automatic actions based on rational interests. In Streeck's terms, it "should be obvious that [the politics of integration are] *not* driven by a logic of 'spill-over' from international market integration to supranational state formation."[25] The logic of seeking advantage is unsuitable as a vehicle for building a political community, because steps toward integration will always appear, at least in the short term, as costs (such as a loss of protection or a reduction in security) and thus will carry with them the temptation to withdraw or block the initiatives of others. Even if economic and monetary union, moreover, were to prove a positive-sum game, the anticipation of such a blessing would not engender any motivational thrust, for as Jacques Delors used to say, "You do not fall in love with a common market."[26] No, progress toward a unity of European intention and action will materialize only when national publics are presented with *normatively* convincing grounds for political integration—reasons they would find sufficiently compelling to warrant their acceptance of the (temporary) disadvantages caused by the integration of states, regions, sectors, and social classes.

NORMATIVE ARGUMENTS FOR EUROPEAN INTEGRATION

Having determined the need for a more intentionalistic paradigm for European integration, we must now examine whether there exists an adequate supporting repertoire of European social norms. These norms must be potentially binding and they must have the motivating power to support the establishment of a federal European organ of governmental rule beyond particularistic and short-term calculations (and eventually in opposition to them).[27] Our examination must also embrace the related question of whether there is such a thing as a European "identity," a totality of binding and obligating traditions originating in European history, and unanimously accepted as valid by present-day Europeans as orienting and legitimating political action at the regional level. The outlook is bleak on both fronts.

Münkler has convincingly demonstrated that the term "Europe" lacks positive content and fails to provide practical convergent points for orienting activity.[28] Rather, it is outward looking and more in the nature of a "counter term." Historically, Europe has defined itself as a community of protection against the Ottoman, Asian, and Soviet "East"; as an internally divided colonial community of "mother countries" in relation to the South; and, from time to time, as a culturally chauvinistic community of traditions set against the Anglo-Saxon "West" and its civilization. When one attempts to formulate a normatively substantive and nonidealistic definition of Europe as an entity in and of itself, however, the term immediately falls apart into groupings of nation-states, whose common history is remembered as one that divides more than it binds.[29]

The roots of these, at times, partially overlapping aggregates of Europe run very deep and impede the development of binding notions of European citizenship and pan-European social solidarity. Greven convincingly develops this observation in his chapter in this book. The truth is that Europeans generally do not view each other as possessing the status of people "like ourselves."[30] Conceptions of family resemblance (historically, economically, geographically, politically, or however substantiated) are typically reserved for selected "neighbors" and generally are not extended to all Europeans. In reality, the term "European" is more a descriptive social-geographic category than a politically instructive category for common reflection and for political will that could become a basis for self-characterization. This has disturbing implications for European integration. As Delanty writes, "European integration must recreate what exists on the level of the nation-state, but this is impossible because Europe is devoid of a cultural framework independent of the nation-state."[31]

Clearly, there is a need for principles that could transform European unification into a hegemonic idea, independent of the balance sheet of positive and negative "payoffs," but the search for such principles has been held back by the absence of a clear conceptual starting point. If peace, human rights, democracy, and economic prosperity and its equitable distribution are the genuine European reference values, then the Maastricht and Amsterdam treaties are hardly documents that could feed a European constitutional patriotism based on these values. In any case, the Commission lacks the jurisdiction, the will, and the financial resources to turn the EU into such a bastion of social justice.[32] As for EMU, the present focus of the integration process, it certainly does not furnish the moral and political motives for a political union of Europe. Instead, widespread fears about its impact on economic stability and unemployment have prompted a backlash, which makes it seem unlikely that a plebiscite on further integration would achieve a positive result.[33] European political elites have endeavored to combat this negative view of closer economic integration by appealing to the symbolic-expressive and moral principles of European identity, but to little avail. "The articulation of a symbolic discourse of Europeanness has . . . had little impact (and even that has often been negative, notably in the anti-Muslim overtones of the idea of a 'Christian' Europe), and the institutions designed to embody it (e.g., European citizenship as created by the Maastricht Treaty, or even direct elections to the European Parliament) have been highly marginal."[34]

There are also practical obstacles to the formulation of a strong normative argument in favor of European integration. Given the size of the EU today and the diversity of economies and cultures it encompasses, it may be inevitable that attempts to transcend national particularities and to achieve a symbolic-moral self-characterization of "Europe" lapse into abstraction.[35] And as fiscal austerity measures undermine the EU's capacity for structural, regional, and agricultural subvention, and eastward expansion admits new members who will be net recipients of EU funds, it seems probable that what little goodwill the European public currently does bear the project of European integration will evaporate.[36] This constellation of European values and nation-state interests is leading to the visible decay of the symbolic *gestalt* of Europe and of the political-moral demands that can be plausibly attached to the EU.[37]

In the worst-case scenario, some observers have suggested that democracy—the quintessential European principle—will be damaged rather than strengthened by political integration. "The principle of democracy is validated in the member states; these, however, see their decision-making powers on the wane. The decision-making powers accrue to the European Community, where the principle of democracy is only weakly developed."[38] The above discussion of strategies to enhance the legitimacy of the European institutions has made clear that institutional reform by itself is an inadequate response to this problem. As Scharpf succinctly points out, "the democratic deficit cannot be reformed away."[39] Grimm, like Greven, contends that the EU's democratic deficit is rooted in its multilingualism and the obstacle this raises to the formation of a European general public capable of holding political parties and legislative institutions accountable in accordance with the standards of western European democracy.[40] In the absence of a European "people," the demand for accountability will have to be addressed within the framework of the nation-state. Since any attempt by the EU to approach a federal state in its structures and functions will weaken democratic principles, the EU's legal basis must remain grounded in a contract binding under international law, not in a European constitution.[41]

The conclusion seems inescapable. A repertoire of social norms capable of supporting a more intentionalistic paradigm of contemporary European integration simply does not exist. Moreover, interdependence and the division of labor will not automatically generate this trust and solidarity any more than social integration, in the sense of the convergence of social norms and cognitive orientations, will flow naturally from the integration of national markets. The horizon of the Single Market coincides

in principle with that of a European political society, conceived as an undivided community of will. If this society is to be brought into being, a
differently motivated process is required. Five possible guiding images to
such a process of political socialization are considered below.

Europe as Guarantor of Peace

The political integration of Europe is to be desired (and the attendant
economic costs and loss of national sovereignty to be accepted) because
this would represent a definitive surmounting of the rivalries between European nation-states that led to this century's most catastrophic military
conflicts. In particular, it would ensure the integration into Europe of the
country of origin of the two World Wars—namely, Germany—which is
also the largest and richest EU member state, and which directly borders
potentially threatened neighboring countries. The attempt to cast Europe
as a guarantor of peace is driven by the twin impulses of European fear of
German dominance and German anxiety about this fear.[42] It is doubtful,
however, that fear is "enough to drive European integration forward."[43]
The experiences of World War II and the Nazi terror are becoming distant
memories, and the prospect of a military confrontation between the stable
democracies of the EU is now highly unlikely. International guarantees
make state borders in Europe effectively inviolable, and, in any case,
states increasingly recognize that gaining access to others' resources is
more easily achieved through such "peaceful" means as trade and the
movement of capital than through the use of military force.

Of course, the inviolability of existing borders is no guarantee against
the more likely danger that separatist civil wars will be fought over part
of a nation-state's territory, possibly with a view to establishing new borders. It is difficult, however, to see how the EU and related regional institutions could respond effectively to threats of this sort. On the contrary,
the spectacular failure of European governments to take decisive action
in Yugoslavia after 1991, and their reliance on American military power
thereafter, discredited the vision of the EU as guarantor-authority of a
European order of peace. In short, the EU reinforces a peace that is not
threatened, but it is powerless in the face of the more immediate danger
of subnational wars within individual EU member states and on the region's periphery.

Europe as Bastion of Freedom

Since 1989, the antithesis of freedom and human rights against the "totalitarian" bloc of the Warsaw Pact and Comecon has no longer func-
tioned as a negative political motivator for Europe. Instead, the sudden

liberation of the countries of central and eastern Europe has created a long waiting list of aspiring EU members, whom the existing member states can no longer demonize for their violations of human rights and their restriction of political and civic freedoms. The EU, however, cannot refer to these candidates for membership in unambiguously positive terms. Whether because of poor economic and political conditions or because of the lack of a strong civil society tradition, many of them fall far short of the European standard, particularly with respect to the treatment of minorities, human rights policies, and restrictions on media liberties. In southeastern Europe and the Baltic states in particular, it is questionable that the principle of freedom truly presents itself as a positive, normatively unifying bond.[44]

Europe as Singular Synthesis of Political Values and Principles

Europe can be idealized from an historical perspective as the place where the tension among the three components of political modernization—namely, equal rights of citizens, sovereignty of the people, and social justice—was resolved in theory and, on occasion, in practice. The institutionalization of that achievement has, however, given rise today to a contradiction. On the one hand, the synthesis has been quite limited in Europe itself, occurring only under the favorable conditions of postwar prosperity in the third quarter of the twentieth century. On the other hand, the normative intention to bring about that synthesis is no longer an exclusively European goal; it has in fact become one of the hegemonic political ideas in the world. At the same time, in Europe itself, it has been eroded in various ways. Today, it is Australia that holds the honor of having achieved the most successful and lasting synthesis of the three principles of political modernization, while in Europe liberals warn of the danger of a "new authoritarianism" that threatens civic freedoms, rights of political participation, and social security.[45]

Present-day Europe can claim a monopoly on neither the idea nor the reality of freedom, democracy, and the social welfare state. If a sharp external distinction can be made between Europe and the rest of the world, it is a practical rather than a normative one, arising from the use of trade and immigration policy to construct a "fortress Europe." The values and principles upon which modern Europe established itself have become, through a synthesis of the legacies of the Judeo-Christian, enlightened liberal and socialist traditions, global common property. They are therefore not suitable (at least not without regression to a cultural and confessional strategy of political confrontation) as the distinguishing *proprium* of Europe. Cliches such as that of a "common intellectual heritage" do nothing to address the problem because they are rooted in the past, when this heritage was in fact unique to Europe. Europe today is a motley collection of languages, cultures, religious denominations, historical traditions, and nation-bound understandings of sovereignty; this heterogeneity will only become more pronounced as the EU expands eastward. One looks in vain for standards and principles that would be authoritative *everywhere* in Europe and *only* in Europe.

Europe as Shared Cultural Space and Way of Life

It is often assumed that the expansion of the EU will make national borders less motivationally and cognitively relevant and lead to a greater homogeneity of lifestyles and consumption patterns. Transnational tourism, media broadcasts of sporting events, an opening of national-linguistic spheres of communication through the spread of foreign language skills, the dissemination across Europe of visual and acoustic (that is, nonverbal) art and entertainment programs, and the extensive media coverage of European themes—all are seen as ways of creating a shared cultural space and way of life. Eventually, a new cognitive framework may emerge, one that protects local and regional traditions while remaining firmly grounded in a positive conception of a unified Europe.

In the meantime, the reality is that self-identification as "European" remains a marginal phenomenon (except in tiny Luxembourg, with its 29 percent share of EU-foreigners in the residential population). Only a small minority of the people living in Europe "think of themselves presently as 'European' in the psychological sense [and] academics think of themselves as 'European' proportionally twice as often as persons with less formal education."[46] The European frame of reference is, therefore, that of a narrow segment of elites, whereas attitudes toward work and politics, religion, family, and education still exhibit clear national and subregional patterns. As for political, educational, and cultural programs aimed at shifting the focus of citizens' worldviews from the national to the European level, skepticism is warranted, especially given the reservations Europeans already have about the implications of economic integration.[47]

Europe as Economy of Scale

Combining the economic, political, technological, scientific, and military resources of the (expanded) EU would create opportunities far surpassing those available to conventional economic world powers, among which would be the formation of an unprecedented potential for solving political and social problems. Less obvious are the solutions for problems meriting a pooling of resources (as differentiated from the simple removal of barriers to the mobility of various resources) and the precise modalities for deploying this formidable problem-solving capacity. The only Europeans with a definite claim on the well-endowed European funds are the candidate countries of central and eastern Europe. For them, the speed and direction of economic and political modernization are dependent upon whether and how soon they can partake, as full members, in the structural and agricultural funds of the EU. Acute budgetary and labor-market crises in many existing EU member states, however, have reduced western European tolerance for transnational redistribution.[48] Furthermore, the long-term contribution that central and eastern Europe could make to the EU's collective resources (new markets, possibilities for investment, military security, control over migration) is much less evident than that expected from Spain and Portugal at the time of the EU's expansion into southern Europe in 1986.

To complicate matters further, the European funds are not the only means of achieving the much-vaunted effects of synergy and economies of scale; these effects can also be realized below the level of the Commission through bilateral and multilateral economic, scientific-technical, and military forms of cooperation. If the full economies of scale of European integration are to be realized, mutually agreed-upon goals and projects will be necessary, to which EU members will have to be sufficiently committed to accept the necessary short-term distributional sacrifices. Such goals and projects are currently in short supply.

The problem would not be so serious if forms of positive integration existed, which could make the European polity into a vehicle for a Europe-wide social and employment pact. Instead, the opposite is the case, with the consequences of the present negative approach to integration— competitive deregulation of national employment and environmental protection standards and rising pressure to consolidate budgets—actively working against the development of a positive vision of integration. The sole remaining argument in favor of conceiving Europe as an economy of scale in political and economic terms is that the continent's political integration as "fortress Europe" could ensure its protection from external competitors, chiefly in North America, Asia, and also within Europe. This is hardly a strong basis for that positive vision.

CONCLUSION

None of the five normative interpretations just considered offers a clear path toward political integration in Europe. Analyzed together, however, they do reveal one important thing. The European public needs a normatively convincing defense of the integration project, and that need grows more pressing as the project moves forward. This is true for both internal and external reasons. At home, Europe confronts the rise of right-wing, populist-nationalist sentiment, primarily in Austria but also in Greece. This remains a localized phenomenon, but to the extent that it represents a backlash against the negative consequences of integration, it may intensify as those consequences become more apparent. Abroad, Europe faces a plethora of problems—involving ecology, economic stability, development, migration, crime, the media, security, and external affairs—that require concerted transnational action. In the face of these pressures, the functionalist approach to European integration, which suggests that the European project—at times haltingly, at times precipitously—will somehow, under the strain of existing interdependencies and emerging elite consensus, make itself complete "on its own," is increasingly barren. Europe provides a framework not just for cooperative problem solving but also for problem diffusion. If the EU is to play its original role—if it is to mount a coherent defense against the disintegrating pressures of globalization and rejuvenate the scope for political action—it will first have to reconstitute itself purposively as an effective and legitimate structure for governance.

I conclude by shifting the focus away from the normative motives for political integration to the social and moral consequences of integration. The optimistic view of Europe is that the European Union will steadily acquire greater legitimacy by virtue of its perceived accomplishments, growing citizen familiarity, and the occasional institutional innovation. The democratic deficit, in other words, will wither away of its own accord. A less optimistic, but perhaps more realistic alternative, can be summed up in the following proposition: the horizons of trust and solidarity, and the potential for creating a community on a civic-societal and republican-political basis, narrow as the frame of reference for relations of competition and interdependence widens. The delimitation of functional interrelations is accompanied by a deliberate decommitment on the part of individuals, groups, regions, and whole states to Europe as a collectivity. When the borders of nation-states become porous, the functional-systematic and social-moral modes of integration develop in opposite directions. Recent events in northern Italy and the Federal Republic of Germany may be adduced to support this claim. Neither the Padanisian fiscal secession efforts nor the German proposal for a regionalization of the social security system can be explained without reference to the budgetary constraints and competitive conditions wrought by the Single Market.

What should we infer from this? Historically, as Greven analyzed in the preceding chapter, the largest social body capable of supporting redistributive sacrifices has been the nation-state. We should therefore not be surprised by increasing resistance when the demands of redistribution are extended beyond that entity. Individuals begin to feel that excessive moral demands are being made of them, and they react by morally under-challenging themselves. As in Banfield's model of "amoral familialism," they become vigilant lest someone outside their social circle profit from their contributions. This decline in the operative horizons of trust and obligation is caused by the opening of nation-state borders, and it can be expected equally from "rich" and "poor"—from the former because they will rationally attempt to evade national and transnational demands on their resources, from the latter because, as beneficiaries of regional and structural funds, they will have a strong incentive to emphasize their sub-national identities. These two strategies, moreover, are obviously in a relation of reciprocal intensification.

In the absence of coextensive efforts to create a political community, borderless systems often overestimate their moral and legitimate power. In the process, they become breeding grounds for postmodern and neo-liberal tendencies, and they jeopardize the dispositions and institutional arrangements that encourage individuals and governments to consider the social, temporal, and practical effects of their actions (and inaction) in the long term. This suggests that the most important of these arrangements—the social welfare state and democracy, but also the corporatist system of comprehensive and far-sighted interest mediation—can be realized only "within borders." This implies a mode of socialization limited to the nation-state, whose protagonists recognize each other as worthy of trust and solidarity and who perceive each other as equal participants in an enduring and authoritative community of law. By disregarding these connections and allowing the polity to be delimited with impunity, we undermine its power to impose duties and open the door to regional and particularist motives and strategies.

NOTES

1. For an earlier treatment in German upon which this chapter is based, see Claus Offe, "Demokratic und Wohlfahrtsstaat: Eine europäische Regimeform unter dem Streß der europäischen Integration," in *Internationale Wirtschaft, nationale Demokratie, Herausforderung für die demokratic Theorie*, ed. Wolfgang Streeck (Frankfurt am Main: Campus Verlag, 1998), 99–136.

2. Dieter Grimm, *Braucht Europa eine Verfassung?* (München: Carl Friedrich von Siemens-Stiftung, 1995), 31.

3. Jürgen Habermas, *Die Einbeziehung des Anderen: Studien zur politischen Theorie* (Frankfurt: Suhrkamp, 1996), 135, 137.

4. Max Weber, *Wirtschaft und Gesellschaft: Grundriß der verstehenden Soziologie*, 4th ed. (Tübingen: Mohr, 1956), 237, 244.

5. A common market, for example, is nothing more than a partial sacrifice of

this power to regulate matters within one's borders. Here, the sacrifice is motivated by the economic (e.g., the economies of scale) and political advantages that are expected to accrue from the suspension of internal borders. However, this does not change the fact that political communities are dependent upon territorial borders and empowered to act only in reference to them.

6. This is in accordance with Jellinek's well-known formula.

7. Claus Offe, *Modernity and the State: East, West* (Cambridge, U.K.: Polity, 1996), 147–182.

8. If citizens regard each other as "hostile" or "malicious," they might, out of this "timorousness" (Weber's *Timidität*), feel that their interests would be better served by an authoritarian regime.

9. Lutz Hoffmann, "Das 'Volk': Zur ideologischen Struktur eines unvermeidbaren Begriffs," *Zeitschrift für Soziologie* 20, no. 3 (1991): 191–208.

10. Fritz W. Scharpf, "Negative and Positive Integration in the Political Economy of European Welfare States," in *Governance in the European Union*, ed. Gary Marks, Fritz W. Scharpf, Philippe C. Schmitter, and Wolfgang Streeck (London: Sage, 1996), 15–39.

11. Grimm, *Braucht Europa eine Verfassung?*

12. Philippe C. Schmitter, "Examining the Present Euro-Polity with the Help of Past Theories," in *Governance in the European Union*, ed. Marks et al. (London: Sage, 1996), 1–14.

13. The "intentionalistic" conception of transnational processes of integration implies that the integration process could be disrupted by a lack of support from the national populations affected. This distinguishes it from

> the functionalistic theory of integration, [which] thinks of European unification as a process controlled by the leading elites of the countries involved, as well as by the functional elites of international organizations. As long as these [elites] . . . are in agreement that the current political and economic challenges demand international solutions, the opinion of the broader population is, to a large extent, without consequence for the course of further integration.

Stefan Immerfall and Andreas Sobisch, "Europäische Integration und europäische Identität: Die Europäische Union im Bewußtsein ihrer Bürger," *Politik und Zeitgeschichte* 10 (1997): 26.

14. Fritz W. Scharpf, "Demokratische Politik in Europa," *in Zur Neuordnung der Europäischen Union: Die Regierungskonferenz 1996/1997*, ed. Dieter Grimm et al. (Baden-Baden: Nomos, 1996/1997), 65.

15. There are certain conditions under which it may be rational for nation-states to cede their sovereignty to supranational institutions. Marks et al. identify two such situations. First, an advantage of cooperation (for example, reduced transaction costs) may come into effect earlier than the disadvantage associated with relinquishing sovereignty. Second, the transfer of decision-making rights to a higher level of government may enable governing elites to shift responsibility for the undesirable consequences of a decision to that level of government. In some circumstances, responsibility for a particular decision is a power to be avoided rather than sought. This is true if any decision on a particular issue brings more costs than benefits. See Gary Marks, Liesbet Hooghe, and Kermit Blank,

"European Integration Since the 1980s: State-Centric Versus Multi-Level Governance," *Journal of Common Market Studies*, 34, no. 3 (1996): 341–378. It is important to note, however, that both scenarios simply involve a trick, whereby problems of legitimation are deferred to a future date.

16. T. H. Marshall, *Class, Citizenship and Social Development* (Garden City, N.Y.: Doubleday, 1964).

17. Nation-states show no signs of being willing to transfer this authority. While the members of a nation-state generally concede to their fellow citizens the right to impose normative duties according to jointly created constitutional and legislative procedural principles, and attribute to them the moral and cognitive competence to do so, they typically extend this recognition only to conationals.

18. Sven S. Andersen and Kjell A. Eliassen, eds., *The European Union: How Democratic Is It?* (London: Sage, 1996).

19. Fritz W. Scharpf, "Economic Integration, Democracy and the Welfare State," unpublished manuscript, Max Planck Institute (1996), 154–155.

20. Keith Middlemas, *Orchestrating Europe: The Informal Politics of European Union 1973–1995* (London: Fontana, 1995), 340–364.

21. Marks et al., "European Integration Since the 1980s."

22. Scharpf, "Negative and Positive Integration."

23. Middlemas, *Orchestrating Europe*, 386, 468, 487ff., and 598; Andersen and Eliassen, *The European Union*, 40–51, 251.

24. Habermas, *Die Einbeziehung des Anderen*, 142. This environment would be conducive to learning when the two requirements formulated by Habermas are met: "The citizens must also be able to experience the practical value of exercising their rights in the form of social security and reciprocal recognition of different cultural ways of life" (143). However, the experience of "social security" is predicated upon the existence of a European governmental authority that has already made itself visible through its ability to act, while that of "reciprocal recognition" can result only from a legitimization process that addresses the fear that European dictates will demolish national institutions and ways of life (for example, the Swedish liquor sales and distribution system or the German public broadcasting corporations).

25. Wolfgang Streeck, "Neo-Voluntarism: A New European Social Policy Regime?" in *Governance in the European Union*, ed. Marks et al. (London: Sage, 1996), 65 (emphasis in original).

26. Cited in Brigid Laffan, "Legitimacy," *Encyclopedia of the EU* (Boulder, Colo.: Lynne Rienner, 1997).

27. It is notable that insistence upon the intrinsic normative value of European integration and related efforts to downplay points of view based on national interests are special peculiarities of the discourse of political and intellectual elites in Germany. Consequently, the objectives that inform this discourse are more "Euro-federal" than "intergovernmental." Although strong arguments can be marshaled in favor of this one-dimensional vision of a Europe grounded in principles rather than interests, they remain vulnerable to two suspicions. Outside observers not unreasonably fear that this vision (1) merely expresses German uneasiness about persistent European fears of renewed German hegemony or, more

seriously, (2) uses "postnational" discourse as a smoke screen to obscure a drive for dominance of a monetarily unified Europe by the German government (and its Bundesbank).

28. Herfried Münkler, "Europa als politische Idee: Ideengeschichtliche Facetten des Europabegriffs und deren aktuelle Bedeutung," *Leviathan* 19, no. 4 (1991): 521–541.

29. Think of the Latin-European Mediterranean states, the Greek-Orthodox countries, the Carolingian countries, the Hapsburg succession states, the German-speaking countries, the British and French model cases of western democracy, the British Isles, Benelux, Scandinavia, the Baltic states, the Allies of World War II, the emerging democracies of central and eastern Europe, the four neutral countries not members of NATO, or the coastal states of the three European seas and oceans.

30. Nor do they view each other as possessing an unconditional right to assistance arising from a European sense of solidarity. When Europeans are moved to altruism, they are far more likely to direct their charitable donations to Bangladesh than to the inhabitants of the Irish Northwest.

31. Gerard Delanty, "Theories of Social Integration and the European Union: Rethinking Culture," unpublished paper (University of Liverpool, 1996), 6.

32. In the mid-1990s, EU social expenditures totaled 0.9 percent of the welfare budgets of member states. Richard Gomà, "The Social Dimension of the European Union: A New Type of Welfare System?" *Journal of European Public Policy* 3, no. 2 (1996): 222.

33. Immerfall and Sobisch, "Europäische Integration und europäische Identität."

34. John Crowley, "European Integration: Sociological Process or Political Project?" *Innovation* 9, no. 2 (1997): 156.

35. Presently, the EU is home to eleven languages, three large Christian and several non-Christian religious communities, growing geographic distance, vastly different member state experiences with Europe, and, above all, disparities in economic development and productive capacity. For example, with respect to the last dimension, the ratio of the per capita production of Luxembourg and Greece in 1995 was 3 to 1. See Richard Rose, *What Is Europe? A Dynamic Perspective* (New York: HarperCollins, 1996), 278.

36. Michael J. Baun, *An Imperfect Union* (Boulder, Colo.: Westview, 1996), 143.

37. The preceding discussion demonstrates that the EU cannot be thought of as a construct analogous to a normal "state." The reason is that the collapse of state socialism and its border with the West has raised questions about the limits of the European state and its "people" that have yet to be definitively answered in the manner required for a normal and proper state.

38. Grimm, *Braucht Europa eine Verfassung?* 34.

39. Scharpf, "Demokratische Politik in Europa," 65.

40. The standard of western European democracy should be thought of here in contrast to what O'Donnell terms the simple "electoralism" of Latin American "delegative democracy." See Guillermo O'Donnell, "Delegative Democracy," *Journal of Democracy* 5, no. 1 (1994): 55–69.

41. Habermas vehemently rejects this conclusion, even if with a few bold normative insinuations, in *Die Einbeziehung des Anderen*. And he is not alone in dissenting from this pessimistic view of the prospects for European integration. Sassoon thinks it imaginable, desirable, and even imperative for the maintenance of the level of integration already achieved in Europe that the integration process be liberated from the shackles of the Common Market and informed instead by the objective of setting goals for a sociopolitically secured "democratic union of citizens." To this end, he proposes anchoring a normative minimum for the whole of Europe in a European *Charta*. This *Charta* would be more abstract than the *acquis*, and at the same time would democratize European legislation and strengthen the protection of basic and social rights in certain member states. Its purpose would be to make the political principles of a "European model of social capitalism" binding on all present and future members of the Union. See Donald Sassoon, *Social Democracy at the Heart of Europe* (London: Institute for Public Policy Research, 1996), 15. A similar call for the political-moral validity of a specifically "European project of modernity," combining an emphasis on productivity with political and institutional checks on the operation of the market, is found in Brian Bercusson et al., *Soziales Europa—ein Manifest* (Hamburg: Rowohlt, 1996), 18.

42. EU member states are suspicious of the fact that Germany is the only EU member to express a national preference for supranational empowerment. Even when this preference is recognized as sincere, distrust can be stirred by the anomaly of a nation-state that has misgivings about its own sovereignty and therefore seeks to abolish it. See Andre Markovits and Simon Reich, *The German Predicament* (Ithaca, N.Y.: Cornell University Press, 1997), on this subject.

43. Ian Buruma, "Fear and Loathing in Europe," *New York Review of Books*, October 17, 1996, 57.

44. Tony Judt, *Große Illusion Europa: Herausforderungen und Gefahren einer Idee* (München: Hanser, 1996), 142–159.

45. Ralf Dahrendorf, "Die Quadratur des Kreises—Freiheit, Solidarität und Wohlstand," *Transit* 12 (1996): 5–28.

46. Immerfall and Sobisch, "Europäische Integration und europäische Identität," 33.

47. Walter Hornstein and Gerd Mutz, *Die europäische Einigung als gesellschaftlicher Prozeß* (Baden-Baden: Nomos, 1993), 22, 249.

48. For instance, it is clearly not feasible to extend the common agricultural policy, as it is presently conceived, to a country such as Poland, where no less than 27 percent of all those employed are still in the agricultural sector.

5

Democratic Governance beyond the Nation-State

Michael Zürn

If the EU were to apply for membership in the EU, "it would not qualify because of the inadequate democratic content of its constitution."[1] Nevertheless, a good 50 percent of the acts passed in, for example, France today are merely the implementation of measures decided upon in the opaque labyrinth of institutions in faraway Brussels.[2] Is France still democratically governed? The picture is similar for other international organizations across the world. The system of agreements associated with the World Trade Organization, for instance, comprises almost 10,000 pages. The last round of trade negotiations lasted for over a decade and included the participation of more than 150 states and thousands of experts. Although these agreements have far-reaching implications for employees in the agricultural and crisis-prone industrial sectors, the German government is generally almost overzealous in implementing the demands stipulated in the agreements. Did German citizens really have a recognizable influence on these decisions?

The problem is clear. Although security and social welfare, two important aims of governance, can be better achieved with international institutions than without them, the mere existence of international institutions is no guarantee of good governance. Apart from producing effective solutions to problems in the fields of security and social welfare, governance must also fulfill certain procedural requirements in order to be perceived as good. From the point of view of democratic theory, international institutions have very shaky foundations. As state competences dwindle, therefore, democratic substance seems necessarily to be draining away.[3]

But what exactly are the problems of democratic legitimation in multilevel decision-making systems, where national representatives formulate policies through international negotiation? In this chapter, I want to argue first that the underlying problem is societal denationalization, not international institutionalization. Framing this problem as a choice between *effective problem-solving through international institutions and democratic political processes* is misconceived. Without international institutions, politics in the OECD countries would not be more democratic. Those who see international institutions as the problem are, however, correct in emphasizing that the connection between nation and democracy is not an accidental one. The civil notion of nation implies a *demos* and thus public discourse. As Greven and Offe observe with respect to Europe, the lack of such a *demos* on a transnational level poses a problem that becomes more acute when combined with the existence of transnational social spaces. Although other forms of transnational interest aggregation—such as intergovernmental bargaining and argumentation among transnational epistemic communities—alleviate the problem, they do not solve it. Second, I contend that in a modern, denationalized society, democratic legitimation can be achieved only with a mixed constitution comprising both majority procedures and negotiation mechanisms. Third, such a solution at the transnational level requires a new perspective, which involves breaking away from a static notion of the so-called prerequisites of democracy and dismantling some of the more cherished analytical concepts of democratic theory.

DEMOCRACY

"Persons should be free and equal in the determination of the conditions of their own lives, so long as they do not deploy this framework to negate the rights of others."[4] On the basis of this principle of autonomy, democracy is, in a very general sense, a form of public-will formation and decision making whereby everybody affected by the decision has the same opportunity to influence and actively participate in the process. Moreover, democracy is required to produce normatively justifiable solutions. This "complex concept of democracy"[5] rejects purely proceduralist or republican interpretations that reduce democracy to a decision-making system and ignore the content of decisions. At the same time, it challenges purely liberalist or constitutionalist definitions that regard individual political rights as prepolitically given and seeks to protect them from the outcomes of the democratic process. A complex concept of democracy is reflective in the sense that the normative fundamentals of the democratic process, such as autonomous individuals with freedom of opinion and information, and the democratic process itself are seen as mutually reproducing one another.[6]

One central requirement for the working of democracy thus understood is congruence, the matching of social and political spaces.[7] For the purposes of democracy, congruence is necessary at two critical junctures: first, between citizens and their representatives (the congruence of input and decision-making systems), and second, between the space in which regulations are valid and the space in which social interactions are dense (output congruence). If there is no input congruence, then a group affected by a decision but not participating in its making can be considered to have been determined by others instead of self-determined. Traditional forms of foreign determination or dominance were asymmetrical—for instance, when a small group of colonial rulers ruled over a large group of people in a colony. Today, however, foreign determination has taken on a different appearance. It tends to be more symmetrical and is based on manifold externalities, as a result of which many political decisions have transboundary effects. For example, the decisions of the British and German governments in the 1960s and 1970s not to implement certain environmental protection measures led to acidic lakes and high fish mortality in Scandinavia. Swedish fishermen, however, were not in a position to participate in public-will formation or relevant decision making with Great Britain or Germany. This constitutes a democratic deficit.

The congruence of the space for which regulations are valid and the boundaries of the relevant social transactions—output congruence—are also significant for democratic legitimation. A *de jure* freedom, that is, the legal authorization to do something or to refrain from doing something, is worth almost nothing without de facto freedom, that is, actual freedom of choice. In a denationalized world ruled by a system of formally independent nation-states, however, there is a danger that political communities will be unable to reach a desired goal owing to conditions outside their jurisdiction. Here, it is not a decision of another government or political actor, but structural pressures growing out of a denationalized economy that causes the deficit. Thus, a social policy desired by the majority of the people in a given political community can become unaffordable for reasons of international competitiveness. In this case, the problem is constituted by so-called non-decisions,[8] a new, non-class-specific type of "selectivity practised by political institutions,"[9] which cannot rationally be justified. If certain governance goals that were traditionally pursued and achieved in the heyday of the democratic welfare state can no longer be attained because of an output incongruence, then there is also a democratic deficit.[10] For instance, if so-called Ordo-Liberals strive for a European economic constitution, which on the one hand fosters European market integration but on the other prevents political interventions in the market, then such a "constitutional division of economic powers"[11] creates a limitation on democracy. Economic liberties, the domestic market, and the system of undistorted competition must be the justifiable results of a process of public-will formation and decision making. They cannot simply be withdrawn from this process and declared to be prepolitical issues.

Although it is necessary to be realistic about setting democratic criteria and to avoid falling victim to the myth of "democratic omnipotence,"[12] it is equally important from a critical perspective not simply to adjust normative standards to political reality without comment. Without question, there is a "need to re-set the standards by which we assess legitimacy."[13] However, the new concept must derive from normative standards that adequately reflect new circumstances and not be purely the result of empirical observations. In this sense, as Greven points out in his chapter, both the growing political externalities of integrated markets (due to input incongruence) and the declining political discretion of nation-states (due to output incongruence) pose a democratic problem. It is important to emphasize in this regard that incongruence between social and political space caused by globalization is therefore prior to international institutions.

DEMOCRATIC PROCESSES IN AND BEYOND THE NATION-STATE

In the age of globalization, governance beyond the nation-state can actually improve social welfare and democracy. To the extent that societal denationalization—in my opinion, a more precise concept than globalization—increases, the effectiveness of national policies in many areas diminishes.[14] This loss of political effectiveness is partially compensated for by international institutions that extend the space in which political regulations are valid in accordance with the density of societal transactions. In this way, they reduce the democratic deficits caused by input and output incongruence. At the same time, however, they produce new democratic deficits. The greater the significance of such international institutions, the greater the need for democratic legitimation of their decisions. At the moment, it is inadequate.[15] Certainly as regards European institutions, I am in agreement with Greven and Offe that the contemporary situation is far from ideal.

It would be wrong, however, to treat complaints about democratic deficits in the European Union as a direct criticism of individual bodies of the EU. Such complaints often reflect a rather general criticism of the manner in which political regulations in Europe come into being and of the content of those regulations. Thus, they typically relate to the European multilevel policy-making system as a whole. The concept of a multilevel system sui generis, however, implies that the European Union has to be seen as a new type of political system made up of national and European institutions that are constituted in relation to each other. It follows from this that western European national institutions and EU institutions are so closely interwoven that they can no longer be conceived as separate political systems.[16] Democratic legitimacy in Europe is therefore less a question of democratizing individual EU bodies than of considering how a complex multilevel system in its totality can be made more democratic.

The logic of multilevel systems and the problems of democratic legitimacy arising from them affect international institutions other than the EU in a similar way.[17] Nevertheless, the multilevel system of the EU differs from conventional international institutions in at least two ways. First, regulations emanating from the different European sectors (European regimes, if you wish) are so closely related to each other that, as a network, they affect a number of political issue areas at once within a defined territory, the borders of which are somewhat loosely specified. This, indeed, is what justifies the use of the terms "European community" and "multilevel system." In contrast, issue-specific international institutions are more functional, and the sum of international regimes does not cover a recognizable territorial space. Here, the term "multilevel politics" (for each specific institution) is more appropriate. Second, in contrast to the European Union, international regimes are to a great extent passive political institutions that are hardly capable of becoming politically autonomous, established as they are by nation-states existing independently of the regimes themselves.

While some observers situate the problem of democratic legitimacy in the workings of the EU and other international institutions, others, like Greven and Offe, question the very possibility of democratic processes beyond the nation-state. In their view, democratic legitimacy is possible only within the framework of a *demos*—that is, a political community expressed in the concept of the nation. Beyond the nation-state, there is no strong sense of public interest, and the potential for political regulation is limited.[18] Peter Graf Kielmansegg eloquently summarizes this point of view: "Collective identities develop, become stable, and are passed into tradition in communities of communication, of experiences, and of memories. Europe, even within the narrower scope of Western Europe, has no communication community, hardly any common memories, and only limited common experiences."[19] Hence, the connection between nation and democracy is not an historical coincidence but is systematic and indissoluble. A European political community extending beyond national borders does not as yet exist, but without such a *demos*, there can be no democracy. That appears to be the essence of the skeptical argument. Let me explain this view more fully.

The skeptical view of the prospects for democratic legitimacy beyond the nation-state seems particularly apt in the case of majority decisions, which are often regarded as the central component of the democratic process. The principle of majority decisions holds that when a collectively binding decision is taken, everyone must comply with it, including those actors who voted against it.[20] As a rule, however, outvoted actors will accept a decision only if the decision-making process is deemed legitimate and sanctions are applied for noncompliance. Typically, a high regard for the legitimacy of the decision-making process and a willingness to establish a system of sanctions develop within the framework of a political community, and so without a *demos*, there seems to be no basis for a democratic majority decision.

In this regard, some theorists have argued that where there is neither a *demos* nor a sufficiently stable collective identity, it is better to give precedence to bargaining and "consociational" procedures over majority decisions. As Gerhard Lehmbruch, one of the foremost analysts of so-called consociational or concordant democracies, writes with regard to countries such as Switzerland or Austria: "In the development phase of culturally fragmented societies, which is characterized by vertically integrated 'factions' or 'pillars', concordant democracies are strategically planned by organisational elites of the rival sides, as they know that they cannot reckon with certain gains in majority decision procedures."[21] Grande considers this political form more fully in the next chapter.

Nevertheless, even negotiation systems that require unanimous decisions can be deficient in the absence of a *demos*. In the first place, without a minimal sense of "togetherness," relations among social units tend to become competitive. Competitive relations, however, encourage participants to be relative gains-seekers, impeding cooperation in the pursuit of longer-term objectives.[22] This means that efforts to coordinate the improvement of welfare often fail before they begin, and this is clearly inconsistent with the democratic requirement that outcomes be justifiable in normative terms. Such efforts are successful only when participants in the negotiating process regard each other positively; if they are indifferent to each other's needs, coordination will usually depend on supplementary factors. And there is another drawback. Without a distinct collective identity, negotiation systems based on unanimity can never lead to redistributive measures, because "rational" factions will veto any measure that requires them to relinquish resources.[23] Thus, without a *demos*, even negotiation systems based on consensus procedures seem to be doomed to failure.

Against this background, it comes as no surprise that more recent analyses of democratic legitimacy focus on international political processes in which aggregative decision-making components are dominated by deliberative components emphasizing arguing over bargaining. In 1996, for instance, in the multilevel system of the European Union, there were 409 committees active in the implementation of general Council decisions. These committees enjoyed extensive interpretative freedom in their work. Their members were mainly experts and representatives of concerned interest groups, as well as national civil servants selected by national governments, and committee decisions typically met with approval.[24] Intensive empirical studies of the food committees, particularly by Joerges and Neyer, conclude with a positive evaluation of this "comitology."[25] These authors maintain that comitology explicitly fulfills the congruence requirement, because it takes the interests of all those affected by an issue into account, not just those within a particular country. They contend, moreover, that it is conducive to deliberative behavior that transcends strategic intergovernmental bargaining. In the same vein, Giandomenico Majone advocates the role of independent agencies as a means of social regulation: "Recent empirical research provides additional evidence in favour of the thesis that non-majoritarian decision-making mechanisms are more suitable for complex, plural societies than are mechanisms that concentrate power in the hands of the political majority."[26]

Related developments can be observed in the field of international environmental politics. After the admission of transnational nongovernmental organizations (NGOs) into the process, intergovernmental negotiations received an impetus that clearly distinguished them from conventional interstate negotiations. The inclusion of NGOs elevated the status of epistemic communities,[27] which has had two salutary effects. It has helped strengthen deliberative elements at the expense of simple bargaining elements, and it has contributed to the relativization of particular interests by public interests.[28] One outcome has been the rise of "sectoral publics," which appear to play a role in the formulation of policies beyond the nation-state that is functionally equivalent to the role played by national publics in domestic policy making.

But if a model of deliberative democracy among public interest–oriented associations does not require a complete *demos*, the deliberation of the representatives in committees at least implies that a common goal exists, one that transcends individual interests. This suggests that deliberative networks, which are a productive form of governing beyond the nation-state, depend on the participating actors being oriented toward the public interest. Such a suggestion, if true, would add more support to the skeptical thesis that, without elements of a transnational *demos*, democratic governance beyond the nation-state is not possible.

A model of deliberative democracy among public interest–oriented associations confronts further problems. If it is to fulfill basic democratic criteria, it must incorporate individual rights and the complementary principle of majority voting. As a rule, however, consensus-oriented deliberations are more successful when held *in camera* and among a small number of actors. Thus, the model of deliberative democracy can create new, and sometimes even more severe, problems for democratic legitimacy. As Benz writes, "Deliberative negotiations and cooperation improve the effectiveness of state activities, but they are at the same time linked with unequal chances of participation and an infringement of the principle of public accessibility."[29]

Consensus-oriented decision making is also not at all conducive to the formulation of redistributive policies, since those actors who would be required to relinquish resources are likely to be resistant to such policies. Majone's response to this problem is to advocate that the EU in general be relieved of responsibility for redistributive policies, and its competence restricted to "social regulation."[30] A closer look at the policies analyzed by Majone reveals, however, that the regulatory agencies recommended actually focus mainly on the regulation of products, not production processes. The regulation of production processes (an important component of regulatory policies and vital for effective governance) always has significant redistributive implications. The strategy of delegating redistribution to such narrowly focused agencies is dubious and likely to exacerbate underlying political and social tensions.

Even within specific fields of regulatory policy, then, nonmajoritarian decision-making processes have only limited applicability. To expect such processes to form the central element of democratic governance beyond the nation-state, as Majone does, is to evade the problem.[31] If the implementation of social and regulatory policies with strong distributive implications is hampered at the national level by international competition and obstructed at the international level by nonmajoritarian decision-making processes, then the initial question reemerges: How can effective and democratically legitimate governance beyond the nation-state be achieved? In part, at least, we have to rely on aggregative democratic elements, because purely consensus-oriented deliberation is unlikely to lead to policies involving redistribution. In short, the democratic quality of a multilevel political system cannot be enhanced by drawing up a "new model" of democracy that downgrades majoritarian decision making.

DISAGGREGATING THE *DEMOS*

Without any form of *demos*, there will always be democratic deficits. There is no law, however, stating that a *demos* beyond the nation cannot exist. In order better to understand the origins of *demos*-formation, it is necessary to deconstruct the all-embracing term. A *demos* is not a prepolitical quantity, the result of cultural or ethnic homogeneity. On the contrary, cultural pluralism is, logically speaking, a precondition for a democratic process. In Gerstenberg's words, "Democratic self-government is not thwarted by, but rather benefits from, a heterogeneity of participants and comprehensive moral outlooks."³² A *demos* is thus necessary only in the sense that, in addition to the plethora of the differences, a basic public-interest orientation must exist. A fully cultivated public-interest orientation, nevertheless, need not obtain from the outset. As the development of democratic nation-states has shown, community and democracy are mutually reinforcing. It is also important to note that the borderlines of a *demos* are not automatically identical with those of social spaces. The theory of nationalism identifies a number of requirements for the development of a *demos*: for example, the increasing density of transactions,³³ the functional requirements arising out of growing interdependencies,³⁴ the existence of an administrative apparatus,³⁵ and sufficient means of communication.³⁶ Clearly, then, the boundaries of a *demos* are not given but are politically defined.

The dynamic relationship between community building and democracy can be appreciated more fully by pulling apart the concept of *demos*. The term itself today comprises several aspects that converged historically in democratic welfare states but that are analytically distinct. The following dissection also makes clear that the different components of a democratic process discussed above are based on different aspects of the term *demos*.

1. The members of a demos acknowledge each other as autonomous individuals, each with a right to personal self-fulfillment. In this sense, civil liberty rights, including the right to physical integrity, are constitutionally embodied in a political community. Within the advanced industrial world, a transnational concern for human rights can largely be assumed to exist. Increasingly, civil society actors sue for human rights and protection from arbitrary violence on a transnational scale, and people organize themselves transnationally to prevent infringements of human rights "abroad." The course of societal denationalization has heightened the significance of these transnational monitoring activities. Even the legally binding incorporation of human rights at the individual level, including the right to bring suit in their defense, is guaranteed by the European Human Rights Commission. There is evidence of similar developments outside of Europe too.³⁷

2. The members of a *demos* mutually acknowledge the right of one another to participate in will formation and decision making. In this sense, political rights to participation are an integral part of a political community. At the same time, the mutual recognition of partici-

pation rights implies that once an obligation has been entered into,
it must be complied with. This aspect of a political community also
appears to be relatively well established in the advanced industrial
world. If problems that have clear transboundary implications arise,
it is more or less accepted that all affected countries are entitled to
have their say as long as they are represented by democratically
elected politicians. It is also generally accepted that agreed-upon international obligations should be fulfilled, and national populations
increasingly demand this. Indeed, if this were not the case, it would
be hard to explain why most western states comply with international contractual obligations.[38] The origins of these principles may
be the mutual obligations that arise in a society of states, and thus
they may be construed as states' rights rather than individual
rights.[39] The critical point, however, is that these principles are
stronger today than ever, fostered as they are by a mutual transnational acknowledgment of the importance of participation in decision-making processes having an impact at the individual level. The
steady increase in election monitoring, for example, demonstrates
that political rights, including those of people in other countries, are
increasingly being defended on a transnational scale.[40]

3. The members of a fully developed *demos* also exhibit a collective
sense of identity if their preferences as individuals include a concern
for the welfare (or the suffering) of the collective. In its weak form,
such a sense of identity is a precondition for public deliberations
about the right solution for the community as a whole, and it is precisely this aspect of a *demos* that does not fully exist on the transnational level, even within the advanced industrial world. There is little
transnational public debate about the "right" policies for the western world as a whole. There definitely exist transnational sectoral
publics, however, in the field of environmental protection, which can
roughly be described as engaging in deliberations about the "right"
policies.

4. In its stronger form, a collective sense of identity provides the basis
for (re)distributive processes within a political community. Although the EU's regional and structural funds reflect some awareness of redistributive obligations on the European level, a recognizable sense of transnational social obligations is barely perceptible.
While redistributive programs to deal with catastrophies exist, they
have an ad hoc character and aim mainly at rescuing people. Hu-
manitarian activities of this sort are more accurately interpreted as
evidence of support for the notion of a transnational concern for
human rights. It is not clear, though, that the strong form of collective identity suggested by the acceptance of redistributive measures

is necessary for democracy. National democracies differ widely in their use of redistributive policies, and, even within individual nation-states, acceptance of such measures varies across geographic regions.

The preceding differentiation of the components of a *demos* shows that the potential for democratic processes beyond the nation-state must not be ruled out as a matter of principle; rather, it indicates that such processes are in their initial stages of development. It is not disputed in the advanced industrial world that all those affected by a denationalized issue must be represented in the process of international policy formulation. Congruence is thus acknowledged as a transnational normative criterion. At the same time, at least in certain issue areas, it is possible to identify sectoral networks that deliberate in a semipublic fashion over the right course of action to take. Elements of a transnational political community with supervisory functions can be seen in the monitoring of national governments' implementation of certain international policies and in the transboundary recognition of basic individual human rights. This in no way means that the democratic legitimacy of governance beyond the nation-state is already sufficient. It does indicate, however, that some aspects of a transnational political community—a transnational *demos*—do exist. There is no reason why this cannot be further developed within a democratic framework.

THE DEMOCRATIZATION OF INTERNATIONAL INSTITUTIONS

What kind of institutional policy would facilitate the development of democratic governance beyond the nation-state? The answer is a policy comprising a mixture of democratic components. In the face of denationalization, neither traditional intergovernmental bargaining nor consensus-oriented forms of decision making by experts nor majority decision alone can do the job. As Benz puts it, it is a question of "finding the right combination."[41] For this purpose, it is necessary to debate a combination of proposals for institutional reform. Two caveats must be kept in mind as the following remarks work to push just such a debate forward. First, my emphasis here is on desirability, not immediate feasibility. Second, brevity is of value at this stage and in the present context; qualifications must wait.

In order to find the right combination, it is necessary to make two categorical distinctions, one pertaining to the constitutive processes of a democracy and the other to the constitutive actors of a democracy. With respect to the first distinction, we must note that a democratic process comprises both aggregative and deliberative elements. Aggregative processes, in which all participants try to assert their interests unconditionally, are not sufficient to constitute a democracy. There is also a need for deliberative processes, in which all participants have to justify their concerns as a matter of public interest. In this respect, they must argue instead of bargain with each other. Nevertheless, it is highly improbable that such deliberative and discursive processes will culminate in a consensual decision. At some point, there will be no alternative but to terminate the deliberations and move on to a process of aggregation. This will involve some sort of voting or coming to a decision by unanimity or the majority principle.

With respect to the second distinction, it is important to see that, although the normative reference points of democracy are ultimately individual, autonomous persons, the actors in a democracy can be of the individual or the corporate variety. In a parliamentary democracy, for example, individuals vote for representatives who are answerable only to their own consciences. Individual democratic actors can also act in so-called direct democratic processes, such as municipal meetings and referenda. In contrast, collective organizations represent the interests of their members as a whole. Representatives of these organizations attend international negotiations as agents of the whole; they are answerable to the organizations as collectives, rather than to their own consciences. Here, organizations function as actors.

Crossing the two types of actors with the two fundamental democratic processes yields four single components of a democratic process, each of which signifies a different form of interest mediation (see Table 5.1).[42] The bracketed terms in each box identify institutional stereotypes associated with a bias in favor of that particular component.[43] The key is to find the appropriate mix of components for a given political community.

Not surprisingly, the appropriate mix depends on historical circumstances. Citizens' meetings in Athenian times, for example, when the low

Table 5.1 Components of a Democratic Process

PROCEDURES	ACTORS	
	Individuals	Organizations (territorial or sectoral)
Deliberative	Direct deliberative democracy ("Talking shops")	Associative democracy (Expertocracy)
Aggregative	Majoritarian democracy (Telecracy)	Bargaining democracy (Eurocracy)

number of potential participants made the proceedings easy to survey, were dominated by direct-deliberative elements. In large, democratic, federal nation-states like contemporary Germany, by contrast, all components are relatively evenly represented. There is majority voting in elections but bargaining within the federal elements of the political system. Meanwhile, the "Verbändestaat" (state dominated and penetrated by interest associations) denounced in 1963 by Eschenburg[44] gave rise not just to bargaining but also to public-interest-oriented deliberations, for instance in corporatist organizations. Finally, the German parliament—in theory, at least—is the locus for public debate about the "right" political course overall.

In the EU and other international institutions, however, there is today a strong bias toward the aggregation of state interests. As Greven pointed out above, intergovernmental negotiations, which are mostly of a strategic nature and follow the principle of unanimity, are usually opaque and far removed from the kind of direct-deliberative democratic components that citizens can experience firsthand.[45] Here, there are clearly democratic deficits. To eliminate them, it is necessary first to democratize the problematic bargaining components of the decision-making process, and then to enhance the other components.

Bargaining Procedures—Democratization of Territorial Representation

A central feature of multilevel politics is that national representatives agree in camera on norms and rules to be implemented on the national level. As a rule, the same government representative conducting the negotiations then also lobbies for the approval of the results by his or her national parliament and public. The problem with having the same agent act on different levels, however, is that he or she is better informed than anyone else. This confers an advantage that can be put to strategic use or abuse. One example: an evident increase in credit-claiming and scapegoating in national politics. Every national economic crisis seems to be caused by global economic forces, and every economic boom is the result of wise national policies; a rising crime rate is a manifestation of international trends, but a drop in crime is brought about by the implementation of national measures. Furthermore, the executive is typically better informed than actors in other branches of government, and this puts the latter at a disadvantage in the agenda-setting process.[46]

In international regimes with a limited range of regulations, the aforementioned problems of multilevel politics are tolerable. Because opportunities for linkage across relatively narrowly defined issue areas are limited, it is comparatively easy to keep track of the affairs of specific international organizations. In such cases simple measures are often suf-

ficient to increase transparency and facilitate the monitoring of executive
activities. For instance, every national negotiating team (which as a rule
is made up of government representatives) could be accompanied by a
small group of observers without the right to speak or vote, whose main
function would be to inform the national public about the government's
point of view, behavior, and bargaining strategy. This group could include members of the parliamentary opposition; to prevent the possibility
of information being strategically abused by the opposition, however, it
could also include well-known and highly credible experts from the relevant issue area.

In the case of the European Union, where government conferences and
the European Council negotiate on almost all internationalized issue
areas, the problem of nontransparency is particularly acute. It is almost
impossible for citizens to hold specific governments or representatives responsible for political outcomes. In multilevel systems with relatively distinct borderlines such as this one (that is, with an identical membership
over a large number of issue areas), different persons, each having legitimacy, could represent different levels of the system. For the EU, this
would mean that the national representatives of the Council of Ministers
could be elected directly by their national constituents in an election separate from that for the national government. This would drastically shorten
the Council of Ministers' chain of legitimation and transform it into a
more responsible collective body. Under this arrangement, both the national governments and the national representatives in the Council of
Ministers would have to account for their policies individually before the
public. This would almost certainly lead to frequent conflicts, which
would have the much desired effect of promoting transparency and clari-
fying for the public its own role in the multilevel system. The public
would then be much better equipped to determine who is responsible for
what policy. The American political system, in which governors are
elected independently from senators, is an example of such an arrangement.[47] Democratizing territorial representation in the European decision-making system in this way would surely encourage the growth of a
European sense of identity. It would also reinforce the deliberative component of the decision-making process, insofar as national representatives
would be forced to emphasize the European dimension of their policies
in order to maintain electoral support.

Majority Voting—Promoting Referenda

Political scientists commonly advise against legitimation by majority
voting in international decision-making systems. If this is a valid warning
against naive conceptions of a European or worldwide state system, it

nevertheless also reflects a static view of political institutions, which are not just founded on the basis of a sense of *demos*, but also generate and reinforce that sense in turn. Schmalz-Bruns correctly notes that "taking a side-entrance (by the bargaining method) seems to sap more potential for a sense of political community than it creates."[48] It thus seems desirable to identify procedures that would strengthen a sense of community. Given the interactive relationship between *demos* and the institutions of democracy, such a strengthening would itself contribute to democratization.

In Europe, the aim must therefore be to introduce majoritarian procedures that function in the absence of a fully developed political community while at the same time fostering its development, and that contain a safety valve against bargaining blockades and nontransparent situations. Within the context of the European multilevel system, European referenda on more general issues could be a useful instrument. Although national referenda on the Maastricht Agreement clearly exposed the legitimacy problems of the EU, they also showed that such significant political events can encourage public discourse.[49] A referendum is more than just a ballot. It differs from pure "telecracy" by virtue of a phase of discourse that is at least as significant as the ballot itself. If referenda were held across Europe, it would be futile to instrumentalize them for national purposes (as happened with the referenda on the Maastricht Agreement). European-wide referenda could then constitute a political decision-making instrument for an extended political arena, with the potential for both community building and even public deliberation. Referenda could be called for the specific purpose of increasing the chances of reversing agreed-upon policies in the EU. They could also be a good mechanism for breaking up real or perceived political cartels.[50] Political systems that feature direct democratic elements seem to have a longer time-horizon as well.[51] Finally, referenda could increase transparency and overcome the difficulty of attributing responsibility for individual policies to specific politicians by restoring complete control to the voters.

This is not as far-fetched as it may seem. Comparative democratic research has shown that referenda help to counterbalance deficits in bargaining democracies.[52] In highly heterogeneous societies, national political systems featuring strong bargaining components often offer considerable possibilities for direct citizen participation as well. One of the best examples is the United States, where strong, direct, democratic elements exist at a local level and in individual states. The case of Switzerland, where more referenda have been held since 1945 than in any other democratic system, is also instructive. Nor do direct democratic elements offer a "premium for demagogues," as former German Federal President Theodor Heuss suspected. Rather, they can act as a stabilizing force by giving the electorate a means of checking the high-handedness and empty actionism of the political class. Referenda are also credited for their integrative effect. To be sure, referenda can increase the cost and duration of decision-making processes. Contrary to popular opinion, however, inefficiency does not seem to be the major problem with EU decision making. Although the time it takes for an EU regulation to come into effect, from the day it is officially proposed by the Commission to the day of the Council's final decision, has increased over the past few years to around 160 days, this is not appreciably longer than analogous processes in most national political systems.[53] Thus, it is not surprising that a number of proposals have been advanced for the introduction of European-wide referenda to counterbalance the dominance of bargaining democracy.[54]

The question that remains to be answered is what decisions should be put to European-wide referenda. Clearly, there are a number of issues for which referenda are not an appropriate form of decision making, at least initially. First, an issue must be significant enough to generate the publicity needed for a referendum. A new milk quota regulation is likely not a suitable subject. Second, the issue to be voted on should not be one that has primarily redistributive implications, as this may give rise to conflicts between member states that could jeopardize the existing level of integration. As discussed above, and in the Greven and Offe chapters, redistributive measures are generally accepted only if the *demos* already has a strong sense of identity; they do not provide a good basis for generating such an identity. Thus, given that a European political community has yet to be fully formed, reform of the common agricultural policy would also not likely be a good candidate for a European-wide referendum.

This leaves policies that are a result of majoritarian politics.[55] Policies of this sort spread costs and benefits evenly across the population and transcend the (ever-present) interests of particular parties. A classic example is a defense measure, which would be quite appropriate for a European referendum—for example, a proposed extension of the common foreign and security policies. Similarly, the results of negotiations for entry into the EU could be decided on by referenda, not only in the countries under consideration but also in the whole of the Union. Environmental policy is a third candidate, inasmuch as environmental measures typically lead to higher consumer prices but generate benefits enjoyed throughout Europe. Where constitutional questions are concerned, however, referenda would be best held only after the application of strong restraints and with a qualified majority—if a qualified majority in the European parliament (EP) were to vote for a referendum, perhaps, or a transnational quorum of 10 percent of the European electorate were reached.[56] For "normal" (as opposed to constitutional) policies, lower, though still transnational, quora could be sufficient to call a referendum.

The European parliament could decide on the policies to be categorized as majoritarian, and these policies could be specified on a list supplemented over time.

One important objection to the oft-heard demands for a strengthening of the European parliament with real political powers is the argument that national cleavages will gain in importance within the EP. The answer is to reinforce party-political orientations. A simple way of doing this would be to eliminate national party lists for elections to the European parliament and have European party associations draw up European lists instead. A vote for the Greens in Berlin would then also benefit the Greens in Athens. Again, it is a question of creating majoritarian procedures that generate rather than sap a community spirit and that relieve some of the pressure on the EU's mammoth negotiating structures. Once the European party associations are consolidated, however, more thought can be given to strengthening the powers of the European parliament.

Institutional policies of this sort that generate a sense of community are not really transferable to multilevel systems other than the EU, because conventional international institutions lack a key feature of the European multilevel system that makes the introduction of majority voting feasible. In the EU, the different sectoral European regulations are interwoven so tightly that they form a kind of network, which constitutes a new political arena (albeit one with rather hazy outlines). Only within such an established political arena does it make sense to introduce majority decision-making procedures aimed at improving public welfare.

Associative Democracy—Increasing the Representativeness of Deliberative Networks

In spite of the arguments against institutionalizing deliberative bargaining networks, using networks to engage in associative democracy does have the potential to enhance democratic governance beyond the nation-state. The democratic quality of deliberative networks of interest groups and epistemic communities is heightened if the participating organizations are representative in two respects. First, they must adequately represent their membership; and second, they must not be an elite group. Decision-making networks must in principle be open and transparent to all groups affected by the regulation; self-selection of the members of a deliberative decision-making network must be ruled out.

Transnational decision-making networks could be strengthened but at the same time subjected to entry criteria. These criteria would be designed to permit all those interest groups to participate that: (1) can offer a satisfactory justification for their concern and thus be helpful in the implementation of the regulation in question; (2) have established organizations in

several of the countries concerned; and (3) have democratic internal structures and procedures open to scrutiny. From the point of view of democratic theory, the last requirement is of central significance if the role of
the interest group or epistemic community in the decision-making process extends beyond merely exerting influence to counteracting other interests. If an interest group, an NGO, or an epistemic community partici-
pates in either the making or the implementation of a collectively binding
decision, or if the exit option is not cost free for its members (that is, the
source of the group's influence), the entity must be democratically organized. This means that its membership must be open to all regardless of
party membership, race, or sex; the organizational leadership must be
freely elected; its political structure, including the disclosure of its income
and expenditure, must be open to all members; and it must not pursue
profit-seeking activities.

As Much Direct Deliberative Democracy as Possible

   In a direct deliberative democracy, collective decisions are made by
public deliberation in local fora in which anyone can participate. Some
theorists see direct deliberative procedures as the core of a future democracy project, because in their view today's crucial issues arise at the local
level.[57] In Germany, for example, the bulk of state activities and about
two-thirds of all state investments are still carried out by towns and districts.[58] Although many transactions cross national borders, often reducing the effectiveness of local policies in the process, it seems appropriate
that for the regulation of social transactions with a more local character,
the direct deliberative component be reinforced. *Ceteris paribus*, it is easier
to democratize decision-making processes in small communities, and it is
easier for individuals to cope with the complexity of governance if there
are clearly defined areas in which their direct participation and influence
can be experienced. In this respect, the strengthening of direct deliberative democratic elements in small regional political units becomes an urgently necessary correlate to the strengthening of bargaining elements beyond the national realm. At the same time, an institutionalized forum for
such small political units should be established where participants could
discuss their experiences with different local policies. The notion of competition among policies could be quite productive here, a lesson that
arises often in consideration of American-style federalism.

INDIVIDUALS AND DEMOCRATIC GOVERNANCE
BEYOND THE NATION-STATE

The nation-state acquired a symbolic framework at an early stage that fa-
cilitated the development of a strong sense of national identity. This made

the nation-state uniquely able to reach beyond face-to-face relations and to serve the collective desires of "imagined" communities.[59] In many instances, the emergence of a strong national collective identity brought great suffering in its wake. In time, however, national identities were matched with civil constitutions in most advanced industrial countries. A fully developed civil political community not only facilitates the democratic process but also is constituted by it—points emphasized by my collaborators in this book. On the basis of this two-way causal relationship, democratic multilevel politics at least potentially could help create an orientation toward a public interest beyond the nation-state. For the time being, however, democratic governance beyond the nation-state must manage without a fully developed, civilly constituted sense of identity comprising all four aspects of a *demos*. In any case, governance beyond the nation-state will satisfy the desire for a collective identity much less completely than did the nation-state of the early twentieth century, and this will simply refer the problem of identity back to the social sphere. Ultimately, democratic governance beyond the nation-state is based on a political and moral vision of reflective self-regulation by self-governing individuals and organizations prepared to forgo their own short term interests if there are good universalistic reasons for public interest–oriented behavior.

Such a vision implies the participation of competent citizens with an unprecedented degree of intellectual capacity, normative tolerance, and solidarity.[60] As far as the first of these elements is concerned, however, individuals are better equipped today than ever before. In 1892, the correspondent of a well-known journal wrote that, as a result of the spread of modern newspapers, the inhabitants of a provincial village knew more about general social and political developments than the head of a government had a hundred years previously.[61] Even more could be claimed today. Anyone who visits a large city only once a year is confronted with a broader array of lifestyles, cultures, and social environments than our great-grandparents could ever have envisaged. In the modern age, and in the last few decades in particular, individuals have achieved new levels of self-determination and competence, enabling them to fulfill better than ever a central requirement of democratic governance beyond the nation-state.

Whether this knowledge revolution is sufficient, however, remains to be seen.[62] "World citizenship with republican intentions" requires moral as well as cognitive competence, and here the outlook is somewhat bleaker.[63] There is a widely held view in sociology that the sense of community is generally decaying. This civil deficit is often attributed to the growing power of market structures, which consume the potential for solidarity, and the prevalence of state welfarism, which strips individuals of

their sense of joint responsibility. There is, however, empirical evidence
that paints a different picture. Robert Wuthnow, for instance, points out
that almost every other American over eighteen years of age does volun-
teer work of some sort, and that this same group of people often displays
a higher degree of individuation than the other half of the population.[64]
So, individuation and community spirit are not mutually exclusive. It is
with this in mind that Ulrich Beck laments: "What astonishes and embit-
ters me is that the conservative mawkishness about the alleged decay of
values is not just utterly wrong, but it also obstructs our view of the
sources and movements which encourage us to tackle our assignments
for the future."[65] Whether he is right or not, the chances for democracy
beyond the nation-state depend purely on people. But that is really nothing new.

NOTES

1. Claus Offe, "Bewährungsproben—Über einige Beweislasten bei der Verteidigung der liberalen Demokratie," in *Die Demokratie am Wendepunkt: Die demokratische Frage als Projekt des 21. Jahrhunderts,* ed. Werner Weidenfeld (Berlin: Sicoller, 1996), 145. (Author's translation.)
2. Giandomenico Majone, ed., *Regulating Europe* (London: Routledge, 1996),
159. For Germany, Beyme focuses on key issues and thus comes to smaller but
still significant shares. See Klaus von Beyme, "Niedergang der Parlamente: Internationale Politik und nationale Entscheidungshoheit," *Internationale Politik* 53, no.
4 (1998): 24–25.
3. Werner Weidenfeld, "Die neue demokratische Frage," in Weidenfeld, *Die
Demokratie am Wendepunkt,* 10.
4. David Held, *Democracy and the Global Order: From the Modern State to Cosmopolitan Governance* (Cambridge, U.K.: Polity Press, 1995), 147.
5. Fritz W. Scharpf, *Demokratietheorie zwischen Utopie und Anpassung* (Kronberg
[Ts.], Germ.: Scriptor, 1975).
6. This formulation takes up one of the central thoughts of deliberative democratic theory. See, among others, Joshua Cohen, "Deliberation and Democratic Legitimacy," in *The Good Polity: Normative Analysis of the State,* ed. Alan Hamlin and
Philip Petitt (Oxford: Oxford University Press, 1989), 18–34; Jürgen Habermas,
Faktizität und Geltung (Frankfurt am Main: Suhrkamp, 1992); Seyla Benhabib, ed.,
Democracy and Difference: Contesting the Boundaries of the Political (Princeton:
Princeton University Press, 1996); and Oliver Gerstenberg, *Bürgerrechte und delib-
erative Demokratie: Elemente einer pluralistischen Verfassungstheorie* (Frankfurt am
Main: Suhrkamp, 1997).
7. Fritz W. Scharpf, "Legitimationsprobleme der Globalisierung: Regieren in
Verhandlungssystemen," in *Regieren im 21: Jahrhundert-Zwischen Globalisierung
und Regionalisierung: Festgabe für Hans-Hermann Hartwich zum 65. Geburtstag,* ed.

Carl Böhret and Göttrik Wewer (Opladen, Germ.: Leske & Budrich, 1993), 165–185; and Held, *Democracy and the Global Order*, 16.

8. Peter Bachrach and Morton S. Baratz, *Macht und Armut: Eine theoretisch-empirische Untersuchung* (Frankfurt am Main: Suhrkamp, 1977).

9. Claus Offe, *Strukturprobleme des kapitalistischen Staates* (Frankfurt am Main: Suhrkump, 1972), 74.

10. Louis W. Pauly, "Capital Mobility, State Autonomy and Political Legitimacy," *Journal of International Affairs* 48, no. 2 (Winter 1995): 369–388.

11. Ernst-Joachim Mestmäcker, "Zur Wirtschaftsverfassung in der Europäischen Union," in *Ordnung in Freiheit: Festgabe für Hans Willgerodt zum 70. Geburtstag*, ed. Rolf H. Hasse, Josef Molsberger and Christian Watrin (Stuttgart: Gustav Fischer, 1994), 274.

12. Fritz W. Scharpf, "Economic Integration, Democracy and the Welfare State," *Journal of European Public Policy* 4, no. 1 (1997): 18–36.

13. Giandomenico Majone, "Europe's 'Democratic Deficit': The Question of Standards" unpublished paper, (1998), 1.

14. Societal denationalization can be defined as a shift in the borders of dense transactions (these borders are defined as the place where a significant reduction in the frequency and intensity of certain interactions occurs) beyond national borders, but not necessarily to the extent of globalization. In a research project funded by the German Research Association, my colleagues and I developed 72 indicators to determine the extent of societal and political denationalization. See Marianne Beisheim et al., *Im Zeitalter der Globalisierung? Thesen und Daten zur gesellschaftlichen und politischen Denationalisierung* (Baden-Baden: Nomos, 1998); a summarized version is found in Gregor Walter, Sabine Dreher, and Marianne Beisheim, "Globalization Processes in the OECD-World," *Institute for Intercultural and International Studies, InIIS-Working Paper* 4–5 (Bremen, Germ.: University of Bremen, 1997), 5–22.

15. For a study of the relationship between societal denationalization and international institutions, see Michael Zürn, "Does International Governance Meet Demand? Theories of International Institutions in the Age of Denationalization," *Institute for Intercultural and International Studies, InIIS-Working Papers*, Nos. 4–5 (Bremen, Germ.: University of Bremen, 1997), 23–54.

16. Markus Jachtenfuchs and Beate Kohler-Koch, "Regieren im dynamischen Mehrebenensystem," in *Europäische Integration*, ed. Markus Jachtenfuchs and Beate Kohler-Koch (Opladen, Germ.: Leske & Budrich, 1996), 15–44.

17. For a survey of discussions on the analysis of international institutions, see Volker Rittberger and Peter Mayer, eds., *Regime Theory and International Relations* (Oxford: Oxford University Press, 1993). For an analysis of multilevel politics in relation to international institutions, see Peter Evans, "Building an Integrative Approach to International and Domestic Politics: Reflections and Projections," in Peter B. Evans, Harold K. Jacobsen, and Robert D. Putnam, eds., *Double-Edged Diplomacy: International Bargaining and Domestic Politics* (Berkeley: University of California Press, 1993), 397–430.

18. Michael Th. Greven, "Der politische Raum als Maß des Politischen: Europa als Beispiel," in *Europäische Institutionenpolitik*, ed. Thomas König, Elmar Rieger, and Hermann Schmitt (Frankfurt am Main: Campus, 1997), 45–65.

19. Peter Graf Kielmansegg, "Läßt sich die europäische Gemeinschaft demokratisch verfassen?" *Europäische Rundschau* 22, no. 2 (1994); 27; my translation.

20. Fritz W. Scharpf, *Games Real Actors Play: Actor-Centered Institutionalism in Policy Research* (Boulder, Colo.: Westview, 1997).

21. Gerhard Lehmbruch, "Konkordanzdemokratie," in *Lexikon der Politik: 3: Die westlichen Länder*, ed. Manfred G. Schmidt (München: C. H. Beck, 1992), 210; my translation.

22. Joseph M. Grieco, *Cooperation among Nations: Europe, America, and Non-Tariff Barriers to Trade* (Ithaca, N.Y.: Cornell University Press, 1990); Scharpf, *Games Real Actors Play*; Michael Zürn, *Interessen und Institutionen in der internationalen Politik: Grundlegung und Anwendungen des situationsstrukturellen Ansatzes* (Opladen, Germ.: Leske & Budrich, 1992).

23. As Scharpf writes, "Negotiation systems will not be able to deal effectively with issues involving high levels of distributive conflict among the parties to the negotiation." *Games Real Actors Play*, 209.

24. For example, see Volker Eichener, "Die Rückwirkungen der europäischen Integration auf nationale Politikmuster," in *Europäische Integration*, ed. Markus Jachtenfuchs and Beate Kohler-Koch (Opladen, Germ.: Leske & Budrich, 1996), 249–280.

25. Christian Joerges and Jürgen Neyer, "Transforming Strategic Interaction Into Deliberative Problem-Solving: European Comitology in the Foodstuff Sector," *Journal of European Public Policy*, 4, no. 4 (1997): 609–625.

26. Majone, *Regulating Europe*, 286.

27. Emanuel Adler and Peter M. Haas, "Conclusion: Epistemic Communities, World Order and the Creation of a Reflective Research Program," *International Organization* 46, no. 1 (1992): 367–390.

28. Thomas Gehring, "Regieren im internationalen System: Verhandlungen, Normen und Internationale Regime," *Politische Vierteljahresschrift* 36, no. 2 (1995): 197–219.

29. Arthur Benz, "Postparlamentarische Demokratie? Demokratische Legitimation im kooperativen Staat," unpublished paper (Universität Halle, 1997), 7; my translation.

30. Majone, *Regulating Europe*, 296–297.

31. Ibid.; and Majone, "Europe's Democratic Deficit."

32. Oliver Gerstenberg, "Law's Polyarchy: A Comment on Cohen and Sabel," *European Law Journal* 3, no. 4 (1997): 350.

33. Karl W. Deutsch, *Nationalism and Its Alternatives* (New York: Knopf, 1969).

34. Ernest Gellner, *Nations and Nationalism* (Ithaca, N.Y.: Cornell University Press, 1983).

35. John Breuilly, *Nationalism and the State*, 2d ed. (Chicago: Chicago University Press, 1994).

36. Benedict Anderson, *Imagined Communities: Reflections on the Origin and Spread of Nationalism*, 2d ed. (London: Verso, 1991).

37. Jack Donnelly, *International Human Rights* (Boulder, Colo.: Westview, 1996); and Tony Evans, "Democratization and Human Rights," in *The Transformation of Democracy*, ed. Anthony McGrew (Cambridge, Mass.: Polity Press, 1997), 122–148.

38. Louis Henkin, *How Nations Behave: Law and Foreign Policy*, 2d ed. (New York: Columbia University Press, 1979); and Abram Chayes and Antonia Handler Chayes, *The New Sovereignty: Compliance with International Regulatory Agreements* (Cambridge: Harvard University Press, 1995).

39. Hedley Bull, *The Anarchical Society* (London: Macmillan, 1977).

40. James N. Rosenau, *Along the Domestic-Foreign Frontier: Exploring Governance in a Turbulent World* (Cambridge: Cambridge University Press, 1997), 259.

41. Benz, "Postparlamentarische Demokratie?"

42. See also Hubert Heinelt, "Zivilgesellschaftliche Perspektiven einer demokratischen Transformation der Europäischen Union," *Zeitschrift für Internationale Beziehungen* 5, no. 1 (1998): 79–108. Heinelt distinguishes between territorial, administrative, civil society, and functional forms of interest mediation within the EU.

43. For a similar typology of democratic components, see Joshua Cohen and Charles Sabel, "Directly-Deliberative Polyarchy," unpublished paper (Cambridge, Mass., 1997). Instead of including constitutive actors in the second dimension, these authors distinguish between direct and representative proceedings.

44. Theodor Eschenburg, *Herrschaft der Verbände?* (Stuttgart: DVA, 1963).

45. But see Harald Müller, "Internationale Beziehungen als kommunikatives Handeln: Zur Kritik der utilitaristischen Handlungstheorien," *Zeitschrift für Internationale Beziehungen* 1, no. 1 (1994): 15–44.

46. Andrew Moravcsik, "Why the European Community Strengthens the State: Domestic Politics and International Cooperation," Center for European Studies, Harvard University, Working Paper Series 52 (1994). Also see Andrew Moravcsik, *The Choice for Europe* (Ithaca, N.Y.: Cornell University Press, 1998).

47. See William H. Riker, "The Senate and American Federalism," *American Political Science Review* 49, no. 2 (1955): 452–469. Riker offers an extremely instructive analysis of the development of the American Senate.

48. Rainer Schmalz-Bruns, "Bürgergesellschaftliche Politik—Ein Modell der Demokratisierung der Europäischen Union," in *Projekt Europa im Übergang? Probleme, Modelle und Strategien des Regierens in der Europäischen Union*, ed. Klaus Dieter Wolf (Baden-Baden: Nomos, 1997), 65; my translation.

49. Wolfgang Luthardt, "European Integration and Referendums: Analytical Considerations and Empirical Evidence," in *The State of the European Community: 2: The Maastricht Debates and Beyond*, ed. Alan W. Cafruny and Glenda G. Rosenthal (Boulder, Colo.: Lynne Rienner, 1993), 53–71.

50. Bruno S. Frey, "Direct Democracy: Politico-Economic Lessons from Swiss Experience," *American Economic Review* 84, no. 2 (1994): 338–342; and Uwe Wagschal, "Direct Democracy and Public Policymaking," *Journal for Public Policy* 17, no. 3 (1997): 223–245.

51. Manfred G. Schmidt, "Das politische Leistungsprofil der Demokratie," in *Demokratie—Eine Kultur des Westens?*, ed. Michael Th. Greven (Opladen, Germ.: Leske & Budrich, 1998).

52. Manfred G. Schmidt, *Demokratietheorien: Eine Einführung* (Opladen, Germ.: Leske & Budrich, 1995), chapters 3, 4.

53. Thomas König and Heiner Schulz, "The Efficiency of European Union Deci-

sion Making," paper presented at the German American Academic Council Young Scholars Workshop, August 5–16, 1996, University of Bremen.

54. See, for example, Heidrun Abromeit, "Überlegungen zur Demokratisierung der Europäischen Union," in *Projekt Europa im Übergang? Probleme, Modelle und Strategien des Regierens in der Europäischen Union,* ed. Klaus-Dieter Wolf (Baden-Baden: Nomos, 1997), 109–123; and Edgar Grande, "Post-nationale Demokratie—Ein Ausweg aus der Globalisierungsfalle," in *Globalisierung und institutionelle Reform: Jahrbuch für Technik und Wirtschaft,* ed. Werner Fricke (Bonn: Dietz, 1997), 353–367.

55. James Q. Wilson and John J. DiIulio, *American Government: Institutions and Policies,* 6th ed. (Lexington, Mass.: D. C. Heath, 1995), chapter 15.

56. The term "constitution" is applied more broadly here than the legal term, which is related to the traditional state concept. In this chapter, "constitutional questions" include all those questions that have implications for any aspect of the structure of the European polity.

57. Cohen and Sabel, "Directly-Deliberative Polyarchy."

58. Roland Roth, "Die Kommune als Ort der Bürgerbeteiligung," in *Politische Beteiligung und Bürgerengagement in Deutschland,* ed. Ansgar Klein and Rainer Schmalz-Bruns (Baden-Baden: Nomos, 1997), 404–447.

59. Anderson, *Imagined Communities.*

60. Herfried Münkler, "Der kompetente Bürger," in Klein and Schmalz-Bruns, *Politische Beteiligung,* 153–172.

61. Anthony Giddens, *The Consequences of Modernity* (Stanford, Calif.: Stanford University Press, 1990), 77.

62. Rosenau, *Along the Domestic-Foreign Frontier.*

63. Ulrich Beck, "Kinder der Freiheit: Wider das Lamento über den Werteverfall," in *Kinder der Freiheit,* ed. Ulrich Beck (Frankfurt am Main: Suhrkamp, 1997), 9–33.

64. Robert Wuthnow, "Handeln aus Mitleid," in *Kinder der Freiheit,* ed. Ulrich Beck, 34–84.

65. Beck, *Kinder der Freiheit,* 17.

6

Post-National Democracy in Europe

Edgar Grande

FULL DEMOCRACY, COSMOPOLITAN DEMOCRACY, AND THE DEMOCRATIC DILEMMA

In the last decade, the study of democracy and democratization has become "a veritable growth industry" in political science.[1] Inspired by the breakdown of authoritarian regimes in Latin America and Eastern Europe, the scholarly literature has produced an abundance of new concepts, competing interpretations, and extreme expectations.[2] Recent analyses of democracy's prospects at the turn of the twenty-first century, for example, run the gamut from euphoria and utopia to skepticism.

The euphoric picture has been painted not by political radicals, but by conservative economists. Indeed, it was the *Economist* that argued in a survey on "Full Democracy"

> that the next big change in human affairs will probably not be a matter of economics, or electronics, or military science; it will be a change in the supposedly humdrum world of politics. The coming century could see, at last, the full flowering of the idea of democracy. The democratic system of politics, which first took widespread root in the 19th century, and then in the 20th century beat off the attacks of both fascism and communism, may in the 21st century realise that it has so far been living, for understandable reasons, in a state of arrested development, but that those reasons no longer apply; and so democracy can set about completing its growth.[3]

As Newman observes in his chapter, this euphoric view finds its most utopian expression in the work of David Held.[4] Held argues that in the face of the globalization of markets and the internationalization of politics, democracy can no longer be realized within the realm of the modern nation-state. In order to provide the basis for "full democracy," the model

115

of modern democracy has to be extended in at least two respects. In the functional dimension, the model must move beyond the realm of politics to that of economics; and in the territorial dimension, it must move beyond the nation-state. "In the contemporary world, democracy can only be fully sustained by ensuring the accountability of all related and interconnected power systems, from economics to politics. These systems involve agencies and organizations that form an element of, and yet often cut across, the territorial boundaries of nation-states. The possibility of democracy today must, accordingly, be linked to an expanding framework of democratic institutions and procedures."[5]

The utopian character of this "cosmopolitan model of democracy" becomes fully apparent when it is confronted with Robert Dahl's skeptical view of the prospects of democracy. Dahl suggests that "a sort of transnational polyarchy" might gradually evolve as a consequence of the increasing internationalization of politics, but he views this development as unlikely:

> Except for the European Union, the prospects for even moderately "democratic" governments of transnational political associations are poor. Even if transnational political systems are greatly strengthened, for a long time to come decisions are likely to be made by delegates appointed by national governments. Thus the link between the delegates and the citizens will remain weak; and the democratic process will be even more attenuated than in existing polyarchies. With respect to decisions on crucial international affairs, the danger is that the third transformation [of democracy] will not lead to an extension of the democratic idea beyond the nation-state but to the victory in that domain of de facto guardianship.[6]

Thus, Dahl advocates maintaining the vitality of the democratic process by strengthening democratic institutions and procedures at the level of the nation-state and below.

The major problem with these and other proposals for the future of democracy in the "age of globalization" is that the models of democracy underlying each argument are either overambitious, as in the case of Held's cosmopolitan model of democracy, or they oversimplify the challenges for democracy, as with the *Economist*'s model of full democracy, which implies a shift from representative democracy back to direct democracy. Hence, the basic questions raised by Dahl still await answers:

> In the same way that the idea and practice of democracy were shifted away from the city-state to the larger scale of the national state, will democracy as an idea and a set of practices now shift to the grander scale of transnational governments? If so, just as democracy on the scale of the national state required a new and unique historical pattern of political institutions radically

different from the ancient practices of assembly democracy that the small scale of the city-state made possible, desirable, and even self-evident, will democracy on a transnational scale require a new set of institutions that are different in some respects, perhaps radically different from the familiar political institutions of modern representative democracy?[7]

In this chapter, I address these questions. I argue, first, that the democratization of politics beyond the nation-state is possible; but, second, that such an extension of democracy requires a shift from the model of representative democracy to a new model of democracy I tentatively call post-national democracy. As I will show in the following sections, this model is less demanding—and, hence, more realistic—than Held's cosmopolitan model, but more complex than the well-known models of direct democracy and representative democracy. I base my argument mainly on the European Union, which appears to have great promise as a case study of the prospects of democracy. Even skeptics like Dahl admit that the European Union offers rather favorable conditions for an extension of democracy beyond the nation-state, for several reasons:

1. First, the European Union is not a state, but it exhibits some statelike features (such as high degree of institutionalization in its decision-making processes and a certain amount of sovereign power vis-à-vis its member states and their citizens).
2. Second, the member states all have democratic constitutions, and twelve of them belong to the group of twenty-one countries that have enjoyed democratic political systems without interruption since World War II.[8]
3. Third, the political elites of the EU's member states and supranational institutions have shown a strong commitment to democratizing the EU. This commitment to strengthen democracy has even been codified in the Maastricht Treaty.
4. Finally, the member states of the EU satisfy what are widely considered to be the economic and social prerequisites for the establishment of democracy on the national level (for example, a high level of economic modernization and tolerant cultural values).[9]

If the assumption guiding contemporary democratic theory holds true—that democracy is "a product that can be manufactured wherever there is democratic craftsmanship and the proper zeitgeist"[10]—it should be possible to transplant democracy within the institutional framework of the European Union rather easily.

In reality, however, the process of European integration has been hindered from the beginning by an aggravating construction flaw. In transferring legal competencies from the national to the supranational level, the democratically elected parliaments in the EU's member states have lost some of their power to shape and control policies. However, there has been no strengthening of democratic legitimacy on the supranational level to compensate for this weakening of democracy on the national level. This "democratic deficit" in European politics has been the subject of much criticism, but it persists to this day.[11] The legal competencies of the European parliament have been extended several times, but they remain quite restricted relative to those of any national parliament in the EU. Meanwhile, other supranational institutions in the EU either lack any democratic legitimacy (like the European Commission) or are legitimized only indirectly (like the Council of Ministers). In sum, EU governance at present "results in a net empowerment of the executive branch of the states."[12]

The democratic deficit of the European policy process has always been problematic, but it was accepted—and maybe even was acceptable—as long as the community's functions were limited and major decisions were still taken at the national level by the parliaments of the member states. With the transfer of additional tasks and competencies through the Single European Act and the Maastricht Treaty, however, the situation has become untenable. The intense public debates on the process of European integration in most member states clearly demonstrate that the period of *benign despotism* associated with the Commission presidency of Jacques Delors is over and that further steps toward an "ever closer union among the peoples of Europe" as envisaged by the Maastricht Treaty can be achieved only if the EU is radically democratized. The crucial question, then, is this: Is there a solution to the "democratic dilemma" on the European level? More concretely, can European politics be made more democratic without jeopardizing the problem-solving capacity of the EU?

THE EUROPEAN DEMOCRATIC DEFICIT AND THE LIMITS OF THE MAJORITARIAN MODEL OF REPRESENTATIVE DEMOCRACY

Any conclusions one might draw about the prospects and problems of democratizing the European Union depend to a large extent on the definition of democracy presupposed. If a "procedural minimum" definition is used, which implies "fully contested elections with full suffrage and the absence of massive fraud, combined with effective guarantees of civil liberties, including freedom of speech, assembly, and association,"[13] the EU already qualifies as a full democracy. Indeed, the democratic quality of its politics would seem to be even higher than that of most of the "democracies with adjectives"[14] established in recent years in Latin America and Eastern Europe.

The picture changes almost completely, however, if we apply an "expanded procedural minimum" definition of democracy, adding the criterion "that elected governments must have effective power to govern."[15] The European Union fails to meet this criterion in several respects. First, governmental functions are fragmented and shared by several institutions, mainly the European Council and the European Commission; second, not all officials at the supranational level actually performing governmental functions are elected by the European parliament (EP), and such electoral powers as the EP has are underdeveloped in any case; and third, the governmental functions of EU institutions are significantly constrained by the member states. If we then add the criterion that elected governments should be fully responsible to the parliament, the democratic quality of the EU becomes even more dubious.

The expanded procedural minimum definition of democracy has formed the basis for most discussions of the democratic quality of the EU. The debate has been highly controversial, and two major competing positions have emerged, which offer fundamentally different expositions of the problem as well as fundamentally different solutions.[16] Mainstream political scientists and policymakers argue that the chief problem in the European Union resides in the limited legal powers of the European parliament. According to this view, an elimination of the democratic deficit is not only possible in principle but also feasible in practice, by means of rather simple institutional reforms to expand the EP's competencies. The proposals for reform, for example, call for the establishment of a two-chamber parliamentary system on the supranational level, in which political and territorial forms of representation coexist. Federal systems, especially the German one, which grant a powerful role to the federal states in national policy-making, are sometimes taken as a model for such a two-chamber system.

This mainstream argument has been vigorously criticized in recent years.[17] Its opponents acknowledge that the European Union suffers from a democratic deficit. Nevertheless, they not only disagree that strengthening the EP would suffice to remove the deficit, but they also maintain that it is impossible in principle to democratize the EU. Like Greven and Offe in this book, their basic argument is that democratic legitimacy is bound to certain substantial presuppositions about the nature of political community and the source of a collective identity. Among these presuppositions are the absence of deep-seated ethnic, linguistic, religious, ideological, or economic cleavages, and the existence of a set of common norms and beliefs. In other words, "the capacity of the majority rule to create legitimacy depends itself on a pre-existing sense of community—of common history or common destiny, and of common identity—which cannot be created by mere fiat."[18] These conditions do not exist within the EU at present, and, in view of the forthcoming enlargement, it is unlikely that they will ever be created. The democratic deficit in the EU is thus a structural deficit, not an institutional one, and consequently it cannot be eliminated by institutional reforms aimed at strengthening the European parliament. This argument implies that the EU is bound to remain a political order of only dubious democratic quality for the foreseeable future.[19]

European citizens seem to be faced with precisely the dilemma between "system effectiveness" and "citizen participation" that Robert Dahl outlined.[20] If they want to meet the normative standards of modern democracy and enhance citizen participation, they have to accept a reduction in the effectiveness of their national political systems caused by the globalization of economic and financial markets; if they want to improve system effectiveness by establishing counterweights to global markets on a supranational level, they must accept a reduction in the democratic quality of the political process. A weakening of the democratic fabric seems to be the inevitable political price for the deplorable fact that collective problems can no longer be solved within the boundaries of the nation-state.

The debate between defenders and critics of institutional reforms to strengthen the democratic legitimacy of European politics is highly instructive mainly in one respect. Both sides are oriented toward the same model of democracy—namely, the majoritarian model of representative democracy. In this sense, critics of institutional reforms do have a point when they emphasize the limited capacity of the majority principle to legitimize political decisions, and when they infer from this that the parliamentary road toward supranational democracy is a dead end. In fact, the debate shows that it is impossible to transfer the majoritarian model of representative democracy to the EU without damaging the Union itself.

The critics carry their argument too far, however, if they conclude that the EU's capacity for democratic legitimacy must remain limited and that its need for legitimacy will have to be met by other, nondemocratic means. The mistake they make is in equating democracy with the majoritarian model of representative democracy. Practically speaking, the identity seems clear, because democracies across Europe are institutionalized according to this model, at least with respect to formal constitutional design (Switzerland being the notable exception). In theory, however, such a tight coupling of the general concept of democracy with a particular type of democracy is highly problematic, inasmuch as it reveals a considerable lack of conceptual differentiation. Theorists must abandon this equation and search instead for nonmajoritarian and nonparliamentary models of democracy applicable to the European Union.

The first step in exploring a "post-national" model of democracy for

Europe is to identify the difficulties of applying a majoritarian model of representative democracy to the multilevel system of policy-making in Europe. The second step is to find alternative solutions to these problems. I do not approach these tasks with yet another democratic thought experiment. Instead, I use comparative empirical research to illustrate my proposal. I take as my starting point the fact that, in its pure form, the model of majoritarian representative democracy exists in scarcely any advanced industrial countries.[21] In most countries, it has been modified, supplemented, or even replaced. On the basis of this observation, I formulate two assumptions. First, I assume that these deviations from the pure model have not come about by mere historical chance; rather, they can be interpreted as appropriate institutional responses to shortcomings of the model revealed by circumstances wherein either the majority rule or the principle of political representation (or both) cannot be sustained at politically acceptable costs. Second, I assume that these deviations and modifications can be integrated into a new model of democracy, which is more suitable for democratizing the EU than existing models. Compared to the model of majoritarian representative democracy, this model of "post-national" democracy is distinct in at least three important respects: (1) its social basis, (2) its mechanism to control political power, and (3) its procedures for citizen participation.

SOCIOCULTURAL HETEROGENEITY, MAJORITY RULE, AND DEMOCRATIC LEGITIMACY

The principal model of modern democracy is based mainly on two principles: majority rule and representation. The crucial weakness of previous discussions of the "democratic deficit" and the prospects for democratizing the EU is that one side overestimates the role of majority rule, while the other ignores the deficits of the principle of representation when it is applied to multilevel systems of decision making.

Majority rule is, in reality, a highly demanding mode of political decision making.[22] It presupposes a stable legal framework of rules and institutions that is isolated from short-term pressures; it assumes that decisions can be reversed and their negative consequences remedied; it assumes that the intensity of preferences can be ignored; and it presupposes a collective identity based on common norms and shared values. The rule contributes to democratic legitimacy only if these preconditions are satisfied; otherwise, it tends to intensify political conflicts and contribute to the disintegration of the political community. In the case of the European Union, most of these prerequisites for the application of majority rule are absent. For example, because of the dynamic nature of the EU, decision making more often than not has been characterized by an intermingling of institutional, procedural, and substantive matters. And the frequent use of commitments and precommitments reflects a clear intention to make decisions about European integration irrevocable.

Most important for the purpose of this discussion are the sociocultural prerequisites of majority rule. As the previous chapters in this book make clear, any extension of democracy beyond the nation-state is confronted with two basic questions: (1) Is there a *demos*? (2) Are there enough substantive commonalities for stable political integration? The first problem has been debated most intensively in Germany as a consequence of the Federal Constitutional Court's Maastricht decision.[23] With respect to the EU, it is argued, primarily on the basis of ethnocultural criteria, "that there is no European *demos*—not a people, not a nation. Neither the subjective element (the sense of shared collective identity and loyalty) nor the objective conditions which could produce these (the kind of homogeneity of the ethno-national conditions on which peoplehood depends) exist."[24] As we have already seen, a rigorous interpretation of this argument would lead to the conclusion "that absent a demos, there cannot, by definition, be a democracy."[25] From the perspective of such an "organic" concept of community, a solution to the EU's problem is indeed hard to imagine. If we employ a less demanding concept of membership, however, the problem becomes far less intractable. A concept of multiple, concentric membership, similar to the concept of multiple citizenship in the horizontal relations between nation-states, could well be introduced to encompass the vertical relationship between the nation-state and the supranational community. In fact, Article 8 of the Maastricht Treaty, which states that "every person holding the nationality of a member state shall be a citizen of the Union," can be interpreted in exactly this way.

If we relax the definition of a *demos* to include an entity with no prepolitical attributes, we must be prepared to accept that this entity will be characterized by a substantial degree of sociocultural heterogeneity. This heterogeneity will raise a serious problem for the application of majority rule: how to avoid structural minorities. The higher the degree of sociocultural heterogeneity, the more likely the development of structural minorities in a political community and the less likely the acceptance of majority decisions as democratically legitimate.[26] In such a constellation, the application of the majority rule as the dominant mode of political decision making may be highly problematic.[27] The Canadian example, treated more fully by Clarkson in this book, highlights some of the ways in which governing by majority rule can intensify conflicts and nourish secessionist movements in socioculturally heterogeneous societies.[28]

Other countries, however, have successfully avoided the development of structural ethnic minorities, despite a high degree of sociocultural heterogeneity. The most interesting cases are those countries that were labeled "consociational democracies" in the late 1960s: the Netherlands, Austria, and Switzerland.[29] The solution these countries found to the problems of deep religious, socioeconomic, or ethnic cleavages was not to give up on democracy but to dispense at least in part with the concept of majority rule. In recent decades, these countries have featured oversized coalitions in government and close cooperation between government and interest groups. Major political decisions have been taken unanimously, and in general the political decision-making process has been characterized by a search for consensus rather than a search for majorities. The most interesting case in this respect is the political system of Switzerland, which is distinguished by a number of institutionalized checks against the tyranny of the majority.[30]

Comparative research has shown that these consociational democracies are not exceptional cases but rather subtypes of a more general and more common type of consensus democracy. In fact, most democracies have complemented or replaced majority rule as the dominant mode of decision making with some form of consensual, political decision making. It is, in truth, consensus democracy and not majoritarian democracy that has become the dominant model of democracy in advanced industrial countries.[31] Without a doubt, one of the reasons for this has been the desire to prevent the emergence of structural minorities and to protect the political integration of communities.

In my view, these national experiences are highly instructive for the debate on the democratization of the EU. They indicate that it is possible to democratize the EU despite its high degree of sociocultural heterogeneity, but they also underscore the limited applicability of majority rule within the institutional framework of the EU. In sum, they suggest that the EU can become a consensus democracy rather than a majoritarian democracy and, with this objection in mind, that it will have to give member states an adequate opportunity to participate in decision making.[32] From an institutional perspective, this means (1) that major decisions will have to be taken unanimously, (2) that political and territorial interests will have to be fairly balanced in decision-making,[33] and (3) that institutional safeguards will have to be introduced to protect minorities in cases of majority decisions.[34]

There is an important caveat, however. The efforts to protect minority rights by introducing the consensus model of democracy could intensify rather than alleviate other aspects of the EU's democratic dilemma. Conventional wisdom holds that "system effectiveness" within the EU can be improved only by replacing unanimous voting with majority rule; otherwise, the EU will be caught in the "joint decision-making trap," and its problem-solving capacity will necessarily remain limited.[35] For this reason, all attempts at institutional reform within the EU currently aim at extending the scope of majority voting, not restricting it. In other words, introducing the consensus model of democracy in the EU might solve one problem only to create another.

At first glance, the consensus approach to decision making in practice does seem to have had a deleterious impact on institutional efficacy within the EU. Decision making in the EU is often characterized by long and cumbersome processes and unsatisfactory outcomes. Nevertheless, any conclusions drawn must be qualified in at least two respects:

1. First, it is premature to blame the model of consensus democracy per se for these problems. The problem could well be that the model has not been properly implemented. In fact, comparative empirical research shows "that majoritarian systems do not perform better in maintaining public order and managing the economy, and hence that the over-all performance of consensus democracy is superior."[36]

2. Second, the tension between the two decision-making rules could be relieved by introducing a "reflexive loop" in the decision-making process, as Claus Offe has suggested.[37] This would mean that, for a number of political matters, the decision rule would not be specified in advance, but left open to (qualified majority) decision. Political actors would then be free to decide how to decide. It would be up to them whether they preferred system effectiveness (and hence the use of majority rule) or political participation and system integration (and hence a more demanding decision rule).

Needless to say, proposals like these will not resolve the democratic dilemma within the EU; at best, they will make it more tolerable. Like any national democracy, the EU cannot escape the challenges of satisfying the criteria of "complex democratic theory" posed by advanced societies.[38]

DEFICITS OF POLITICAL REPRESENTATION IN MULTILEVEL SYSTEMS OF GOVERNANCE

The other major weakness of most current proposals to improve the democratic legitimacy of European politics is their adherence to the principle of political representation. Despite their theoretical differences, advocates of consensus and majoritarian democracy alike believe that the model of representative democracy, with its strong emphasis on individual control and accountability, is the appropriate model for the EU. This reflects the fact that representation is regarded as an immovable pillar of democracy in modern nation-states.[39] In fact, the shift from direct participation (as practiced in the ancient city-states) to an indirect mode of political participation based on the principle of representation has been the decisive precondition for applying the idea of democracy to the modern nation-state.[40] The problem now is that if we want to extend democracy from the nation-state to a multilevel system of governance like the EU, some of the premises of political representation no longer hold.

The principle of political representation can be defined by two formal and two substantive premises.[41] Representation implies:

1. the authorization of a representative to act on behalf of others
2. the accountability of the representative toward his/her constituency
3. the responsiveness of the representative to the interests and preferences of that constituency
4. the relative abilities and capacities of the representatives to act, on the one hand, and of the constituents to articulate their interests and preferences and to control the activities of their representative, on the other hand.

Like the majority rule, the principle of political representation is highly demanding, and its application in modern societies has met with a number of serious problems. Elitist theories of democracy, for example, argue that citizens are not able to articulate their preferences unequivocally and consistently, and that they lack the competences and the capacity to control the activities of their elected representatives.[42] Consequently, elitist theories of democracy suggest lowering the standards for representation and focusing only on formal aspects of authorization and accountability.

In the multilevel system of governance of the EU, the principle of representation encounters several additional problems. First and most obvious is the lack of responsiveness of the elected members of the European parliament to the preferences and interests of their constituents. This is a common problem in parliamentary democracies, but in the case of the EU it has a unique cause. In the ideal model of representative democracy, it is mainly the function of intermediary organizations (especially political parties) to link representatives and their constituents by identifying and aggregating citizens' preferences and interests. We may doubt whether political parties actually perform this function properly in national democracies, but, in the EU, comparable intermediary organizations do not yet exist. There is no integrated European party system—only national parties that have joined up in very loosely coupled political federations. Hitherto, elections to the European parliament have been organized on the basis of national electoral laws; they have featured national parties with national manifestos, and election campaigns have been dominated by national issues.[43] Analysis of the 1989 EP election, for example, shows that European issues, such as the political integration of Europe or the completion of the internal market, were almost irrelevant in the electoral decisions of German voters.[44] Moreover, the links between members of the EP and their constituents are weak, and they are likely to remain so for the foreseeable future.[45] For this reason, strengthening the EP would do little to improve the democratic legitimacy of European politics.

The second and more basic difficulty is that applying the principle of representation to the multilevel system of European decision making leads to structural gaps of accountability and deficits of individual control. Difficulties of control and accountability are inherent in any complex organization.[46] They are far more acute in the case of the EU, however, because the multilevel structure of the decision-making system greatly increases the complexity of the policy process (with respect to the levels of decision making, the number of actors and institutions involved, and the diversity of interests and preferences articulated). The result is long and complicated decision-making chains with inextricable problems of control and accountability. One such problem is known as The Problem of Many Hands.[47] As Thompson notes, "Many acts of complex organizations cannot be blamed on one person in particular—no matter whether he belongs to the top or to an outpost unit—because they are the result of a great number of partial acts of a great number of officials at different levels. This will make it impossible, both practically and for reasons of equality and fairness, to hold one person, or a few, accountable for the eventual total outcome."[48] Another problem arises from the multilevel structure of the decision-making process. If the decision-making process is not organized hierarchically and controlled from the top, and in the EU it is not, then the parliament of the respective level is able to control only part of the decision-making chain. Hence, irrespective of the scope of the legal competencies of a European parliament, it will not be able to control the entire policy process in a multilevel decision-making system. The consequences are obvious. If the democratic legitimacy of the policy process were to be based exclusively on the accountability of parliament, representatives would be held responsible for decisions over which they did not have complete control. In brief, one of the major premises of the principle of representation would not be fulfilled.

A lack of transparency and openness in the European policy process intensifies problems of control and accountability. In recent years, this has become an issue of major concern.[49] Criticism has focused mainly on the secrecy of Council meetings and on the opacity of the community bureaucracy, with its proliferating system of committees. Thus, demands for a strengthening of parliamentary power within the EU are usually combined with calls for more publicity of Council meetings and improved public control of the Council's deliberations. Both of these proposals are consistent with the logic of parliamentary democracy and accountability; in fact, openness of Council meetings and transparency of Council decisions are essential preconditions for effective parliamentary control of EU policies. The problem is that demands for transparency and openness are incompatible with the functional requirements of consensus democracy, which, as I contend, is the appropriate model for the EU. For example, EU committee decision making is highly dependent on the informality and intimacy of negotiations; otherwise, decision-making costs would explode.[50] Increasing the transparency of the European decision-making process by making Council meetings public would either necessitate an introduction of the majority rule or would weaken the effectiveness of the policy process considerably. Since both of these alternatives are undesirable, we are forced to conclude that a lack of transparency and openness will remain a structural feature of the European decision-making process.

Under these institutional conditions, it is unrealistic to expect a European citizen to be capable of identifying political responsibilities correctly, let alone assessing them adequately. Again, the consequences are clear. If control of public decisions were to be based exclusively on individuals' control of elected representatives who, in turn, would control a European government, the European policy process would in reality inevitably suffer from a structural lack of accountability and effective control, and the democratic legitimacy of political decisions would be irremediably poor.

In sum, transferring the model of representative democracy from the nation-state to the multilevel system of European decision making produces two structural deficits. First, the system's lack of responsiveness to the preferences and interests of the citizens hampers the democratic process; second, the system's lack of control and accountability weakens democratic legitimacy. And within the logic of representative democracy, these problems cannot be rectified without threatening some functional prerequisites of consensus democracy. In my view, the solution to this problem is to modify and extend the model of representative democracy in two respects: (1) by reducing the requirements for individual control of power, and (2) by introducing alternative modes of political participation to improve the responsiveness of the system.

POSSIBLE SOLUTIONS: INSTITUTIONAL CONTROL AND DIRECT POLITICAL PARTICIPATION

As we have seen, the multilevel system of European policy making exhausts the capacity of individual citizens to control political power effectively. Thus, to satisfy the requirement for individual checks on political

power in a democratic political system, alternative mechanisms of control
have to be found. Two options for easing the burden on citizens present
themselves: strengthening organizational capacities to control political
power, and introducing institutional checks and balances. These approaches are partly complementary.

The first proposal is based on the assumption that private organizations
have far greater resources at their disposal than do individual citizens,
and that these resources can be deployed for public purposes, either as a
by-product of an organization's pursuit of its private interests or as a direct consequence of its altruism. If the evidence were to bear this out, as
Zürn points out in his chapter, the political power of nongovernmental
organizations could be strengthened by giving them organizational assistance or by granting them privileged access to the political decision-
making process.[51] On the other hand, this strategy has several drawbacks.
It is not self-evident that private vices turn into public virtues as soon as
they are given wider public attention and quasi-official status. As is the
case in the postpluralist, U.S. political system, the result of such a reform
might well be that "both private and public organizations have little incentive to look beyond short-term interests."[52] Furthermore, the control
of political power by nongovernmental organizations tends to remain in-
complete and insufficient. Whereas some supranational institutions, especially the Commission, are known for being open to interest groups, other
institutions (mainly the Council and the Court) are much less accessible—
and rightly so.[53] Hence, strengthening the role of private organizations in
order to improve control of political power in the European policy process at best would solve only part of the problem.

The second approach focuses not on the organizational capacities of
civil society but rather on the capacities for institutional self-control
within the political system. This approach has deep roots in democratic
theory, relying on concepts of political power formulated by Montesquieu
and Tocqueville. The idea of a system of institutionalized control of political power finds its most popular expression in James Madison's famous
fifty-first "Federalist" paper published in February 1788. Madison outlined therein a system of integrated powers whose main purpose is the
mutual institutional control of political power. The problem of how to
avoid an abuse of political power was not laid at the door of individual
citizens or private organizations. Instead, Madison argued that the internal structure of the governmental system should be organized in such a
way that its constitutive elements, by their very interdependence, put
their respective counterparts in their proper place.[54] In my view, this principle of institutional checks and balances to political power should be the
basis not only for the "compound Republic of America" but also for the
complex political system of the European Union. In both cases, effective

control of political power is possible only through the institutionalization of counterbalancing forces.

This implies that proposals for institutional reform of the EU should aim not only to improve the effectiveness of the European policy process but also to address the problem of control. These two objectives may well be incompatible with each other, and resolving the contradictions will be one of the most important and delicate challenges for the EU. The project should be guided by two principles:

1. the principle of equal powers, which states that the major institutions of the governmental system should be equal in power in order to allow effective mutual control
2. the principle of interdependence, which states that there should be no institution outside the governmental system of institutionalized checks and balances.

Recent proposals to strengthen the legal competencies of the European parliament and to transform the existing system of supranational institutions into an effective two-chamber system of power are sensible and accord fully with the principle of equal powers. Such a two-chamber system seems to offer an auspicious approach to balancing the political interests of citizens and the territorial interests of member states within the governmental system of the EU. Conversely, proposals to increase the independence of the Commission or to establish independent agencies at the supranational level should be viewed with suspicion. These proposals to improve the problem-solving capacity of the EU, although well intentioned, conflict with the two principles enunciated above, especially the principle of interdependence.

The second major problem that arises from the application of the principle of representation to the multilevel system of European policy making is the underdeveloped responsiveness of supranational institutions (including the EP) to the preferences and interests of citizens. Since the nascent European party system is ill-equipped to bridge the gap between the supranational level of decision making and the citizenry, democratization of the EU will have to be based on additional procedures of political participation that complement the established channels of parliamentary democracy. In recent years, two key proposals for strengthening the role of European citizens in the political process have been presented: (1) the establishment of an "associative democracy" based on the integration of voluntary private interest groups into the decision-making process,[55] and (2) the introduction of direct forms of citizen participation.

The model of associative democracy tries to reinterpret the role of private-interest groups from the perspective of democratic theory. The model assumes that interest groups can be both instruments to improve the effectiveness of public policy making and tools for citizen participation. In situations where political parties fail to provide adequate venues for citizens to articulate their interests and preferences and to participate in the decision-making process, interest groups could fill the gap by offering opportunities for "the more explicit engagement of citizens in social problem-solving."[56] Compared to the model of representative democracy, the model of associative democracy offers several advantages:

1. It allows for the flexible combination and recombination of functionally based forms of action and their integration into plural networks of policy making.
2. It is much better able to mobilize available social capital and channel it effectively into decision-making processes.
3. It improves citizens' inclusion in the policy process and strengthens the willingness and the capacity of both public and private actors to argue in the policy process.[57]

As a result, associative governance can potentially contribute to the effectiveness of public policies and provide additional democratic legitimacy to public policy making.

The model, however, also has some well-known disadvantages.[58] The first is that citizens' capacities to organize are distributed unevenly. This makes the associational democracy more vulnerable to special interests than are competing models. In multilevel, decision-making systems, this problem is aggravated by the increased diversity of interests and the greater heterogeneity of organizations. The second disadvantage is that participation in the policy process tends to be limited to small numbers of delegates. These "representatives" of private-interest groups have no authorization that meets the requirements of democratic theory. Their involvement in the public-policy process may be justified for reasons of system effectiveness, but the democratic quality of their activities is dubious from the perspective of both representative and participatory models of democracy.

In my view, a more promising solution to the lack of responsiveness of supranational institutions to the preferences and interests of European citizens is the introduction of forms of direct participation into the European policy process.[59] I am not suggesting that the indirect, representative model of democracy should be replaced completely by a direct model of democracy. Rather, like Zürn, I advocate complementing the existing institutions of representative democracy with additional opportunities for political articulation and participation that would allow citizens to intervene directly in the policy process on issues of outstanding importance.

In short, the objective is to establish a mixed system of political participation and decision making within the EU, in which elements of direct and indirect democracy are combined pragmatically.

Comparative observation supports the notion of such a mixed system. Despite the fact that the constitutions of western democracies are designed according to the model of representative democracy, most allow for some form of direct citizen participation by means of referenda. Indeed, these constitutions reveal a multitude of different combinations of representative and plebiscitarian forms of participation.[60] Furthermore, although in most countries direct forms of political participation are clearly subordinated to the procedures and institutions of representative democracy, these forms are most prevalent in countries characterized by a high degree of sociocultural heterogeneity (for example, Switzerland and many U.S. states).[61] Quite obviously, the standard argument against direct forms of political participation via referenda—that they would exacerbate political conflicts and contribute to the disintegration of political communities—has a weak empirical basis.[62] Rather, it would seem to be precisely the elements of direct political participation that contribute most decisively to the political integration of multicultural and multiethnic societies.

In Europe, most EU member states already make use of direct forms of political participation on the national level (with Belgium, Germany, and the Netherlands being the only exceptions),[63] and, for the most part, these national referenda have been called to deal with issues of European significance. Empirical analyses of the national referenda on the ratification of the Maastricht Treaty, however, indicate that the outcomes did not reflect "European" attitudes but were rather a function of the popularity of national governments, regardless of the reasons for this popularity.[64]

On the basis of these experiences and of existing typologies of referenda,[65] and somewhat differently from Zürn, I would draw at least five institutional guidelines for the introduction of direct forms of political participation within the EU:

1. Referenda on European issues should be organized on the European level, and not as a series of national referenda.
2. European referenda should be allowed on any subject held important by a qualified number of European citizens.
3. European referenda should be organized on the initiative of the voters; they should not be initiated by a supranational institution or a national government.
4. The outcome of European referenda should be binding for the relevant supranational institutions.
5. Supranational institutions should have the opportunity to respond

to initiatives of European citizens and to integrate them into their own proposals.

Designed in this way, European referenda could become effective instruments with which European citizens could intervene in the European decision-making process. Of course, the role of active citizens in political decision making tends to be highly ambiguous; they can be a source of political innovation or, as in the Swiss case, an element of conservatism. Nevertheless, inasmuch as the possibility of direct citizen intervention in policy making can serve as a threat to public officials, elected representatives, and formal institutions, it can increase institutional responsiveness to citizens' preferences and interests and thus enhance the democratic quality of the decision-making process.

POST-NATIONAL DEMOCRACY: A SUMMARY OF THE MODEL

Applying the majoritarian model of representative democracy to the multilevel system of European policy making creates at least three structural problems: (1) the emergence of structural minorities and the greater sociocultural heterogeneity of the EU; (2) the lack of political accountability and control; and (3) the underdeveloped responsiveness of supranational institutions to the preferences and interests of European citizens, both of which result from the poor fit between the demands of the principle of representation and the reality of the EU. This does not mean that it is impossible to democratize the EU. Rather, it implies that the majoritarian model of representative democracy is unsuited to the EU and, by extension, that most of the proposals to eliminate the EU's "democratic deficit" that are based on this model (for example, extending majority rule, strengthening the European parliament, and increasing the transparency of the decision-making process) are misconceived.

In fact, Robert Dahl's hunch "that democracy on a transnational scale [will] require a new set of institutions that are different in some respects, perhaps radically different from the familiar institutions of modern representative democracy," turns out to have been prescient.[66] My analysis has shown that there are solutions to the problems associated with the extension of representative democracy beyond the nation-state, and that these solutions can be integrated into a consistent model of democracy. This model of "post-national democracy" is, however, fairly distinct from our conventional understanding of modern democracy. First, because of the EU's heterogeneous social base, decision-making processes cannot be based mainly on majority rule. Instead, a consensual mode of decision-making has to play a major role. Second, because of the complexity of the

EU's multilevel system of institutions, political power has to be controlled mainly by means of institutional checks and balances, not by relying on the skills and capacities of individual citizens. And third, because of the weakness of intermediary institutions and the consequent unresponsiveness of European institutions to the preferences and interests of European citizens, existing channels of indirect political participation have to be complemented by direct forms of political participation via European referenda.

This post-national model of democracy is much better suited to the supranational level than the model of democracy most closely tied to the modern nation-state, the majoritarian model of representative democracy. But identifying some of the basic principles of post-national democracy is only part of the solution to the problem of democratizing Europe. There are still a number of difficulties to overcome in theory and in practice. Among these are the problem of embeddedness, the problem of compatibility, and the problem of uncertainty.

The first difficulty results, as Greven and Offe noted, from the fact that political institutions are deeply embedded in their national political systems. The consequences of direct forms of political participation are not only dependent upon their institutional design, which may vary considerably, but they are also highly sensitive to the broader political context (such as the structure of the party system, the strength of interest groups, and the power of social movements). This implies that the experiences of national political systems may not have direct analogies at the EU level. The problem is complicated by the fact that the European Union has to be considered a political system sui generis.[67] Hence, even if proposals to democratize the EU are soundly based on national experiences, there is no guarantee that they will function as anticipated in the supranational environment.

The second difficulty arises from the fact that European countries are home to a wide variety of democratic forms. Some, mainly the consensus democracies, strongly resemble the model of post-national democracy. Others, such as Britain's parliamentary democracy, contrast sharply. It remains to be seen whether these different types of democracy can be integrated into a single, multilevel system of policy making. The task of democratizing the European Union, in short, requires finding a model that is not just suited to the supranational level but is also consistent with the types of democracy that currently exist on the national level.

Finally, there are serious problems of uncertainty. While this is always a peril in constitutional "redesign," the European case is once again unique.[68] Democratizing the European Union involves transforming already existing and (more or less) functioning democratic systems, not replacing untenable authoritarian regimes. In order to redress their democratic deficits, European citizens are confronted with yet another democratic dilemma: choosing between a still acceptable but worsening status quo and a potentially far brighter but uncertain future.

NOTES

1. Scott Mainwaring, "Transition to Democracy and Democratic Consolidation: Theoretical and Comparative Issues," in *Issues in Democratic Consolidation*, ed. Scott Mainwaring, Guillermo O'Donnell, and J. Samuel Valenzuela (Notre Dame: Notre Dame University Press, 1992), 195; and Doh Chull Shin, "On the Third Wave of Democratization: A Synthesis and Evaluation of Recent Theory and Research," *World Politics* 47, no. 1 (1994): 138.

2. David Collier and Steven Levitsky, "Democracy with Adjectives: Conceptual Innovation in Comparative Research," *World Politics* 49, no. 3 (1997): 430–451.

3. "Happy 21st Century, Voters! A Survey of Democracy," *The Economist*, December 21, 1996, 3.

4. See especially David Held, "Democracy, the Nation State and the Global System," in *Political Theory Today*, ed. David Held (Stanford, Calif.: Stanford University Press, 1991), 197–235; David Held, "Democracy: From City-States to a Cosmopolitan Order?" in *Prospects for Democracy*, ed. David Held (Cambridge, U.K.: Polity Press, 1992), 13–52; and David Held, *Democracy and the Global Order: From the Modern State to Cosmopolitan Governance* (Stanford, Calif.: Stanford University Press, 1995).

5. Held, *Democracy and the Global Order*, 267.

6. Robert A. Dahl, "A Democratic Dilemma: System Effectiveness versus Citizen Participation," *Political Science Quarterly* 109, no. 1 (1994): 33.

7. Ibid., 27.

8. See Arend Lijphart, *Democracies: Patterns of Majoritarian and Consensus Government in Twenty-One Countries* (New Haven, Conn.: Yale University Press, 1984), 38.

9. See Seymour Martin Lipset, "Some Social Requisites of Democracy," *American Political Science Review* 53, no. 1 (1959): 69–105.

10. Shin, "On the Third Wave of Democratization," 141.

11. For an example of the standard version of the "democratic deficit" argument presented by a former president of the European parliament, see Klaus Hänsch, "Europäische Integration und parlamentarische Demokratie," *Europa-Archiv* 41, no. 7 (1986): 191–200.

12. J.H.H. Weiler, Ulrich R. Haltern, and Franz C. Mayer, "European Democracy and Its Critique," *West European Politics* 18, no. 3 (1995): 7.

13. Collier and Levitsky, "Democracy with Adjectives," 434.

14. Ibid.

15. Ibid.

16. See Edgar Grande, "Demokratische Legitimation und Europäische Integration," *Leviathan* 24, no. 3 (1996): 339–360.

17. Dieter Grimm, "Mit einer Aufwertung des Europa-Parlaments ist es nicht

getan: Das Demokratiedefizit der EG hat strukturelle Ursachen," in *Jahrbuch zur Staats- und Verwaltungswissenschaft*, vol. 4, ed. Thomas Ellwein et al. (Baden-Baden: Nomos, 1993), 13–18; Dieter Grimm, *Braucht Europa eine Verfassung?* (München: Carl Friedrich von Siemens-Stiftung, 1995); Fritz W. Scharpf, "Europäisches Demokratiedefizit und deutscher Föderalismus," *Staatswissenschaften und Staatspraxis* 3, no. 3 (1992): 293–306; Fritz W. Scharpf, "Demokratische Politik in Europa," *Staatswissenschaften und Staatspraxis* 6, no. 4 (1995): 565–591; Fritz W. Scharpf, "Economic Integration, Democracy and the Welfare State," *Journal of European Public Policy* 4, no. 1 (1997): 18–36; Peter Graf Kielmansegg, "Läßt sich die Europäische Gemeinschaft demokratisch verfassen?" *Europäische Rundschau* 22, no. 2 (1994): 23–33; Peter Graf Kielmansegg, "Integration und Demokratie," in *Europäische Integration*, ed. Markus Jachtenfuchs and Beate Kohler-Koch (Opladen, Germ.: Leske & Budrich, 1996), 47–71.

18. Scharpf, "Economic Integration, Democracy and the Welfare State," 20.

19. In recent publications, Grimm (*Braucht Europa eine Verfassung?*) and Scharpf ("Economic Integration, Democracy and the Welfare State") have modified their argument, dissociating themselves from organic concepts of community based on ethnocultural criteria and emphasizing the social construction of collective identities instead. As a result of this "constructivist turn," both now admit that the democratic deficit can in fact be overcome in principle. However, since the social construction of collective identity is the product only of long-term historical processes, the practical implications of this reformulation of the argument are extremely limited.

20. Dahl, "A Democratic Dilemma." For a first systematic analysis of this dilemma in the field of domestic politics, see Fritz W. Scharpf, *Demokratietheorie zwischen Utopie und Anpassung* (Kronberg/Ts., Germ.: Scriptor, 1970).

21. Arend Lijphart, "Majority Rule in Theory and Practice: The Tenacity of a Flawed Paradigm," *International Social Science Journal*, no. 129 (1991): 483–493.

22. See Claus Offe, "Politische Legitimation durch Mehrheitsentscheidung?" *Journal für Sozialforschung* 22, no. 3 (1982): 311–336.

23. For a summary and critique, see Weiler, Haltern, and Mayer, "European Democracy and Its Critique."

24. Ibid., 13.

25. Ibid.

26. Joseph Weiler's often cited example of the Danes joining a larger state like Germany has to be interpreted in this way. If the only, or at least the major, commonality of the minority in a political decision is their Danish nationality and if the Danes lose out time and again for only this reason, there is no reason for them to accept majority decisions as democratically legitimate. See J.H.H. Weiler, "Does Europe Need a Constitution? Reflections on Demos, Telos and the German Maastricht Decision," *European Law Journal* 1, no. 3 (1995): 219–258; also Scharpf, "Economic Integration, Democracy and the Welfare State."

27. Graham Smith, ed., *Federalism: The Multiethnic Challenge* (London: Longman, 1995); and Renaud Dehousse, "Constitutional Reform in the European Community: Are There Alternatives to the Majority Avenue?" *West European Politics* 18, no. 3 (1995): 118–136.

28. See also Colin H. Williams, "A Requiem for Canada?" in Smith, *Federalism,* 31–72; and Rainer-Olaf Schultze, "Interessenrepräsentation und Westminster-Modell: Kanada—ein abweichender Fall?" *Staatswissenschaft und Staatspraxis 7,* no. 2 (1996): 163–193.

29. Gerhard Lehmbruch, *Proporzdemokratie* (Tübingen, Germ.: J.C.B. Mohr, 1967); Arend Lijphart, *The Politics of Accommodation: Pluralism and Democracy in the Netherlands* (Berkeley: University of California Press, 1968).

30. Wolf Linder, *Swiss Democracy: Possible Solutions to Conflict in Multicultural Societies* (New York: St. Martin's, 1994).

31. Lijphart, *Democracies,* and "Majority Rule in Theory and Practice"; and Manfred G. Schmidt, *Demokratietheorien: Eine Einführung* (Opladen, Germ.: Leske & Budrich, 1995).

32. Dimitris N. Chryssochoou, "Democracy and Symbiosis in the European Union: Towards a Confederal Consociation," *West European Politics 17,* no. 4 (1994): 1–14; Dehousse, "Constitutional Reform in the European Community"; Heidrun Abromeit, "Überlegungen zur Demokratisierung der Europäischen Union," in *Projekt Europa im Übergang?,* ed. Klaus Dieter Wolf (Baden-Baden: Nomos, 1997), 109–124.

33. One mechanism for achieving this balance would be to require a double majority of both the member states and the Union's population in political decisions.

34. A promising solution to this problem would be Renaud Dehousse's suggestion for the introduction of an "alarm bell mechanism" that would enable a significant minority of member states (say, three) to block a proposal that would, in their opinion, threaten their vital interests; see Dehousse, "Constitutional Reform in the European Community," 133. Compared to giving a single member state simple veto power, this approach has the advantage of reducing the potential for blackmail while still protecting minority positions rather effectively. In essence, it forces the member state to convince another state that its claims are legitimate; this means that the state must argue its position, instead of relying on bargaining or blackmail alone.

35. Fritz W. Scharpf, "The Joint Decision Trap: Lessons from German Federalism and European Integration," *Public Administration 66* (Autumn 1988): 239–278.

36. Arend Lijphart, "Democracies: Forms, Performance, and Constitutional Engineering," *European Journal of Political Research 25,* no. 1 (1994): 1. However, we have to consider Lijphart's own view that his findings on the superiority of consensus democracy are only "a partially proven hypothesis instead of a fully proven proposition."

37. Offe, "Politische Legitimation durch Mehrheitsentscheidung?" 332.

38. Scharpf, *Demokratietheorie zwischen Utopie und Anpassung.*

39. Giovanni Sartori, *Demokratietheorie* (Darmstadt: Wiss. Buchgesellschaft, 1992).

40. Dahl, "A Democratic Dilemma."

41. Hanna F. Pitkin, *The Concept of Representation* (Berkeley: University of California Press, 1967).

42. See Joseph A. Schumpeter, *Capitalism, Socialism and Democracy* (New York: Harper & Brothers, 1942).

43. Oskar Niedermayer, "Die Europäisierung der Parteienlandschaft," in *Legitimationsprobleme und Demokratisierung der Europäischen Union*, ed. Andreas Maurer and Burkard Thiele (Marburg: Schüren, 1996), 85–96.

44. Hermann Schmitt, "Was war 'europäisch' am Europawahlverhalten der Deutschen? Eine Analyse der Europawahl 1989 in der Bundesrepublik," in *Wahlen und europäische Einigung*, ed. Oskar Niedermayer and Hermann Schmitt (Opladen, Germ.: Westdeutscher Verlag, 1994), 63–83.

45. Any enlargement of the EU would aggravate the problem of responsiveness, for several reasons. The differences between east and west European parties and party systems would make the evolution of an integrated European party system vastly more difficult. In addition, an enlargement of the EU would require either an increase in the size of the EP or an enlargement of the electoral districts (or both), and the latter would weaken the links between members of the European parliament and their constituencies even further.

46. See Mark A. P. Bovens, "The Social Steering of Complex Organizations," *British Journal of Political Research* 20, no. 1 (1990): 91–117. Thirty years ago, Anthony Downs formulated several "laws" that express these difficulties: "The first is the Law of Imperfect Control: No one can fully control the behavior of a large organization. The second is the Law of Diminishing Control: The larger any organization becomes, the weaker is the control over its actions exercised by those at the top. The third is the Law of Decreasing Coordination: The larger any organization becomes, the poorer is the coordination among its actions." Downs, *Inside Bureaucracy* (Boston: Little, Brown, 1967), 143.

47. Dennis F. Thompson, "Moral Responsibility of Public Officials: The Problem of Many Hands," *American Political Science Review* 74, no. 4 (1980): 905–916.

48. Bovens, "The Social Steering of Complex Organizations," 115.

49. Juliet Lodge, "Transparency and Democratic Legitimacy," *Journal of Common Market Studies* 32, no. 3 (1994): 343–368.

50. Giovanni Sartori, "Will Democracy Kill Democracy? Decision-Making by Majorities and by Communities," *Government and Opposition* 10, no. 2 (1975): 131–158; Edgar Grande, "Konfliktsteuerung zwischen Recht und Konsens," in *Sozialpartnerschaft in der Krise: Leistungen und Grenzen des Neokorporatismus in Österreich*, ed. Peter Gerlich, Edgar Grande, and Wolfgang C. Müller (Wien: Böhlau, 1985), 225–254.

51. See Michael Zürn, "Über den Staat und die Demokratie im europäischen Mehrebenensystem," *Politische Vierteljahresschrift* 37, no. 1 (1996): 27–55; and Rainer Schmalz-Bruns, "Bürgergesellschaftliche Politik—ein Modell der Demokratisierung der Europäischen Union," in *Projekt Europa im Übergang?*, ed. Klaus Dieter Wolf (Baden-Baden: Nomos, 1997), 63–90.

52. John Heinz, Edward O. Laumann, Robert L. Nelson, and Robert H. Salisbury, *The Hollow Core: Private Interests in National Policy Making* (Cambridge: Cambridge University Press, 1993), 412.

53. Sonia Mazey and Jeremy Richardson, eds., *Lobbying in the European Community* (Oxford: Oxford University Press, 1993); and Edgar Grande, "The State and Interest Groups in a Framework of Multi-Level Decision-Making: The Case of the European Union," *Journal of European Public Policy* 3, no. 3 (1996): 318–338.

54. James Madison, "Federalist Nr. 51, 6 February 1788," in *Die Amerikanische Revolution und die Verfassung 1754–1791*, ed. Angela Adams and Willi Paul Adams (München: Deutscher Taschenbuch Verlag, 1987), 403–408.

55. Joshua Cohen and Joel Rogers, "Secondary Associations and Democratic Governance," *Politics & Society* 20 (December 1992); 393–472; Joshua Cohen and Joel Rogers, "Solidarity, Democracy, Association," in *Staat und Verbände*, ed. Wolfgang Streeck (PVS-Sonderheft 25) (Opladen, Germ.: Westdeutscher Verlag, 1994), 136–159. See also Rainer Schmalz-Bruns, *Reflexive Demokratie: Die demokratische Transformation moderner Politik* (Baden-Baden: Nomos, 1995); and Schmalz-Bruns, "Bürgergesellschaftliche Politik."

56. Cohen and Rogers, "Solidarity, Democracy, Association," 157.

57. Schmalz-Bruns, "Bürgergesellschaftliche Politik," 83.

58. Claus Offe, "Korporatismus als System nichtstaatlicher Makrosteuerung? Notizen über seine Voraussetzungen und demokratischen Gehalte," *Geschichte und Gesellschaft* 10, no. 2 (1984): 234–256.

59. Grande, "Demokratische Legitimation und Europäische Integration"; and Zürn, "Über den Staat und die Demokratie im europäischen Mehrebenensystem."

60. David Butler and Austin Ranney, eds., *Referendums: A Comparative Study of Theory and Practice* (Washington, D.C.: American Enterprise Institute, 1978); Winfried Steffani, *Pluralistische Demokratie* (Opladen, Germ.: Leske & Budrich, 1980); Wolfgang Luthardt, *Direkte Demokratie: Ein Vergleich in Westeuropa* (Baden-Baden: Nomos, 1994); Silvano Möckli, *Direkte Demokratie: Ein internationaler Vergleich* (Bern: Verlag Paul Haupt, 1994); Michael Gallagher and Vincenzo Uleri, eds., *The Referendum Experience in Europe* (Basingstoke, U.K.: Macmillan, 1996); and Rainer Grote, "Direkte Demokratie in den Staaten der Europäischen Union," *Staatswissenschaften und Staatspraxis* 7, no. 3 (1996): 317–363.

61. David Butler and Austin Ranney, eds., *Referendums around the World: The Growing Use of Direct Democracy* (Basingstoke, U.K.: Macmillan, 1994).

62. See, for example, Sartori, *Demokratietheorie*, 128.

63. However, in Germany and the Netherlands, direct participation at the local and regional levels has been strengthened in recent years, and debate has intensified in both countries on the introduction of a national referendum.

64. Mark N. Franklin, Cees van der Eijk, and Michael Marsh, "Referendum Outcomes and Trust in Government: Public Support for Europe in the Wake of Maastricht," *West European Politics* 18, no. 3 (1995): 101–117.

65. See Pier Vincenzo Uleri, "Introduction," in *The Referendum Experience in Europe*, ed. Michael Gallagher and Pier Vincenzo Uleri (Basingstoke, U.K.: Macmillan, 1996), 8–10.

66. Dahl, "A Democratic Dilemma."

67. Markus Jachtenfuchs, "Die Europäische Union—ein Gebilde sui generis?" in Wolf, *Projekt Europa im Übergang?* 15–36.

68. Jon Elster and Rune Slagstad, eds., *Constitutionalism and Democracy* (Cambridge: Cambridge University Press, 1988).

7

Do Deficits Imply Surpluses?
Toward a Democratic Audit of North America

Stephen Clarkson

It would be a mistake to infer from the preceding chapters' intense debate on the democratic deficit in Europe that the EU is the site of globalization's most acute challenge to twentieth-century liberal and national notions of democracy. Granted, when states coalesce in a continental grouping, bent on achieving goals unachievable on their own—military, political, economic, or cultural—they necessarily sacrifice some degree of self-control. Granted, too, the EU is the most advanced, sophisticated, and seasoned continental regime. It is, however, no longer the only one. Nor is it necessarily the least friendly to democratic norms. Several other state groupings have in the contemporary period been cobbled together in response to the pressures of global competition. Mercosur, the Southern Common Market in Latin America, leans toward the European model. ASEAN, the Association of South-East Asian Nations, is its antithesis in institutional simplicity.

North of South America and east of Asia lies a continent whose three constituent states, along with the many aboriginal nations they have displaced, have been involved for several centuries in a tortuous history of integration and differentiation in their economies, their cultures, and their civil societies. Canada participated ambivalently in this contested process for over a century, endeavoring to profit from the advantages of proximity to the world's most powerful economy while retaining enough autonomy for its fragmented polity to limp along as a separate state. The signing of the Canada–United States Free Trade Agreement (CUFTA) on January 1, 1989, seemed to many to mark the abandonment of this struggle.

For many decades, Mexico offered a valiant contrast to this story of ac-

139

commodation by pursuing an autonomous, import-substituting, development model strategy. Since the early 1980s, however, it has been playing
a high-risk game of catch-up, turning its laws, regulations, market incentives, and even its constitution upside down in order to intensify its already considerable degree of integration in the American system. This
surrender to the American model was formally recognized and radically
intensified in 1994 by Mexico's signing a broadened and deepened version of CUFTA, the North American Free Trade Agreement (NAFTA).

NAFTA is a fascinating object for study less because of the size of its
economy (which, for the moment at least, is virtually identical to that of
the fifteen-member EU)[1] than because of the peculiarity of its composi-
tion. This membership consists of the globe's unrivaled superpower
(which enjoys grossly asymmetrical relations with its two neighbors), a
rich but relatively underpopulated state to the north, and a large but still
developing country to the south. Still in its infancy, NAFTA is an institutionally flimsy regime about which few predictions can be made with
confidence. Some hope and others fear that it is the embryo for a supranational regime. Another view relegates NAFTA to a low rank in the global
lineup of continental systems. Whatever its future potential, auditing its
democratic accounts in light of the EU debate outlined in the previous
four chapters may yield some helpful insights into the thorny question
with which this volume is grappling—the analysis of democracy beyond
national boundaries.

Long before Canadians became conscious of a debate among Europeans about the political ramifications of the postwar effort to build a transnational community, they were concerned with the threat to their sovereignty—and ipso facto the democratic quality of their institutions—posed
by their country's growing integration in the economy and culture of
their overwhelmingly dominant neighbor. A tough Rooseveltian "open
door" policy had proven entirely unnecessary in Canada's regard in the
early years of the twentieth century. The portals of the Dominion were
not just ajar; they were already off their hinges, given the unrestricted
flows of capital back and forth across the Canadian-American border. By
the 1950s, when the St. Lawrence Seaway was finally built with American
participation, this common engineering feat was thought of as a "giant
zipper" linking the two economic spaces together.[2] The "longest unde-
fended border in the world"—sometimes considered the most over-
worked cliche in the lexicon of political rhetoric—applied to a host of phenomena, such as the extraterritorial application to Canada of the U.S.
Trading with the Enemy Act, which prevented Canadian subsidiaries of
U.S. corporations from exporting to such commercial partners (but American ideological foes) as Castro's Cuba or the People's Republic of China.

In the opinion of most political scientists, Canada's prospects for survival as a recognizably sovereign democracy were even more severely jeopardized by CUFTA[3]. In obvious contrast, Mexico's incorporation into NAFTA was considered by many to be a prelude to its long-blocked transitions from autocracy to democracy. The institutionalization of the existing bilateral Canadian-American and Mexican-American dependencies into a trilateral structure has been trumpeted as the harbinger of a transformed political economy for the North American continent. The set of rules for trade and investment between its members and the wide range of new policy-making norms affecting these states' freedom of action will surely shift the previous loci of political power and alter the processes of decision making, with consequent implications for democracy.

Considering its elementary institutional form, compared to the EU—no parliament, no commission, no council of ministers, no court—it might seem to be a relatively simple, empirical task to draw up a balance sheet of NAFTA's democratic deficit. But such an operation in political accountancy presupposes agreed-upon conventions for deciding what counts as an asset and what counts as a liability. Since the discourse on democracy is plagued by the widely differing meanings with which the concept is endowed, applying it to NAFTA requires some preliminary agreement on which definitions to adopt.

MEASURING DEMOCRACY

For more than two millennia, thinkers trying to puzzle out what would make the best form of government have traced their intellectual roots back to how a few thousand men in Athens strove to organize their political affairs. Over the centuries, as this small, ethnically homogeneous, slave-based polity was reified into the paradigmatic utopia from which later thinkers deduced their prescriptions, political philosophy became polarized into two normatively opposed channels. On the left, emphasis on participation and self-fulfillment characterizes what we might call today an egalitarian, social-democratic, or developmental current. Contending with it from the right is a more explicitly elitist, individualistic, even hierarchical view of what makes a good society. Whether it was Jean-Jacques Rousseau's deductive ruminations on what process would generate a social contract, or John Locke's inductive reflections on how best to protect property via representative forms of government, such political ideas had revolutionary impacts, provoking bourgeois revolutions first in England, then in its American colonies, and soon after in France, where notions of citizenship and human rights were linked to those of nation and sovereignty.

The advent of industrialization and the emergence of a mass society whose proletariat demanded political inclusion presented political thought with a frontal challenge. Democracy, which had long been dismissed, in C. B. Macpherson's memorable phrase as "class rule, rule by the wrong class,"[4] now acquired a new potency as a legitimate political desideratum. For mid-nineteenth-century optimists like John Stuart Mill, the extension of education and the franchise to working people and to women offered hope for a new, emancipatory variant of representative government based on citizen participation organized by political parties. For early twentieth-century pessimists like Roberto Michels, an "iron law" decreed the impossibility of democracy in a mass society: "Who says organization, says oligarchy."[5] Shortly after these words were written, a world war was fought to make the world "safe for democracy." Two decades later a second global cataclysm erupted to save democracy from fascism. In the midst of that struggle, the economic historian Joseph Schumpeter tried to make sense of the competing appeals of capitalism, socialism, and democracy. He argued that the Greek city-state should be discarded for being an inappropriate model from which relevant notions of democracy could be derived. Citizens in the modern world could not continually deliberate over the affairs of state in the same way that the free males of Athens could convene in the agora to discuss in plenary session the great and small issues of the day. Periodic elections would suffice, Schumpeter suggested, if they were fair and offered competing teams of candidates, leaders, and platforms from which the sovereign voters could choose their governors.[6]

We then labored until the 1990s under the shadow of a possible third global conflagration that would be triggered by the threat that communism presented the industrial democracies. Now that we have entered a new era characterized by some as the end of history, by others as the end of geography, and by still others as the end of time, democracy is triumphant. Or so it seems, depending on the meaning we give this much used but rarely defined nine-letter word. If we set the bar low enough, almost any state can qualify. If we set it too high, none can pass.

Low

By the 1950s, all countries claimed the mantle of democracy, whatever their actual institutional characteristics. Indeed, to see the word "democratic" in the name of a country was virtually to guarantee its negation: the "People's Democracies" of Soviet-occupied central and eastern Europe made the point. Until recently, Indonesia's claim to membership among the ranks of the democratic was also more than slightly dubious.

In any event, a low standard of democracy would center on a basic procedural minimum—some system of voting and periodic electoral activity, with at least some linkage to the actual process through which definitive policies are made. The more attenuated that linkage, the lower the quality of a democracy.

Medium

More interesting than such universally inclusive and therefore meaningless claims are the aspects of good governance now generally considered to be defining characteristics of democratic politics.

- Peaceful transition—Assuring the transfer of power without violence from one leadership group to another is considered to be one of the great triumphs of election-based political systems.
- Equality—When defined as nominal egalitarianism, which requires giving all adults such rights as the franchise and access to the courts, equality is a standard that is relatively easily met. If actual *égalité* in economic terms is made the precondition for meaningful democratic life, it is a standard that no political system based on a capitalist economy has ever achieved.
- Citizenship—Understood as membership in a national community, the quality of citizenship can be a measuring rod for distinguishing acceptable, and therefore "democratic," regimes from unacceptable ones.
- Rights—A deceptively simple approach has been to equate democracy with rights, but these have multiplied over time from political and legal rights to the ever-extending domain of social and identity rights.
- Minority guarantees—Even the more literal view of democracy as decision on the majority principle is routinely balanced by the requirement to defend minorities against abuse by superior numbers.

In all these categories, a democratic deficit exists when power is transferred at the barrel of the gun; when the gap between rich and poor makes a mockery even of nominal equality; when citizens do not have the right to emigrate; when courts do not enforce constitutionally prescribed freedoms; when basic social services are not provided; and when minorities suffer oppression at the hands of majorities. Since most countries in the industrialized world do not exhibit these attributes in egregious degrees, political philosophers—who, not coincidentally, hail mainly from these lands—tend to assume without much question that their own systems are democratic.

High

When we take a narrower, process-centered conception of democracy as the standard, few industrial societies score very high. Such a standard would require extensive opportunities for most of a defined population to participate in actual policy making. In fact, several of modern society's characteristics make high levels of direct participation by all citizens in political life extremely difficult to attain. For instance:

- The division of labor—Politics, like other vocations, has become professionalized. Salaried politicians work at their jobs on a full-time basis in political parties and parliaments. These and their related institutions have subcultures, behavioral codes, and career paths that elevate the putative servants of the people to such a superior status that their "political masters" are virtually excluded from the process of government.
- Policy specialization—While politics becomes an all-consuming occupation for the gladiators of the system, the rest of the citizenry become mere spectators, devoting little time to the bewilderingly complex dossiers that governments handle.
- Information overload—The amount of knowledge available about the ramifications of most policy problems defies the intellectual capacity of the nonspecialist.
- Sociological hierarchy—If, as behavioral analysts assure us, political efficacy varies positively with socioeconomic status, then the uneven distribution of educational resources is one more factor contributing to low actual levels of political participation in most countries. If the well-educated, the well-off, and the well-positioned participate most, then the majority does not rule in most countries that call themselves democratic.

EVALUATING THE MEMBER STATES OF NAFTA

Before we attempt a balance sheet of NAFTA's democratic credentials as a continental regime, we need a rough, national accounting of each member state. Once these benchmarks are established, we can assess the quality of democracy at the collective level.

Canada

If Canada were charged with practicing democracy, would there be enough evidence to convict her? The evidence for answering this question turns out to be mixed, providing ample material for heated debate between any would-be prosecution and defense lawyers at an imaginary global court. Even at the local level of government, where citizen oversight of city hall is thought to be the most intimate, an observer in Toronto recently expressed grave doubts:

> A full-time commitment plus additional hours in the evening are required for anyone wanting to keep up with the number of meetings, issues, reports and changes happening just in the Toronto community. The community councils, city council, committees, citizen meetings, and all of the accompanying reams of paper, reports, deputations, etc. mean the possibility of real democratic input can only realistically be in the hands of a few committed citizens.[7]

Beyond being overwhelmed by heavily loaded policy agendas at the less accessible levels of the provincial and federal governments, where electoral politics is appropriated by oligarchic parties, Canadians have lately been experiencing the removal of politics to a completely different arena. The judicialization of politics has engendered a decline in such traditional forms of democratic expression as public debate, demonstrations, and interest-group lobbying focused on legislative decisions. Whether this transposition of political issues to the courts reflects an increased democratic deficit is a matter of considerable controversy. If minority rights are better protected through the decisions of unelected judges—as seems to be the case in Canada as far as native peoples, homosexuals, and women are concerned—then we are driven by this logic to conclude that the democratic deficit has decreased at the same time as the capacity of elected representatives to pass legislation has been curtailed.

United States of America

If the United States were charged with practicing democracy, the prosecution would surely focus on what so famously caught Alexis de Tocqueville's attention: the vibrant life of interest groups and voluntary associations at the local level, and the active use they make both of the electoral and of the judicial process in state and federal politics. A second string for a prosecutor's bow would be the legislature, where representatives and senators, free of the constraints of party discipline, can serve the interests of their supporters with near-complete autonomy—and a sometimes near-anarchic impact on the coherence of an administration's policies.

The defense case that the United States not be convicted of democratic practices would rest on more specific evidence, such as:

- the practical disenfranchisement of the poor, the imprisoned, and racial minorities, most of whom do not even register to vote
- the low electoral turnout even among those who are registered
- the enormous power that business exerts through the provision of funds to finance the election campaigns of aspiring politicians, who, when elected, serve the interests of their patrons
- the virtually uncontrolled use of negative advertising in election campaigns, which so demeans political discourse as to delegitimize the very process of democracy
- the homogeneity of a two-party system, which, thanks to low voter turnout and high business funding, often offers electors only a pseudo-choice at the polls.

Returning to a key theme in Newman's chapter, democracy in America is still a vision far from realization.

Mexico

It is not poverty that has characterized the political system of Mexico in the decades preceding NAFTA as much as single-party dictatorship. The Partido Revolucionario Institucional (PRI) has long secured its hold on power through a corporatist network of business associations, government-controlled trade unions and peasant organizations, along with a patronage system of employment throughout an extensive network of the public and parastatal institutions. During the course of its reign as the effective government of Mexico, the PRI became a political monolith in stark and shocking defiance of the noble ideals and progressive positions entrenched in the country's revolutionary constitution. A democratic audit in the years leading up to NAFTA would have found very little to put on the asset side of the ledger. Opposition parties did exist. A right-wing party had split off from the PRI, as had a left-wing faction, but blatant corruption in electoral practices ensured that, however the public voted, the government party would win. Peaceful transition to non-PRI rule was unthinkable. Formal freedom of the press and the great variety of newspapers and periodicals available to the reading public, moreover, belied the considerable control that the government exerted through physical and personal intimidation of dissenting journalists and financial pressure on individual newspapers. While far from being a totalitarian system, Mexico was equally far from meeting either our medium or our high standards of democracy.

AUDITING NAFTA

A healthy sense of skepticism about the claims to democratic virtue in each of the North American states gives us an appropriate point of departure for examining the democratic qualities of the new continental regime ushered in by NAFTA. Now that the regime has been in force for more than half a decade, three issues need to be addressed to begin our assessment. To start with, we need to know what has been the impact on each signatory state, first of negotiating and then of ratifying the new agreement. Next we have to determine what democratic qualities the nascent polity created by the agreement has developed. Given the extent to which trade blocs are interconnected with a multilateral economic regime, we need, finally, to examine how the emerging global order of governance affects the new continental system and the democratic norms of the member states.

The Impact of NAFTA on Its Member States

For this first part of a democratic accounting of the new North America, we must carefully distinguish the two roots of our key concept, democracy: *demos* (people) and *kratos* (power).[8] Like my collaborators in this book who debate the content of the former term in the European context, we have so far focused on assessing the limited capacity of the *demos* in Canada, the United States, and Mexico to wield political power in each of these states. Here, we turn to the question of *kratos* to examine how the creation and implementation of a new North American economic agreement has affected the power of the three partners. A treaty can increase or decrease the *kratos* of a signatory state and so enhance or contract the scope of its *demos*. By creating a new level of governance, a continental economic agreement may also create a new locus of *kratos*, which raises questions about its control by the enlarged collective *demos*, a question we address in the subsequent section.

Negotiation

Let us consider each participant in turn, starting with the one most generously endowed with power at the outset of the process.

United States of America   In *Democracy's Discontent*, Michael Sandel asked if globalization in effect disempowered the nation-state. "One of the major tasks of democratic government," he concluded, "is to maintain the conditions in which its citizens have a sense of command over their destiny."[9] The extent to which American citizens sensed they had "command over their destiny" before 1988 would have been considerable if they knew anything about their government's long-standing capacity to command the destiny of its neighbors. When Canadian policies did not suit American interests, Washington generally showed itself able to nudge or, if necessary, strong-arm them in the desired direction. Historically high levels of economic integration, combined with the twelve-to-one imbalance in the size of the two systems, gave the United States, quite simply, power over Canada.

Even though Mexico was economically weaker than Canada, its fierce nationalism supported a revolutionary tradition that kept the United States at arm's length for decades. But in the early 1980s, when the PRI decided that import substitution was doomed as an industrialization strategy and economic liberalization was the only alternative, Washington started to enjoy an even greater level of command over Mexico's governors than it did over Canada's. The U.S. government pushed the PRI to liberalize its investment regime, deregulate its banking system, and privatize its parastatal corporations, all in accordance with a set of criteria designed to meet the needs of leading U.S. corporations interested in extending their participation in the Mexican economy. In sum, even before North American free trade was actively considered, the United States enjoyed a power surplus, exerting extensive "command" over the destiny of its two neighbors.

When we look at the actual trade negotiations that led to CUFTA, we find that the American agenda prevailed over the Canadian one. The United States gained major concessions in energy (guaranteed export levels), industrial policy (national treatment), and many other areas. Just as important, the United States was able to block the achievement of the key Canadian objective, a subsidies code and exemption from U.S. trade remedy legislation that would have impinged on the sovereignty of the U.S. Congress. We can infer that America's *kratos* surplus was increased by virtue of the greater command over the destiny of Canadians that CUFTA yielded to Washington. At the same time, it conceded virtually no Canadian command over American destiny in return.

The same conclusion follows from a look at the NAFTA negotiating process. Once again, the United States emerged from the bargaining having made no concessions on a subsidy code that could have restrained its unilateral capacity to impose antidumping or countervailing duties on its continental trade partners. NAFTA contained a chapter on intellectual property rights, which was at the top of the major American drug companies' wish list, and broadened stipulations on investment, greatly increasing the rights of foreign investors—benefiting American transnational corporations disproportionately—in the signatory states. U.S. labor and environmental groups also managed to have their government address their concerns, which focused on the danger of a regulatory race to the bottom. The resulting North American agreements on labor and environmental cooperation showed that NAFTA helped to increase the American democratic surplus both on the left and the right.

Canada   After months of frustrating discussions, in which it was faced with renouncing substantial instruments of government power without gaining an exemption from U.S. trade remedy legislation, Canada threatened to break off the CUFTA negotiations. The deal was saved by inserting in the draft text a number of bilateral dispute settlement mechanisms (DSMs). Highly touted by government spokespeople at the time, the DSM has turned out to be of little value, since its capacity to restrain the excesses of American trade harassment is limited to verifying whether American trade law has been correctly applied in any particular case. Since it was the discriminatory substance of these laws, and not their application, that was the main bone of contention, Washington's concession in accepting a bilateral dispute process was minimal. Even when a trade determination has been remanded, Congress can change the relevant policy and so enable the particular protectionist interest to return to its attack against Canadian exports.[10]

Apart from not achieving its major objective, the Canadian government also failed to resist making concessions on those issues it wished to keep off the agenda: agriculture, energy, culture, the Auto Pact, inter alia. In terms of simple sovereign *kratos*, then, CUFTA augmented the already considerable asymmetry with the United States and so represented an increase in Canada's democratic deficit.

Mexico   As with one neighbor, so with the other. When it came to negotiating NAFTA, Mexico was the party that had to make the bulk of concessions if it wanted to achieve the deal it felt was crucial for its economic recovery. Many changes had already been made to Mexico's laws and regulations, but further adaptations to U.S. demands were required in the energy and banking sectors, and with regard to foreign direct investment norms, intellectual property rights, and rules of origin. Following his election, President Clinton insisted on further concessions that would give the United States (and Canada) levers to pressure Mexico to implement its already legislated high environmental and labor standards. The United States set the criteria; Mexico's only choice was to adopt them in practice if it wanted admission to the new club. If the negotiation of free trade for Mexico can be fairly summarized as the incorporation of U.S. legal norms in its governing systems, then a first answer in our inquiry is that NAFTA increased an already considerable democratic surplus in the United States and deepened the corresponding democratic deficit in Mexico.

Once a consideration of *demos* is added to that of *kratos*, the same issues take on a slightly different cast. To the extent that trade liberalization willingly weakened state structures in Canada and Mexico, the reduction of policy-making autonomy moved NAFTA from democracy's liability to its asset column. It is true that CUFTA was a highly contested issue in Canada, favored only by the governing party and opposed by the other two national parties as well as by the vast majority of the public, according to opinion polls of the day. Nevertheless, by the norms of Canadian electoral practice, Brian Mulroney's Progressive Conservative party won 57 percent of the seats in the 1988 federal parliament (with 43 percent of the votes). In signing the free trade agreement, it can be said to have legitimately executed its democratically sanctioned program. Furthermore, the polarization of Canadian politics over free trade in the 1986–1988 period caused a significant increase in the intensity of political discourse in the country. The long months of debate spawned extraordinarily high levels of public discussion about the implications of this dramatic new initiative. Major coalitions were constructed by interest groups supporting and resisting signature of the agreement. Seeing free trade in this light presents us with a conundrum: in terms of *kratos*, Canada's external deficit increased with CUFTA, but in terms of deliberative *demos*, its internal deficit decreased.

Mexico lost considerable sovereignty with NAFTA as well, but the agreement was happily signed by the PRI leadership, which believed that this radical change in economic strategy was urgently needed and in the best interests of the Mexican economy and the Mexican people. Public debate on NAFTA was negligible, however, because of the tight control that the government exerted over the issue's treatment by the media. Free trade was presented as an unquestionable bonanza and contrary positions were systematically suppressed.

Implementation

To assess the democratic consequences of free trade we need to consider once again the asymmetrical relations connecting NAFTA's three members.

United States of America   For the United States, NAFTA presented only a minor problem. The American implementation legislation specifically asserted the precedence of American law over the trade agreement.[11] Indeed, when American farming, forestry, or fishing interests considered that NAFTA's rules-based system was affecting their bottom lines, they prevailed on Washington to ignore the agreement altogether and return to the tried-and-true methods of power-based protectionism. The continuing irritant of Canada's increasing softwood lumber exports was dealt with by a highly political show of U.S. force. Mexico had similar experiences when its exports of tomatoes and brooms were halted in response to the demands of U.S. producers and when its truckers were prevented from delivering their loads to American destinations. Such incidents indicate that American sovereignty remained virtually unrestricted by the continental agreement. If the new rules proved not to be working in their favor, U.S. customs officials were able to alter their impact by changing their regulations, just as U.S. farmers could thumb their noses at the agreement by blocking the border with their trucks and tractors.

An apparent deviation from Congress's capacity to maintain control over its own destiny was precipitated by the Mexican currency crisis of late 1994. So serious was the threat of a "tequila effect," in which speculative hysteria could jeopardize the stability of other currencies (including the U.S. dollar), that the administration felt compelled to step in and help prop up the peso. Bolstered by a supportive contribution from Ottawa, the United States supplied massive short-term funding to the Bank of Mexico to help it weather the financial storm. In effect, Washington found that NAFTA had created a new vulnerability with respect to Mexico that required United States assistance.

Canada In Canada's case, although "free trade" has now existed with the United States for over ten years, it is remarkably difficult to offer an authoritative analysis of its impact. This is not for lack of hypotheses. The intense debate during the period of negotiation and ratification of the original CUFTA yielded many predictions about how free trade would affect Canadian politics. Proponents of the agreement argued that wealth creates power: because free trade would dramatically increase Canadian prosperity, Canadian governments would necessarily be more autonomous, not less. They would be more capable of playing any independent role in the world to which they aspired. Because each region would profit from free trade, the traditional animosity between the peripheral provinces and central Canada would also diminish. By extension, the quality of Canadian democracy would improve.

Arguing in the opposite direction, critics of free trade predicted that the Canadian state would be hollowed out as a result of the remorseless corporate pressure to harmonize public policy standards down to U.S. levels. Because of such constraints as the "national treatment" principle for foreign investment and restrictions on the entrepreneurial activities of crown corporations, Canadian government efforts to support nationally controlled firms with microeconomic policies would no longer be possible.

The chilling effect of the free trade agreements is not easily documented: nondecisions are difficult for scholars to observe. If policymakers know that a proposed line of action will lead to trouble with Washington because of a clause in a NAFTA annex, they will not contemplate it for very long. In one known case, Ontario's New Democratic government decided not to keep its 1990 electoral promise to introduce public auto insurance in large part because it was advised that CUFTA would require astronomically high levels of compensation to the expropriated U.S. insurance companies.[12]

Since CUFTA obligates the Canadian government to inform Washington of any policy change that might affect the working of the agreement, Washington has in effect been admitted into the decision-making chambers of both the federal and the provincial governments. The federal government withdrew proposed film-distribution legislation under severe U.S. pressure linked to the negotiating process. As for the U.S. drug industry's long campaign to undo Canada's generic drug legislation, the free trade negotiations did not at first succeed. But U.S. firms kept trying, first in the Uruguay Round discussions and then in the NAFTA negotiations, where they succeeded in having intellectual property rights enshrined in the agreement. As a result, they obtained near-complete satisfaction from the Mulroney government, which brought in legislation to give branded drugs intellectual property rights protection for twenty years.[13] The financial viability of Canada's universal health care system, secured only through decades of political struggle, has thus been jeopardized by rising costs flowing in part from NAFTA's empowerment of foreign-controlled pharmaceutical corporations, to the detriment of their indigenous competitors.

The endowment of their partners' corporations with greater rights than those effectively enjoyed by nationally based firms adds an extraordinary twist to the notion of democratic deficit in the signatory states. Among the investment provisions in NAFTA's chapter 11 is the clause protecting foreign investors against governmental measures that constitute or are "tantamount to" expropriation. This stipulation gives a U.S. or, more improbably, a Mexican company with interests in Canada a right not enjoyed by a Canadian company—the power to compel the arbitration of its complaint by a private international body, which decides the case in secret according to international definitions of what constitutes expropriation. This provision, the implication of which does not seem to have been understood by Canada's representatives when the free trade agreements were being negotiated, marks a significant increase in the vulnerability of democratically enacted policies to corporate attack. *Mutatis mutandis,* the same deficit exists in Mexico with respect to U.S. and Canadian corporations. Since this notion of expropriation is an American norm, and since the relative weight of Canadian and Mexican corporations in the U.S. economy is low, chapter 11 does not constitute as great a derogation of governmental powers for the United States as it does for its partners.

Apart from the stark example of the now-notorious chapter 11, what makes it difficult to prove or disprove the proponents' hypotheses about NAFTA is a new factor—the drive to control federal and provincial deficits. This preoccupation, which took over from trade liberalization as the

Canadian governments' priority in the late 1990s, was the immediate cause of cutbacks to the country's social programs. We have witnessed a reduction in the quality of the universal health care system, public education, and other government services in Canada, with precisely the downward convergences toward U.S. levels that critics of free trade predicted. Because free trade cannot be shown to be the direct cause of these deficit-cutting actions, however, the decline in citizens' social rights cannot easily be laid at the door of NAFTA.

Other expected outcomes of free trade remain as hypothetical today as they were ten years ago. Provincial capitals feared that Ottawa would use the agreements' requirement that the federal government ensure provincial conformity with CUFTA's and NAFTA's terms as a new means of interfering in their jurisdictions. To date there has been neither a showdown nor a supreme court ruling to suggest that free trade has generated any such power shifts to the federal from the provincial levels of government and so altered the federation's carefully balanced distribution of *kratos*.

Expectations that accelerated continental integration prompted by the new trade agreements would further aggravate the disintegration of the federal system have not been realized either. Efforts by the Progressive Conservative government in 1987 and 1992 to amend the Canadian constitution in favor of greater decentralization proved unsuccessful. Neither the Meech Lake Agreement nor the Charlottetown Accord was implemented. And while provincial trade with the United States has increased rapidly on an interregional basis, evidence of federal economic disintegration must be balanced against other evidence showing recentralization, specifically through supreme court judgments on issues relating to the 1982 Charter of Rights and Freedoms and the division of powers.

To some extent, the debate over the impact of free trade on Canadian economic policy capacity is moot. The argument that the principle of national treatment would make it impossible for Canadian governments to support Canadian-owned enterprises through subsidies and incentives falls on barren ground because of a paradigm shift: Canadian politicians and bureaucrats no longer believe that such policies are desirable. If governments are prevented by NAFTA from doing what they do not intend to do in any case, has the democratic deficit increased? The answer is "No" for the present, while governments have no intention of intervening in the economy, but could conceivably be "Yes" in the future, when more interventionist legislators could find themselves shackled by neoconservative policy norms that have in effect been constitutionalized.

Mexico   Since the question of implementation deals more with *demos* than with *kratos*, the Mexican case has a story to tell that is both similar to and different from Canada's. NAFTA obligated Mexico to make changes in its legislation, its regulatory systems, and its constitution. Since the PRI leadership, like the Mulroney Conservatives in Ottawa, had already become radically neoconservative, a movement toward privatization, deregulation, and downsizing cannot on the face of it be taken as evidence of an increased democratic liability.

The Mexican differs from the Canadian case in the assumption that a reduction of sovereignty necessarily entails a restriction of democracy, an equation that may not hold for authoritarian regimes. If trade liberalization norms require a nondemocratic government to increase transparency, reduce corruption, and lessen procedural arbitrariness, then the nation's citizens may, as an unintended yet happy consequence, gain greater knowledge about government policy and greater confidence in the judicial system. If Mexican workers find that illegal, repressive acts by their trade union or employer can be challenged by American or Canadian comrades through the North American Agreement on Labor Cooperation, their sense of disempowerment may be mitigated. If their government is subject to court action by aggrieved foreign investors, Mexican citizens may by the same token be emboldened to seek judicial validation of their own rights.

Beyond such theoretical considerations, actual changes can be seen as enhancing democracy. NAFTA-induced increases in U.S.-Mexican trade and investment flows have manifested themselves on a regional basis, with winning states near the U.S. border increasing their autonomy from the federal government in Mexico City.[14] This expansion of state power at the subnational level is in turn coinciding with increased levels of democratic struggle and a growing number of electoral successes by parties challenging the political monopoly of the PRI.

From the uprising in Chiapas to the election of a non-PRI mayor in Mexico City and non-PRI governments in a number of state capitals, Mexican politics is clearly showing signs of popular political effervescence. The Chiapas uprising was deliberately scheduled by Subcomandante Marcos to break out on the very day that free trade was signed by the three governments. The insurgents regarded NAFTA with hostility because it was directly linked to the alienation of communal lands and the promotion of large-scale agribusiness oriented toward export to the American market, thereby threatening the viability of traditional *ejido* agriculture. It may seem perverse to argue that, in worsening the plight of Mexico's indigenous and laboring peoples to the point where they are goaded to revolt, NAFTA contributed to an increase in democratic practice. In an autarchy, however, insurrection may be the ultimate means of legitimate political expression.

In sum, the impact of continental free trade on the democratic quality of each member state has varied from minimal in the most powerful, the United States of America, to mixed in Canada, to maximal in the weakest, the United States of Mexico. The story is far less complicated when we look at the new system as a polity in its own terms.

NAFTA as a Polity

Because the concept of a democratic deficit first emerged from among critics of the European Union, it is appropriate to look to the Old World's newest political experiment for criteria by which to judge the far less articulated continental regime created by NAFTA. The debate over the quality of democracy at the EU level is instructive. For those like Greven and Offe, who set the bar very high in this book, the EU can never expect to make the grade. Its political space is not really a public space. Its citizenship is less a matter of membership in a new community than an extension of member-state citizenship. A European identity is claimed by only a handful of the continent's elite. The European Commission, the European Council, and the European Court of Justice (ECJ) are substantial institutions, but the European parliament lacks effective control. Political parties are strategic alliances rather than genuine continental organizations, and elections resemble national by-elections more than proper pan-European affairs. In short, though the EU has an impressive institutional structure with real and growing powers, this new continental *kratos* is not adequately balanced by an equivalent continental *demos*. Without a public agora in which deliberations, identity formation, and public decision making can create a genuine sense of continental community, the EU's democratic deficit is doomed to persist.

More optimistic observers, such as Grande and Zürn in this volume, would be more prone to give the benefit of the doubt to a set of institutions that has been only five decades in the making and that is certain to evolve further. A clear trend has increased the authority of the European parliament, which now can even force the resignation of the Commission's president and commissioners. Greater links of accountability and transparency are also developing between member-state delegations in Brussels and their constituents. In effect, Europe already has a constitution in the form of its various treaties and agreements, and Europeans do have a nascent identity and sense of citizenship linked to the considerable judicial scope of the ECJ, which has expanded individual rights against their member-state governments.

However this argument fares for Europe, its great utility for the study of North America is the striking contrasts it provokes. If, as my colleagues point out above, the EU's democratic deficit is attributable to a lack of *demos* within powerful institutions, then NAFTA's deficit is a function of a lack of *kratos*. CUFTA has no supranational institutions at all. NAFTA has only a small secretariat, and two commissions for labor and environmental cooperation, which have minimal supranational autonomy from the member states that created them and hold their purse strings. Even NAFTA's modest dispute-settlement process is set up without supranational capacity. Panelists are drawn from a roster of available national trade experts and judges; they do not form a tenured corps of jurists mandated to develop a transcendent corpus of continental legal norms.

Given the three member states' refusal to devolve sovereignty from themselves to a continental *kratos*, one cannot speak of a "people" of North America as if it were a community endowed with rights by a constitution. There is no possibility of a representative assembly to which this North American people could elect representatives organized in continentwide political parties. To the extent that there is a continental consciousness at all, it has less to do with NAFTA than with the marketing of Taco Bell franchises from the Gulf of Mexico to the Arctic Ocean.

Nor is there any sense of a continental citizenship. The two northern member states have moved actively not to lower national borders, but to raise barriers to the free flow of people from the south. A chief objective of the United States in negotiating NAFTA was to reduce, not increase, the immigration of Mexicans into Texas and California. In a similar vein, Canada has been toughening its border regulations to lower demographic inflows as a whole, with a consequent reduction of immigration from Mexico.

The political capital of the European Union—the locus for most EU policy making—is Brussels, which, as the capital of one of its smallest member states, symbolizes the community's efforts to offset inherent asymmetries. NAFTA has a virtual capital, that of its largest member. But there is little about Washington that would make one suspect that its political life has been transformed by the rise of a new North American polity. Indeed, NAFTA has been remarkably unpopular in Washington ever since the peso crisis showed how unstable the Mexican economy was and what a potential albatross it could be around Uncle Sam's neck. American bad feelings toward Mexico have been exacerbated by continuing evidence of political corruption in the southern member, linked to the unchecked flow of narcotics into the American market.

NAFTA was a solution for the 1980s, when Americans had convinced themselves that they were in the process of hegemonic decline. A decade later, when the new dragons of Asia were the ones in the grip of economic crisis, Washington had little time for NAFTA. Congress could not even see fit to give the administration fast-track authority to negotiate a Free Trade Agreement for the Americas. In other words, NAFTA's deficit is double: it lacks *kratos* and it lacks a *demos*.

This is not to say that there are no signs of political development at the continental level. As Newman noted above, the dramatic continentalization of the economy that has seen corporations restructure their operations on a borderless, continentwide basis represents a strengthening system of market governance and a weakening of public government.[15] Some scholars have also written about "continentalization from below," the development of alliances among social movements and political activists in the three countries in areas such as human rights, trade union solidarity, academic research, and environmental lobbying.[16] Other researchers have shown that some trilateral decision making is happening in specialized areas, such as the development of standards for the transport of dangerous chemicals.[17]

In those areas where continental integration between Canada and the United States had been proceeding for over a century, trade liberalization does not seem to be having a particularly significant effect on political identity. In Mexico, where continental integration was resisted until recently, NAFTA may have a more substantial effect. It tells Mexicans that they belong to the larger North American whole. Rather than "Norteamericanos" being the gringos and their snowy neighbors further north, Norteamericanos are now "us." Still, the extent and importance of this shift should not be exaggerated. Mexicans may adjust their self-definition, speaking English to a greater extent and becoming more like Americans and Canadians in their consumption patterns. They may develop a sense that they belong to a greater whole, just as Canadians are starting to realize that they now have a special relationship with Mexicans. But such changes are modest when compared with the much larger and symbolically significant steps taken toward the development of a European identity, such as the common format for passports, the EU flag, and the EU anthem.

Greven may be highly critical of the EU's democratic practice, but these shortcomings seem trifling to anyone who had hoped that NAFTA would institute a supranational regime that could restrain its dominant member's headstrong unilateralism. Taming the United States has also been a theme in the march toward developing a global system of economic governance. How the emerging world trade order affects our democratic audit of North America is the last question we need to consider.

Rebalancing Continental with Global Governance

The interaction between the national, continental, and global orders in North America is best illustrated by the processes leading to the foundation and activation of the World Trade Organization. Had prospects for the eighth round of trade liberalization negotiations under the General

Agreement on Tariffs and Trade (GATT) appeared rosy in the mid-1980s, it is probable that neither CUFTA nor NAFTA would have seen the light of day. The original Canada–United States agreement was the offspring of a mutual frustration with the gridlock apparently bedeviling the prenegotiations leading up to what later became the spectacularly successful Uruguay Round.

The United States had a long trade policy agenda. It wanted agricultural subsidies and trade in services included within the ambit of global trade rules, as well as a tougher, more comprehensive, and more easily enforceable set of intellectual property rights than the World Intellectual Property Organization contained. With Europe stonewalling on the food side lest its Common Agricultural Policy be jeopardized, and Brazil and India firmly opposed to a new intellectual property (IP) regime that threatened to lock them into permanent technological dependence on western transnationals, the prospects for a successful and timely conclusion of the negotiations seemed bleak. If the multilateral arena was blocked, however, Washington saw in bilateral negotiations with an obliging Canada a tactically useful means of setting precedents that could subsequently be applied in global negotiations. A CanAm agreement would create a stick with which to threaten other trading partners: either agree to negotiate multilaterally or we will sign deals on the CUFTA model with our competitors one by one, starting with the most docile, until we have isolated the most obdurate. The stratagem succeeded. Once CUFTA, then NAFTA, and even the Asia Pacific Economic Cooperation (APEC) initiative established potential fortresses from which the EU might be excluded, Brussels agreed to consider previously unthinkable concessions.

The United States was not the only North American country to achieve its objectives through the Uruguay Round. Canada took the lead in proposing a reform of the functioning of the GATT system.[18] This important initiative led to the GATT's transmogrification into the World Trade Organization (WTO), a membership institution with legal personality and far greater scope, coherence, and muscle than its predecessor. If it was in Canada's interests as a medium-sized trading state to have a rules-based, rather than a power-based system, in whose ongoing norm-making it could participate as a full member, then the creation of the WTO represented a major gain in its international *kratos* and by extension an important extension of its democratic assets. A further gain for Canada was the incorporation in the WTO of a dispute-settlement mechanism far superior in every respect to that of CUFTA, which was further degraded at American insistence when translated into NAFTA. In the WTO's dispute-settlement mechanism, the rules on which cases would be decided were international, not national, and the panelists would be nationals of countries other than those in contention on a particular case. The expertise, consistency, and rigor of adjudication were expected to be greater, rooted as the process was in developing a global common law. Panel decisions could be appealed to an appellate body, but that group's findings would be final and authoritative.[19]

The WTO also included something Canada had failed to achieve bilaterally in CUFTA or trilaterally in NAFTA: a subsidy code. The global agreement spelled out a triple set of policy categories—red light (forbidden), green light (permitted), and orange light (contestable). These definitions go a long way toward taking the uncertainty out of economic policy making for member states. If this code becomes accepted in the North American context, it will reassure Canadian decision makers worried about American countervailing and antidumping actions.

In principle, a member state's transfer of sovereignty to an intergovernmental organization is balanced through its participation in that organization's institutional life. The extent to which a shift of *kratos* to a higher level is balanced by *demos* is an empirical question, which must be approached with care. Even though Canadian negotiators were jubilant, it did not follow that a rules-based system would work to their advantage—especially if the rules reflected the interests of the most powerful states that had taken part in the negotiations. The passage of time and the actual resolution of specific conflicts will reveal which country's sovereignty has been or will be reinforced or eroded by the new global trade regime. In the short history of the WTO since 1995, four cases have provided important grist for this academic mill.

1. Hormones. The WTO ruling in the case brought by the United States and Canada against the EU's ban on the import of beef containing growth hormones suggests that the internationally developed Sanitary and Phytosanitary Standards incorporated in the WTO have provided a new scientific standard for dealing with health-related trade issues—in this case, to North America's advantage. To the extent that Canadian officials take part in the definition of standards in the international Codex Alimentarius, Canadian *demos* can be seen to have increased. And in the hormone case, at least, Canadian *kratos* grew as well, since the case went Canada's way.

2. Tariffication. In response to the agricultural section of the WTO agreement requiring signatory states to transform quantitative restrictions on food imports into tariffs that are to be reduced progressively over time, the United States challenged Canada's tariffication as a violation of its NAFTA commitment not to increase tariffs on its imports of foodstuffs. A panel set up under NAFTA's dispute-settlement mechanism ruled that the WTO agreement had precedence over NAFTA in this case. Here, Canadian participation in the

global order broke the restraints imposed on it by the continental regime. For Canadian farmers, this may spell bad news, as the WTO agreement calls for reduced protectionism. For Canadian consumers, it may mean cheaper food. For Canadian democracy, it suggests that Canadian state participation has greater vitality in the multilateral forum of the WTO than in the bilateral forum of NAFTA.

3. Cultural policy. Although Canada had negotiated a grandfathering of its cultural protection measures in CUFTA, Washington took advantage of the WTO's trade rules to challenge a number of measures Ottawa had implemented to preserve the Canadian magazine industry from being overwhelmed by its American competitors. The WTO panel on the *Sports Illustrated* case ruled against Canada, and the appellate body judgment made things still worse from Ottawa's point of view. While claiming that they were not passing judgment on the validity of cultural protection in principle, the WTO panel and appellate body rulings have jeopardized Canada's capacity to sustain a niche for the production of national cultural material aimed at nourishing the population's need for information and stories about itself.[20] Unlike the hormone case, in which the WTO panel showed considerable political sensitivity to the EU's position, there was no sense in the *Sports Illustrated* case that either the panelists or the appellate body understood what was at stake for Canada's politically sensitive problems of identity.[21]

It would not be appropriate to judge every country's loss at a WTO panel as a diminution of its democracy. Nevertheless, the *Sports Illustrated* decision does point out a disturbing reality. Democratically generated laws that had been on Canada's books for years, even decades, were dismissed as violating the new, 1995 set of global trade rules. This letter-of-the-law approach to an issue central to the country's sense of national security should be considered in relation to the treatment of an issue of comparable sensitivity in the United States—American policy toward Cuba.

4. Helms-Burton. The EU decided to drop its case against Washington's Helms-Burton legislation, which attempted to extend U.S. proscriptions against Cuba, for fear that the United States would boycott the panel and jeopardize the WTO's dispute-settlement system. This raises the disturbing prospect that, for all the hope that the WTO had created a new, rules-based system, it was still subject to the hegemon's moods. For its part, Canada chose not to request that a NAFTA panel be convened to deal with this extraterritorial violation of its rights, lest an American boycott of the panel threaten the operation of the NAFTA dispute-settlement mechanism. The Cana-

dian government's reluctance to take a stand in this matter under-lines the extent to which NAFTA operates ultimately at the pleasure of Uncle Sam, whatever the formal rules.

CONCLUSION

What constitutes democracy in an environment overshadowed by global and continental rule-making and dispute-settlement processes is certain to remain a contested subject. Those who look forward to a new era of global citizenship will find little evidence in the regime created by NAFTA of what Richard Falk called a "growth of human solidarity aris-ing from an extension of democratic principles as a result of the exertion of peoples and their voluntary associations."[22] Nevertheless, to the extent that the nation-state remains the central player on the world stage, its in-teraction with continental and global regimes is not having a necessarily degenerative effect on their democracy. The effective public protest pro-voked around the world by negotiations on a Multilateral Agreement on Investment shows that democracy beyond national limits is still rooted within national boundaries.

If God is in the details, we must continue to pay attention to the ongo-ing process of international negotiation and the extent to which nations are able to project and defend their values continentally and globally. At the same time, we must monitor the extent to which implementation of the resulting new norms respects or violates the sovereignty of signatory states. *Demos* does not always move in step with *kratos*. As the localization of the continental and the global is accompanied by the continentalization and globalization of the local, the need to continue auditing each coun-try's democratic accounts will become increasingly important. The WTO's dynamism as a locus for dispute settlement and as a site for nego-tiating further trade rules suggests that the asymmetry, which NAFTA deepened, between a democratic deficit in Canada and Mexico and a democratic surplus in the United States, may actually be mitigated as a global legal order becomes successfully embedded in international prac-tice.

NOTES

1. In 1995, the three NAFTA countries had a population of 384 million and a combined gross domestic product (GDP) of U.S. $8.5 trillion. By 1996, the fifteen EU countries had a population of 373 million and a combined GDP of U.S. $8.6 trillion.

2. Gordon Stewart, "A Special Contiguous Country Economic Regime: America's Canadian Policy," *Diplomatic History* 6, no. 4 (fall 1982): 339–357.

3. David Leyton-Brown and Mark Gold, eds., *Trade-Offs on Free Trade: The Canada-U.S. Free Trade Agreement* (Toronto: Carswell, 1988).

4. C. B. Macpherson, *The Life and Times of Liberal Democracy* (Oxford: Oxford University Press, 1977), 10.

5. Roberto Michels, *Political Parties: A Sociological Study of the Oligarchical Tendencies of Modern Democracy* (New York: Dover, 1959 edition of the English translation of 1915), 401.

6. Joseph Schumpeter, *Capitalism, Socialism and Democracy* (New York: Harper, 1943), 250–283.

7. Evelyn Ruppert, "Who Can Afford Democracy?" *The Annex Gleaner*, March 19, 1998, 5.

8. The connotations of the Greek word *kratos* were physical strength, naked force, might, and power. Zeus, for example, was *krateros*, the mighty one. A *demokratia* was a political system in which the people wielded the power.

9. Michael J. Sandel, *Democracy's Discontent* (Cambridge: Harvard University Press, 1996), 317.

10. Charles Doran, "Trade Dispute Resolution on Trial: Softwood Lumber," *International Journal* 51, no. 4 (autumn 1996): 710–733.

11. Daniel Drache, "Dreaming Trade or Trading Dreams: The Limits of Trade Blocs," in *International Regulatory Competition and Coordination: Perspectives on Economic Regulation in Europe and the United States*, ed. William W. Bratton, Joseph McCahery, Sol Picciotto, and Colin Scott (Oxford: Clarendon Press, 1996).

12. Chuck Rachlis and David Wolfe, "An Insider's View of the NDP Government of Ontario: The Politics of Permanent Opposition Meets the Economics," in *The Government and Politics of Ontario*, ed. Graham White (Toronto: University of Toronto Press, 1997): 344–347.

13. Christopher Kent, "The Uruguay Round GATT TRIPS Agreement & Chapter 17 of the NAFTA: A New Era in International Patent Protection," *Canadian Intellectual Property Review* 10 (1994): 711–733.

14. Teresa Gutiérrez-Haces and Nicolas Hiernaux, "Economic Changes and the Need for a New Federalism: Lessons from Mexico's Northern States," *American Review of Canadian Studies* 26, no. 2 (summer 1996): 233–244.

15. Stephen Blank and Stephen Krajewski, "US Firms in North America: Redefining Structure and Strategy," *North American Outlook* 5, no. 2 (February 1995).

16. Teresa Gutiérrez-Haces, "Globalization from Below: The Awakening and Networking of Civil Societies in North America," paper presented to the Association of Canadian Studies in the United States conference, Toronto, November 1996.

17. CEC (Commission for Environmental Cooperation), *NAFTA's Institutions: The Environmental Potential and Performance of the NAFTA Free Trade Commission and Related Bodies* (Montreal: CEC, 1997).

18. Sylvia Ostry, *The Post–Cold War Trading System: Who's on First?* (Chicago: University of Chicago Press, 1997), 193.

19. Robert Howse, "Settling Trade Remedy Disputes: When the WTO Forum Is Better Than NAFTA," *C. D. Howe Institute Commentary* 111 (June 1998).

20. Ted Magder, "Franchising the Candy Store: Split-Run Magazines and a New International Regime for Trade in Culture," *Canadian-American Public Policy* 34 (April 1998).

21. Joseph Weiler, "Juridification of Dispute Settlement and the Institutional Culture of the World Trade Organization," paper presented to the University of Toronto Faculty of Law, April 1, 1998.

22. Richard Falk, "The Making of a Global Citizenship," in *Global Visions: Beyond the New World Order*, ed. Jeremy Brecher et al. (Boston: South End Press, 1993), 41.

8

Democratic Foundations for a Global Economy
The European Experience and the Call to Imagination

Louis W. Pauly

The issues addressed in this book will be with us for many years to come. At the dawn of a new millennium, the technological, financial, and informational changes driving global and regional economic integration show little sign of dissipating. Even major environmental crises and episodes of turmoil in now deeply interlinked capital markets provide no clear harbingers of a countertrend.

Despite the inequities, unfairness, and injustices that global capitalism leaves in its wake, an intentional disintegration of the world economy offers a low probability of leading to better outcomes. Despite its incompleteness, the experiment in European economic integration looks like an historic success, especially if we can remember the way Europe looked in 1945. Despite its uneven effects, NAFTA was not imposed on unwitting publics by unelected governments. In short, it is not implausible to argue that the citizens of advanced industrial states live in a world they themselves collectively created in the years since 1945. It remains true that the vast majority of humanity finding itself outside that gilded sphere, and even important segments of the populations within it, bear little personal responsibility for the character of a system now constraining them. Barring systemic catastrophe on the scale of the 1930s, however, the prospect of rolling back global capitalism lacks a compelling rationale, an attractive alternative vision, and a powerful constituency. We are left to deal, therefore, with the unintended consequences of prior strategic choices.

The authors of this book address one of the most important of those

165

consequences. Each chapter in its own way reminds us that a lack of attention to the political structures undergirding regional and global markets could well lead, by accident, to a much less attractive world. Global capitalism requires solid political foundations, and citizens grown used to democratic norms in an era of national capitalism cannot be counted upon supinely to abandon them. Even if, as Newman pointed out, democracy-in-practice remains far from ideal, it is difficult to envisage a more effective and just replacement. Even if, as Offe and Greven fear, the advances associated with the historic move from formal to social democracy are increasingly tenuous, a reversion to authoritarian or bureaucratic systems of governance offers no self-evidently promising mechanism for defending them.

There seems, in short, no easy resolution to the key dilemma highlighted throughout this book. The bolstering of governing power beyond the nation-state is implied by the exigencies of economic integration, but ultimate political authority today remains grounded in the nation-state. In the absence of a transnational *demos*, coercive power can in principle flow to the global level, but the legitimacy of its exercise will remain profoundly questionable. And in the absence of a shared sense of legitimate governance, even the obvious winners in the global capitalist resurgence will have cause to worry about the durability of their gains. At a minimum, the willing acquiescence of the losers will continue to be required, especially if they comprise more than small minorities.

Europe's responses to the political challenges of economic integration may turn out to be idiosyncratic and not easily generalizable. The project of stabilizing global capitalism and rendering its outcomes more just may well prove immensely more complicated. But the terrain explored by Greven, Offe, Zürn, and Grande provides an important empirical template for beginning to understand the larger challenge. As Clarkson demonstrates, at the very least it provides a tangible basis for contrasting and comparing the political implications of the integrative project under way in North America. As all of the authors suggest, the EU constitutes an arena wherein new solutions to the democratic dilemma can and must be imagined.

The body of political theory surveyed most explicitly in the Newman, Greven, and Offe chapters stimulates that work of imagination. By engaging with it, scholars have an important role to play. The trajectory of global capitalism is already creating a world where rising tensions surround basic issues of political identity, social obligation, and governmental efficiency. The need to find new ways of rendering decision-making authority both effective and legitimate is already pressing. In advanced industrial states, as well as in a widening array of states aspiring to that status, democratic theory has been crucial to addressing such tensions in the past. Even if democracy-in-practice has rarely lived up to the expectations of romantics or perfectionists, it has not been as hollow as cynics often suggest.

This book highlights two key dimensions of the challenge posed by globalizing capitalism for the structures in which the world's leading states have, both in theory and in fact, grounded political authority. Through those structures, they have arguably rendered that authority relatively more stable, effective, and just than had antecedent structures. One dimension of the challenge centers on the apparently rising power of corporations and a class of skilled individuals capable of spanning national boundaries. Economic globalization seems necessarily to increase the influence of those firms and individuals enjoying potential mobility. It both gives them greater voice in actual policy-making processes and provides them with new options for credibly threatening to exit from defined political jurisdictions. By reshaping their own identities and giving them new ideological tools, moreover, it gives them new responsibilities in principle but releases them from old obligations in fact. In short, economic globalization plausibly chips away at the solidarity of existing political communities without providing a sure replacement. This is the essence of the democratic deficit diagnosed by Greven and Offe in the European Union, a situation likely to be exacerbated as the Union is enlarged. It is also the essence of the democratic deficits seen by Clarkson to be confronting Canada and Mexico as long as NAFTA remains without an adequate political superstructure.

The other dimension of the challenge is directly related to the first. In order to construct the technical capacity to govern increasingly integrated markets for labor, capital, and technology, political authority of a larger-than-national scale seems logically to be required.[1] Power is shifting in that direction, my colleagues concede, but its ultimate legitimation seems to depend upon the prior existence of a political community capable of reconstituting that authority. Such a community does not exist, either at the regional level in Europe and North America, or at the global level. Both dimensions of the challenge translate into an insidious erosion of formal procedures of democracy and of concomitant social institutions as they have heretofore developed across much of the industrial world.

The dilemma is a sobering one, and none of the authors in this book seeks to underestimate it. None of them, however, counsels despair. Newman, Greven, and Offe force us to confront the dilemma squarely. Zürn, Grande, and Clarkson open the door to pragmatic solutions. The empirical cases examined in this book suggest two basic lines of response, both on the part of scholars and practitioners.

In the short run, democratic practice may be adapted in ways precluded only by an overly idealistic approach to popular representation and deliberation. Here, the discussion between Zürn and Grande on combining carefully conceived referenda with new experiments in consensual decision-making procedures is highly suggestive. Of course, it is all too easy to imagine such measures degenerating into plebiscites that simply make opaque a system of rule by corporations or special interests. At the same time, such measures could easily translate into new kinds of barriers to effective participation by women and by social groups disadvantaged in the past and only recently beginning to find their voices in various local contexts. But such difficulties do not obviate the hard work of thinking such ideas through and experimenting with them. Indeed, Zürn and Grande give us some hope that just such an effort is under way within Europe. Democratic theorists would seem to have an obligation to follow that effort, to criticize its results, and to expand the conceptual space for improvements. Students of the phenomenon of globalization, in turn, should seize the opportunity further to probe the limits of lessons drawn from the European case. As Dahl recently pointed out, the difficult and still quite open challenge is "to make sure that the costs to democracy are fully taken into account when decisions are shifted to international levels, and to strengthen the means for holding political and bureaucratic elites accountable for their decisions."[2] Theory and practice must develop together.

In the longer run, the evidence examined by the authors suggests the need to continue the work of reconceptualizing democratic citizenship, effective representation, and political community. Much of the cutting-edge theoretical and empirical research they cite explores the essential malleability of political identity. That identity cannot plausibly be seen as fixed and unchangeable is acknowledged throughout this book in its allusions to the bidirectional process through which most contemporary nations and states were actually created in history. That process suggests the limitations of extrapolating a constitutional model of political legitimation drawn too closely from the unusual experience of the United States. Offe and Greven do not completely foreclose the possibility that the national identities now dominant in Europe can be reconstructed, even as they highlight the continuing social importance of boundaries. If and as such reconstruction occurs, the implications for reconceiving the real world of democracy could be far-reaching. Grande and Zürn anticipate some of those implications in their discussions of denationalizing or post-national societies. At the same time, Zürn and Clarkson begin addressing concrete consequences at the global level, especially with regard to the building of truly representative and accountable international institutions.[3] Continuing discussion and continuing research on all of these points are vital.

As Greven concludes, the pressing need now is to combine history and theory in imagining what global democracy could look like. Scholarly discipline, creativity, and extended debate will all be required. So too will close observation of policymakers seeking to muddle through the ideological and practical conflicts underlined in this book. The alternative would be to deploy that same creative imagination to the task of reversing the accelerating movement toward a global economy. Given the robustness of the nation-state at the end of the twentieth century, such a task may not really be as heroic as today's liberals may think.[4] A truly global economy itself remains a dream, and outside of Europe significant political momentum seems to remain in many national projects aimed at maximizing feasible degrees of policy autonomy without vitiating the benefits of external economic engagement. For leading democracies, however, that engagement is clearly intensifying, and reversing course is becoming more difficult to conceive. Few historians would altogether preclude such a reversal, and only analysts blinded by ideology would ignore its possibility. But to pretend that deep political dilemmas do not already confront us is passively to accept the evisceration of democracy in both its liberal and social forms, and to increase the risk that the great postwar experiment in international economic interdependence will ultimately fail. Globalization cannot be left on autopilot.

NOTES

1. This prospect lies at the center of much current research and debate among scholars of international relations. See, for example, Robert Keohane and Helen Milner, eds., _Internationalization and Domestic Politics_ (New York: Cambridge University Press, 1996); Susan Strange, _The Retreat of the State_ (Cambridge: Cambridge University Press, 1996); and Philip G. Cerny, "Globalization and the Changing Logic of Collective Action," _International Organization_ 49, no. 4 (1995): 595–625.

2. Robert Dahl, _On Democracy_ (New Haven: Yale University Press, 1999), 183.

3. In this regard, see, for example, Robert Keohane, _After Hegemony_ (Princeton: Princeton University Press, 1984); Robert Gilpin, _The Political Enemy of International Relations_ (Princeton: Princeton University Press, 1987); Robert Cox, _Production, Power and World Order_ (New York: Columbia University Press, 1987); Ernst Haas, _When Knowledge Is Power_ (California: University of California Press, 1990); John Gerard Ruggie, _Constructing the World Polity_ (London: Routledge, 1998); Craig N. Murphy, _International Organization and Industrial Change_ (New York: Oxford University Press, 1994); and Vinod Aggarwal, _Institutional Designs for a Complex World_ (Ithaca, N.Y.: Cornell University Press, 1998).

4. On the durability of the nation-state and political identities rooted therein, see, for example, David Laitin, _Identity in Formation_ (Ithaca, N.Y.: Cornell University Press, 1998); Suzanne Berger and Ronald Dore, eds., _National Diversity and Global Capitalism_ (Ithaca, N.Y.: Cornell University Press, 1996); Paul N. Doremus

et al., *The Myth of the Global Corporation* (Princeton, N.J.: Princeton University Press, 1998); Linda Weiss, *The Myth of the Powerless State* (Ithaca, N.Y.: Cornell University Press, 1998); Geoffrey Garrett, *Partisan Politics in the Global Economy* (Cambridge: Cambridge University Press, 1998); and Stephen D. Krasner, *Sovereignty* (Princeton: Princeton University Press, 1999).

Bibliography

Abromeit, Heidrun. "Überlegungen zur Demokratisierung der Europäischen Union." In *Projekt Europa im Übergang? Probleme, Modelle und Strategien des Regierens in der Europäischen Union*, edited by Klaus-Dieter Wolf. Baden-Baden: Nomos, 1997.

Adler, Emanuel, and Peter M. Haas. "Conclusion: Epistemic Communities, World Order and the Creation of a Reflective Research Program." *International Organization* 46, no. 1 (1992).

Aggarwal, Vinod. *Institutional Designs for a Complex World*. Ithaca, N.Y.: Cornell University Press, 1998.

Andersen, Sven S., and Kjell A. Eliassen, eds. *The European Union: How Democratic Is It?* London: Sage, 1996.

Anderson, Benedict. *Imagined Communities: Reflections on the Origin and Spread of Nationalism*, 2d ed. London: Verso, 1991.

Arendt, Hannah. *The Human Condition*. Chicago: University of Chicago Press, 1958.

———. *On Revolution*. New York: Viking, 1963.

———. *The Origins of Totalitarianism*. New York: Harcourt, 1951.

Bachrach, Peter, and Morton S. Baratz. *Macht und Armut: Eine theoretisch-empirische Untersuchung*. Frankfurt am Main: Suhrkamp, 1977.

Barber, Benjamin. *Jihad vs. McWorld: How Capitalism and Tribalism Are Reshaping the World*. New York: Ballantine, 1996.

———. *Strong Democracy: Participatory Democracy for a New Age*. Berkeley: University of California Press, 1984.

Baun, J. Michael. *An Imperfect Union*. Boulder, Colo: Westview, 1996.

Baylis, John, and Steve Smith, eds. *The Globalization of World Politics*. Oxford: Oxford University Press, 1997.

Beck, Ulrich. "Kinder der Freiheit: Wider das Lamento über den Werteverfall." In *Kinder der Freiheit*, edited by Ulrich Beck. Frankfurt am Main: Suhrkamp, 1997.

Beisheim, Marianne, Sabine Dreher, Gregor Walter, Bernhard Zangl, and Michael Zürn. *Im Zeitalter der Globalisierung? Thesen und Daten zur gesellschaftlichen und politischen Denationalisierung*. Baden-Baden: Nomos, 1998.

Bell, Daniel A., et al. *Towards Illiberal Democracy in Pacific Asia*. Oxford: St. Martin's, 1995.

Bendix, Reinhard. *Kings or People*. Berkeley: University of California Press, 1978.

Benhabib, Seyla, ed. *Democracy and Difference: Contesting the Boundaries of the Political*. Princeton: Princeton University Press, 1996.

Benz, Arthur. "Postparlamentarische Demokratie? Demokratische Legitimation im kooperativen Staat." Unpublished paper. Universität Halle, 1997.

Bercusson, Brian, and Dt. von Ulrike Bischoff. *Soziales Europe—ein Manifest*. Hamburg: Rowohlt, 1996.

Berger, Suzanne, and Ronald Dore, eds. *National Diversity and Global Capitalism*. Ithaca, N.Y.: Cornell University Press, 1996.

Beyme, Klaus von. "Niedergang der Parlamente: Internationale Politik und nationale Entscheidungshoheit." *Internationale Politik* 53, no. 4 (1998).

Blank, Stephen, and Stephen Krajewski. "US Firms in North America: Redefining Structure and Strategy." *North American Outlook* 5, no. 2 (February 1995).

Bovens, Mark A. P. "The Social Steering of Complex Organizations." *British Journal of Political Research* 20, no. 1 (1990).

Breuilly, John. *Nationalism and the State*, 2d ed. Chicago: University of Chicago Press, 1994.

Bull, Hedley. *The Anarchical Society*. London: Macmillan, 1977.

Buruma, Ian. "Fear and Loathing in Europe." *New York Review of Books*, October 17, 1996, 57.

Butler, David, and Austin Ranney, eds. *Referendums: A Comparative Study of Theory and Practice*. Washington, D.C.: American Enterprise Institute, 1978.

————. *Referendums around the World: The Growing Use of Direct Democracy*. Basingstoke, U.K.: Macmillan, 1994.

CEC (Commission for Environmental Cooperation). *NAFTA's Institutions: The Environmental Potential and Performance of the NAFTA Free Trade Commission and Related Bodies*. Montreal: CEC, 1997.

Cerny, Philip G. "Globalization and the Changing Logic of Collective Action." *International Organization* 49, no. 4 (1995).

Chapman, J. W. Murray, and I. Shapiro, eds. *NOMOS XXXV: Democratic Community*. New York: New York University Press, 1993.

Chayes, Abram, and Antonia Handler Chayes. *The New Sovereignty: Compliance with International Regulatory Agreements*. Cambridge: Harvard University Press, 1995.

Chryssochoou, N. Dimitris. "Democracy and Symbiosis in the European Union: Towards a Confederal Consociation." *West European Politics* 17, no. 4 (1994).

Clark, Caryl L. "Forging Identity: Beethoven's 'Ode' as European Anthem." *Critical Inquiry* 23 (Summer 1997).

Cohen, Joshua. "Deliberation and Democratic Legitimacy." In *The Good Polity: Normative Analysis of the State*, edited by Alan Hamlin and Philip Petitt. Oxford: Oxford University Press, 1989.

Cohen, Joshua, and Joel Rogers. "Secondary Associations and Democratic Governance." *Politics & Society* 20 (December 1992).

————. "Solidarity, Democracy, Association." In *Staat und Verbände (PVS-Sonderheft 25)*, edited by Wolfgang Streeck. Opladen, Germ.: Westdeutscher Verlag, 1994.

Cohen, Joshua, and Charles Sabel. "Directly-Deliberative Polyarchy." Unpublished paper. Cambridge, Mass., 1997.

Collier, David, and Steven Levitsky. "Democracy with Adjectives: Conceptual Innovation in Comparative Research." *World Politics* 49, no. 3 (1997).

Cox, Robert. *Production, Power and World Order*. New York: Columbia University Press, 1987.

Crowley, John. "European Integration: Sociological Process or Political Project?" *Innovation* 9, no. 2 (1997).

Dahl, Robert A. *Democracy and Its Critics*. New Haven, Conn.: Yale University Press, 1989.

———. "A Democratic Dilemma: System Effectiveness versus Citizen Participation." *Political Science Quarterly* 109, no. 1 (1994).

———. *On Democracy*. New Haven: Yale University Press, 1999.

———. "Why Free Markets Are Not Enough." *Journal of Democracy* 3, no. 3 (July 1992).

Dahrendorf, Ralf. "Die Quadratur des Kreises—Freiheit, Solidarität und Wohlstand." *Transit* 12 (1996).

Dehousse, Renaud. "Constitutional Reform in the European Community." In *Projekt Europa im Übergang?*, edited by Klaus Dieter Wolf. Baden-Baden: Nomos, 1997.

———. "Constitutional Reform in the European Community: Are There Alternatives to the Majority Avenue?" *West European Politics* 18, no. 3 (1995).

Delanty, Gerard. "Theories of Social Integration and the European Union: Rethinking Culture." Unpublished paper. University of Liverpool, 1996.

Deutsch, Karl W. *Nationalism and Its Alternatives*. New York: Knopf, 1969.

Donnelly, Jack. *International Human Rights*. Boulder, Colo.: Westview, 1996.

Doran, Charles. "Trade Dispute Resolution on Trial: Softwood Lumber," *International Journal* 51, no. 4 (Autumn 1996): 710–733.

Doremus, Paul N., William W. Keller, Louis W. Pauly and Simon Reich. *The Myth of the Global Corporation*. Princeton: Princeton University Press, 1998.

Downs, Anthony. *Inside Bureaucracy*. Boston: Little, Brown, 1967.

Drache, Daniel. "Dreaming Trade or Trading Dreams: The Limits of Trade Blocs." in *International Regulatory Competition and Coordination: Perspectives on Economic Regulation in Europe and the United States*, edited by William W. Bratton, Joseph McCahery, Sol Picciotto, and Colin Scott. Oxford: Clarendon Press, 1996.

Eichener, Volker. "Die Rückwirkungen der europäischen Integration auf nationale Politikmuster." In *Europäische Integration*, edited by Markus Jachtenfuchs and Beate Kohler-Koch. Opladen, Germ.: Leske and Budrich, 1996, 249–280.

Elster, Jon, and Rune Slagstad, eds. *Constitutionalism and Democracy*. Cambridge: Cambridge University Press, 1988.

Eschenburg, Theodor. *Herrschaft der Verbände?* Stuttgart: DVA, 1963.

Evans, Peter B., Harold K. Jacobsen, and Robert D. Putnam, eds. *Double-Edged Diplomacy: International Bargaining and Domestic Politics*. Berkeley: University of California Press, 1993.

Evans, Tony. "Democratization and Human Rights." In *The Transformation of Democracy*, edited by Anthony McGrew. Cambridge, U.K.: Polity Press, 1997.

Falk, Richard. "The Making of a Global Citizenship." In *Global Visions: Beyond the New World Order*, edited by Jeremy Brecher, John Brown Childs and Jill Cutler. Boston: South End Press, 1993.

Fishkin, James S. *The Voice of the People: Public Opinion and Democracy*. New Haven: Yale University Press, 1997.

Franklin, Mark N., Cees van der Eijk, and Michael Marsh. "Referendum Outcomes and Trust in Government: Public Support for Europe in the Wake of Maastricht." *West European Politics* 18, no. 3 (1995).

Frey, Bruno S. "Direct Democracy: Politico-Economic Lessons from Swiss Experience." *American Economic Review* 84, no. 2 (1994).

Friedman, David. *The Machinery of Freedom*. New York: Harper & Row, 1973.

Gallagher, Michael, and Vincenzo Uleri, eds. *The Referendum Experience in Europe*. Basingstoke: Macmillan, 1996.

Garcia, Soledad, ed. *European Identity and the Search for Legitimacy*. London: Pinter, 1993.

Garrett, Geoffrey. *Partisan Politics in the Global Economy*. Cambridge: Cambridge University Press, 1998.

Gehring, Thomas. "Regieren im internationalen System: Verhandlungen, Normen und internationale Regime." *Politische Vierteljahresschrift* 36, no. 2 (1995).

Gellner, Ernest. *Nations and Nationalism*. Ithaca, N.Y.: Cornell University Press, 1983.

Gerstenberg, Oliver. *Bürgerrechte und deliberative Demokratie: Elemente einer pluralistischen Verfassungstheorie*. Frankfurt am Main: Suhrkamp, 1997.

———. "Law's Polyarchy: A Comment on Cohen and Sabel," *European Law Journal* 3, no. 4 (1997).

Giddens, Anthony. *Beyond Left and Right: The Future of Radical Politics*. Cambridge, U.K.: Polity Press, 1994.

———. *The Consequences of Modernity*. Stanford, Calif.: Stanford University Press, 1990.

Gilpin, Robert. *The Political Economy of International Relations*. Princeton: Princeton University Press, 1987.

Gomà, Richard. "The Social Dimension of the European Union: A New Type of Welfare System?" *Journal of European Public Policy* 3, no. 2 (1996).

Grande, Edgar. "Demokratische Legitimation und Europäische Integration," *Leviathan* 24, no. 3 (1996).

———. "Konfliktsteuerung zwischen Recht und Konsens." In *Sozialpartnerschaft in der Krise: Leistungen und Grenzen des Neokorporatismus in Österreich*, edited by Peter Gerlich, Edgar Grande, and Wolfgang C. Müller. Wien: Böhlau, 1985.

———. "Post-nationale Demokratie—Ein Ausweg aus der Globalisierungsfalle." In *Globalisierung und institutionelle Reform: Jahrbuch für Technik und Wirtschaft*, edited by Werner Fricke. Bonn: Dietz, 1997.

———. "The State and Interest Groups in a Framework of Multi-Level Decision-Making: The Case of the European Union." *Journal of European Public Policy* 3, no. 3 (1996).

Greider, William. *One World, Ready or Not: The Manic Logic of Global Capitalism*. New York: Simon and Schuster, 1997.

Greven, Michael Th. "Der politische Raum als Maß des Politischen: Europa als Beispiel." In *Europäische Institutionenpolitik*, edited by Thomas König, Elmar Rieger, and Hermann Schmitt. Frankfurt am Main: Campus, 1997.

————. "Political Institutions and the Building of Democracy." *European Journal of Political Research* 27, no. 4 (1995).

————. "Political Parties Between National Identity and Eurofication." In *The Idea of Europe: Problems of National and Transnational Identity,* edited by Brian Nelson, David Roberts, and Walter Veit. New York and Oxford: Berg, 1992.

————. *Systemtheorie und Gesellschaftsanalyse: Kritik der Werte und Erkenntnismöglichkeiten in Gesellschaftsmodellen der kybernetischen Systemtheorie.* Darmstadt and Neuwied, Germ.: Luchterhand, 1974.

————, ed. *Demokratie—eine Kultur des Westens.* Opladen, Germ.: Leske & Budrich, 1998.

Grieco, Joseph M. *Cooperation among Nations: Europe, America, and Non-Tariff Barriers to Trade.* Ithaca, N.Y.: Cornell University Press, 1990.

Grimm, Dieter. *Braucht Europa eine Verfassung?* München: Carl Friedrich von Siemens-Stiftung, 1995.

————. "Mit einer Aufwertung des Europa-Parlaments ist es nicht getan: Das Demokratiedefizit der EG hat strukturelle Ursachen." In *Jahrbuch zur Staats- und Verwaltungswissenschaft,* vol. 4, edited by Thomas Ellwein et al. Baden-Baden: Nomos, 1993.

Grote, Rainer. "Direkte Demokratie in den Staaten der Europäischen Union." *Staatswissenschaften und Staatspraxis* 7, no. 3 (1996).

Gutiérrez-Haces, Teresa. "Globalization from Below: The Awakening and Networking of Civil Societies in North America." Paper presented to the Association of Canadian Studies in the United States conference, Toronto, November 1996.

Gutiérrez-Haces, Teresa, and Nicolas Hiernaux. "Economic Changes and the Need for a New Federalism: Lessons from Northern States." *American Review of Canadian Studies* 26, no. 2 (Summer 1996).

Haas, Ernst. *The Uniting of Europe.* Stanford, Calif.: Stanford University Press, 1958.

————. *When Knowledge Is Power.* California: University of California Press, 1990.

Habermas, Jürgen. *Die Einbeziehung des Anderen: Studien zur politischen Theorie.* Frankfurt am Main: Suhrkamp, 1996.

————. *Faktizität und Geltung.* Frankfurt am Main: Suhrkamp, 1992.

————. *Legitimationsprobleme im Spätkapitalismus.* Frankfurt am Main: Suhrkamp, 1973.

Hamlin, Alan, and Philip Petitt, eds. *The Good Polity: Normative Analysis of the State.* Oxford: Oxford University Press, 1989.

Hänsch, Klaus. "Europäische Integration und parlamentarische Demokratie." *Europa-Archiv* 41, no. 7 (1986).

Hansen, Mogens H. *The Athenian Democracy in the Age of Demosthenes: Structure, Principles and Ideology.* Oxford and Cambridge: Basil Blackwell, 1991.

Hayek, Friedrich. *The Road to Serfdom.* Chicago: University of Chicago Press, 1944.

Haynes, Jeff. *Democracy and Civil Society in the Third World: Politics and New Political Movements.* Cambridge, U.K.: Polity Press, 1997.

Heberle, Rudolf. *Social Movements: An Introduction to Political Sociology.* New York: Appleton-Century-Crofts, 1951.

Hedetoft, Ulf. "National Identities and European Integration 'From Below': Bringing the People Back In." *Journal of European Integration* 28, no. 1 (1993).

Heinelt, Hubert. "Zivilgesellschaftliche Perspektiven einer demokratischen Transformation der Europäischen Union." *Zeitschrift für Internationale Beziehungen* 5, no. 1 (1998).

Heinz, John P., Edward O. Laumann, Robert L. Nelson, and Robert H. Salisbury. *The Hollow Core: Private Interests in National Policy Making.* Cambridge: Cambridge University Press, 1993.

Held, David. *Democracy and the Global Order: From the Modern State to Cosmopolitan Governance.* Stanford, Calif.: Stanford University Press, 1995.

———. "Democracy: From City-States to a Cosmopolitan Order?" In *Prospects for Democracy*, edited by David Held. Cambridge, U.K.: Polity Press, 1992.

———. "Democracy, the Nation State and the Global System." In *Political Theory Today*, edited by David Held. Stanford, Calif.: Stanford University Press, 1991.

Henkin, Louis. *How Nations Behave: Law and Foreign Policy.* 2d ed. New York: Columbia University Press, 1979.

Hix, Simon, and Chris Lord. "Partisanship and Party Formation in European Union Politics." *Comparative Politics* 24 (1997).

Hobbes, Thomas. *Leviathan.* Oxford: Basil Blackwell, 1960.

Hoffmann, Lutz. "Das 'Volk': Zur ideologischen Struktur eines unvermeidbaren Begriffs." *Zeitschrift für Soziologie* 20, no. 3 (1991).

Holmes, Stephen. *Passions and Constraint: On the Theory of Liberal Democracy.* Chicago: University of Chicago Press, 1995.

Hooghe, Liesbet. "Cohesion Policy and European Integration." In *Europäische Integration*, edited by Markus Jachtenfuchs and Beate Kohler-Koch. Opladen, Germ.: Leske & Budrich, 1996.

———, ed. *Cohesion Policy and European Integration: Building Multi-Level Governance.* Oxford: Oxford University Press, 1996.

Hornstein, Walter, and Gerd Mutz. *Die europäische Einigung als gesellschaftlicher Prozeß.* Baden-Baden: Nomos, 1993.

Howse, Robert. "Settling Trade Remedy Disputes: When the WTO Forum Is Better Than NAFTA." *C. D. Howe Institute Commentary* 111 (June 1998).

Huntington, Samuel P. *The Clash of Civilizations and the Remaking of World Order.* New York: Simon & Schuster, 1997.

———. *The Third Wave: Democratization in the Late Twentieth Century.* Norman: University of Oklahoma Press, 1991.

Ignatieff, Michael. *Blood and Belonging: Journeys into the New Nationalism.* Toronto and London: Penguin, 1994.

Immerfall, Stefan, and Andreas Sobisch. "Europäische Integration und europäische Identität: Die Europaische Union im Bewußtsein ihrer Bürger." *Politik und Zeitgeschichte* 10 (1997).

Jachtenfuchs, Markus. "Die Europäische Union—ein Gebilde sui generis?" In *Projekt Europa im Übergang*, edited by Klaus Dieter Wolf. Baden-Baden: Nomos, 1997.

Jachtenfuchs, Markus, and Beate Kohler-Koch. "Regieren im dynamischen Mehrebenensystem." In *Europäische Integration*, edited by Markus Jachtenfuchs and Beate Kohler-Koch. Opladen, Germ.: Leske & Budrich, 1996.

Joerges, Christian, and Jürgen Neyer. "Transforming Strategic Interaction into Deliberative Problem-Solving: European Comitology in the Foodstuff Sector." *Journal of European Public Policy* 4, no. 4 (1997).

Judt, Tony. *Große Illusion Europa: Herausforderungen und Gefahren einer Idee*. München: Hanser, 1996.

Kaplan, Robert D. "Was Democracy Just a Moment?" *The Atlantic Monthly* 280, no. 6 (December 1997).

Katzenstein, Peter, and Takeshi Shiraishi, eds. *Network Power*. Ithaca, N.Y.: Cornell University Press, 1997.

Kennon, Patrick E. *The Twilight of Democracy*. New York: Doubleday, 1995.

Kent, Christopher. "The Uruguay Round GATT TRIPS Agreement & Chapter 17 of the NAFTA: A New Era in International Patent Protection." *Canadian Intellectual Property Review* (1994).

Keohane, Robert. *After Hegemony*. Princeton: Princeton University Press, 1984.

Keohane, Robert, and Helen Milner, eds. *Internationalization and Domestic Politics*. New York: Cambridge University Press, 1996.

Kielmansegg, Graf Peter. "Integration und Demokratie." In *Europäische Integration*, edited by Markus Jachtenfuchs and Beate Kohler-Koch. Opladen, Germ.: Leske & Budrich, 1996.

———. "Läßt sich die Europäische Gemeinschaft demokratisch verfassen?" *Europäische Rundschau* 22, no. 2 (1994).

Kohler-Koch, Beate. "Changing Patterns of Interest Intermediation in the European Union." *Government and Opposition* 29, no. 2 (1994).

König, Thomas, and Heiner Schulz. "The Efficiency of European Union Decision Making." Paper presented at the German American Academic Council Young Scholars Workshop, August 5–16, 1996, University of Bremen.

Korten, David. *When Corporations Rule the World*. West Hartford, Conn.: Kumarian Press, 1995.

Krasner, Stephen D. *Sovereignty: Organized Hypocrisy*. Princeton: Princeton University Press, 1999.

Laffan, Brigid. "Legitimacy." In *Encyclopedia of the EU*. Boulder, Colo.: Lynne Rienner, 1997.

Laitin, David. *Identity in Formation*. Ithaca, N.Y.: Cornell University Press, 1998.

Lehmbruch, Gerhard. "Konkordanzdemokratie." In *Lexikon der Politik*, Vol. 3, *Die westlichen Länder*, edited by Manfred G. Schmidt. München: C. H. Beck, 1992.

———. *Proporzdemokratie*. Tübingen: J.C.B. Mohr, 1967.

Leibfried, Stephan, and Paul Pierson, eds. *European Social Policy: Between Fragmentation and Integration*. Washington, D.C.: Brookings, 1995.

Leyton-Brown, David, and Mark Gold, eds. *Trade-Offs on Free Trade: The Canada-U.S. Free Trade Agreement*. Toronto: Carswell, 1988.

Lijphart, Arend. "Democracies: Forms, Performance, and Constitutional Engineering." *European Journal of Political Research* 25, no. 1 (1994).

———. *Democracies: Patterns of Majoritarian and Consensus Government in Twenty-One Countries*. New Haven, Conn.: Yale University Press, 1984.

———. "Majority Rule in Theory and Practice: The Tenacity of a Flawed Paradigm." *International Social Science Journal*, no. 129 (1991).

————. *The Politics of Accommodation: Pluralism and Democracy in the Netherlands.* Berkeley: University of California Press, 1968.

Lindblom, Charles. *Politics and Markets.* New York: Basic Books, 1977.

Linder, Wolf. *Swiss Democracy: Possible Solutions to Conflict in Multicultural Societies.* New York: St. Martin's, 1994.

Lipset, Martin Seymour. "Some Social Requisites of Democracy." *American Political Science Review* 53, no. 1 (1959).

Lodge, Juliet. "Transparency and Democratic Legitimacy." *Journal of Common Market Studies* 32, no. 3 (1994).

Lowi, Theodore J. *The End of Liberalism,* 2d ed. New York: W. W. Norton, 1979.

————. "Think Globally, Lose Locally." *Boston Review* (April/May 1998): 4-10.

Luthardt, Wolfgang. *Direkte Demokratie: Ein Vergleich in Westeuropa.* Baden-Baden: Nomos, 1994.

————. "European Integration and Referendums: Analytical Considerations and Empirical Evidence." In *The State of the European Community,* Vol. 2, *The Maastricht Debates and Beyond,* edited by Alan W. Cafruny and Glenda G. Rosenthal. Boulder, Colo.: Lynne Rienner, 1993.

Macpherson, C. B. *The Life and Times of Liberal Democracy.* Oxford: Oxford University Press, 1977.

Madison, James. "Federalist No. 51, 6 February 1788." In *Die Amerikanische Revolution und die Verfassung 1754–1791,* edited by Angela Adams and Willi Paul Adams. München: Deutscher Taschenbuch Verlag, 1987.

Magder, Ted. "Franchising the Candy Store: Split-Run Magazines and a New International Regime for Trade in Culture." *Canadian-American Public Policy* 34 (April 1998).

Mainwaring, Scott. "Transition to Democracy and Democratic Consolidation: Theoretical and Comparative Issues." In *Issues in Democratic Consolidation,* edited by Scott Mainwaring, Guillermo O'Donnell, and J. Samuel Valenzuela. Notre Dame, Ind.: Notre Dame University Press, 1992.

Majone, Giandomenico. "Europe's 'Democratic Deficit': The Question of Standards." Unpublished paper, 1998.

————, ed. *Regulating Europe.* London: Routledge, 1996.

Mansfield, Edward, and Helen Milner, eds. *Political Economy of Regionalism.* New York: Columbia University Press, 1997.

Markovits, Andre, and Simon Reich. *The German Predicament.* Ithaca, N.Y.: Cornell University Press, 1997.

Marks, Gary, Liesbet Hooghe, and Kermit Blank. "European Integration Since the 1980s: State-Centric Versus Multi-Level Governance." *Journal of Common Market Studies* 34, no. 3. (September 1996).

Marks, Gary, Fritz Scharpf, Philippe Schmitter, and Wolfgang Streeck, eds. *Governance in the European Union.* London: Sage, 1996.

Marshall, Thomas H. *Class, Citizenship and Social Development.* Garden City, N.Y.: Doubleday, 1964.

Mattli, Walter. *The Logic of Regional Integration.* Cambridge: Cambridge University Press, 1999.

Mazey, Sonia, and Jeremy Richardson, eds. *Lobbying in the European Community.* Oxford: Oxford University Press, 1993.

Meier, Christian. *Die Entstehung des Politischen bei den Griechen.* Frankfurt am Main: Suhrkamp, 1983.

Mestmäcker, Ernst-Joachim. "Zur Wirtschaftsverfassung in der Europäischen Union." In *Ordnung in Freiheit: Festgabe für Hans Willgerodt zum 70. Geburtstag,* edited by Rolf H. Hasse, Josef Molsberger, and Christian Watrin. Stuttgart: Gustav Fischer, 1994.

Michels, Roberto. *Political Parties: A Sociological Study of the Oligarchical Tendencies of Modern Democracy.* New York: Dover, 1959.

Middlemas, Keith. *Orchestrating Europe: The Informal Politics of European Union 1973–1995.* London: Fontana, 1995.

Mittelman, James H., ed. *Globalization: Critical Reflections.* Boulder, Colo.: Lynne Rienner, 1997.

Möckli, Silvano. *Direkte Demokratie: Ein internationaler Vergleich.* Bern: Verlag Paul Haupt, 1994.

Moravcsik, Andrew. *The Choice for Europe.* Ithaca, N.Y.: Cornell University Press, 1998.

———. "Why the European Community Strengthens the State: Domestic Politics and International Cooperation." Center for European Studies, Harvard University. Working Paper Series 52 (1994).

Müller, Harald. "Internationale Beziehungen als kommunikatives Handeln: Zur Kritik der utilitaristischen Handlungstheorien." *Zeitschrift für Internationale Beziehungen* 1, no. 1 (1994).

Münkler, Herfried. "Der kompetente Bürger." In *Politische Beteiligung und Bürgerengagement in Deutschland,* edited by Ansgar Klein and Rainer Schmalz-Bruns. Baden-Baden: Nomos, 1997.

———. "Europa als politische Idee: Ideengeschichtliche Facetten des Europabegriffs und deren aktuelle Bedeutung." *Leviathan* 19, no. 4 (1991).

Murphy, Craig N. *International Organization and Industrial Change.* New York: Oxford University Press, 1994.

Niedermayer, Oskar. "Die Europäisierung der Parteienlandschaft." In *Legitimationsprobleme und Demokratisierung der Europäischen Union,* edited by Andreas Maurer and Burkard Thiele. Marburg, Germ.: Schüren, 1996.

Nugent, Neil. *The Government and Politics of the European Union.* London: Macmillan, 1994.

O'Donnell, Guillermo. "Delegative Democracy." *Journal of Democracy* 5, no. 1 (1994).

Offe, Claus. "Bewährungsproben—Über einige Beweislasten bei der Verteidigung der liberalen Demokratie." In *Die Demokratie am Wendepunkt: Die demokratische Frage als Projekt des 21. Jahrhunderts,* edited by Werner Weidenfeld. Berlin: Sicoller, 1996.

———. "Demokratie und Wohlfahrtsstaat: Eine europäische Regime form unter dem Streß der europäischen Integration," in *Internationale Wirtschaft, nationale Demokratie, Herausforderung für die Demokratie theorie,* edited by Wolfgang Streeck. Frankfurt am Main: Campus Verlag, 1998.

———. "Korporatismus als System nichtstaatlicher Makrosteuerung? Notizen über seine Voraussetzungen und demokratischen Gehalte." *Geschichte und Gesellschaft* 10, no. 2 (1984).

————. *Modernity and the State: East. West.* Cambridge, U.K.: Polity, 1996.

————. "Politische Legitimation durch Mehrheitsentscheidung?" *Journal für Sozialforschung* 22, no. 3 (1982).

————. *Strukturprobleme des kapitalistischen Staates.* Frankfurt am Main: Suhrkump, 1972.

Ostry, Sylvia. *The Post-Cold War Trading System: Who's on First?* Chicago: University of Chicago Press, 1997.

Pauly, Louis. "Capital Mobility, State Autonomy and Political Legitimacy." *Journal of International Affairs* 48, no. 2 (1995).

————. *Who Elected the Bankers?* Ithaca, N.Y.: Cornell University Press, 1997.

Pitkin, Hanna F. *The Concept of Representation.* Berkeley: University of California Press, 1967.

Polanyi, Karl. *The Great Transformation.* New York: Farrar and Rinehart, 1944.

Rachlis, Chuck, and David Wolfe. "An Insider's View of the NDP Government of Ontario: The Politics of Permanent Opposition Meets the Economics." In *The Government and Politics of Ontario*, edited by Graham White. Toronto: University of Toronto Press, 1997.

Richter, Melvin. "Europe and 'The Other' in Eighteenth-Century Thought." In *Politisches Denken: Jahrbuch 1997*, edited by Karl Graf Ballestrem et al. Stuttgart and Weimar, Germ.: J. B. Metzler, 1997.

Riker, William H. "The Senate and American Federalism." *American Political Science Review* 49, no. 2 (1955).

Rittberger, Volker, and Peter Mayer, eds. *Regime Theory and International Relations.* Oxford: Oxford University Press, 1993.

Rose, Richard. *What Is Europe? A Dynamic Perspective.* New York: HarperCollins, 1996.

Rosenau, James N. *Along the Domestic-Foreign Frontier: Exploring Governance in a Turbulent World.* Cambridge: Cambridge University Press, 1997.

Roth, Roland. "Die Kommune als Ort der Bürgerbeteiligung." In *Politische Beteiligung und Bürgerengagement in Deutschland*, edited by Ansgar Klein and Rainer Schmalz-Bruns. Baden-Baden: Nomos, 1997.

Rothbard, Murray. *For a New Liberty: The Libertarian Manifesto.* New York: Collier, 1978.

————. *Man, Economy and State.* Los Angeles: Nash, 1962.

Rueschemeyer, Dietrich, Evelyne Huber Stephens and John D. Stephens. *Capitalist Development and Democracy.* Cambridge: Polity Press, 1992.

Ruggie, John Gerard. *Constructing the World Polity.* London: Routledge, 1998.

Ruppert, Evelyn. "Who Can Afford Democracy?" *The Annex Gleaner*, March 19, 1998.

Sandel, Michael. *Democracy's Discontents: America in Search of a Public Philosophy.* Cambridge: Harvard University Press, 1996.

Sartori, Giovanni. *Demokratietheorie.* Darmstadt: Wissenschaft Buchgesellschaft, 1992.

————. "Will Democracy Kill Democracy? Decision-Making by Majorities and by Communities." *Government and Opposition* 10, no. 2 (1975).

Sassoon, Donald. *Social Democracy at the Heart of Europe.* London: Institute for Public Policy Research, 1996.

Saul, Ralston John. *Voltaire's Bastards: The Dictatorship of Reason in the West*. New York: Free Press, 1992.

Scharpf, Fritz W. *Demokratietheorie zwischen Utopie und Anpassung*. Kronberg (Ts.), Germ.: Scriptor, 1975.

———. "Demokratische Politik in Europa." *Staatswissenschaften und Staatspraxis* 6, no. 4 (1995).

———. "Demokratische Politik in Europa." In *Zur Neuordnung der Europäischen Union: Die Regierungskonferenz 1996/1997*, edited by Dieter Grimm et al. Baden-Baden: Nomos, 1996/1997.

———. *Economic Integration, Democracy and the Welfare State*. Köln: Max Planck Institute, 1996.

———. "Economic Integration, Democracy and the Welfare State." *Journal of European Public Policy* 4, no. 1 (1997).

———. "Europäisches Demokratiedefizit und deutscher Föderalismus." *Staatswissenschaften und Staatspraxis* 3, no. 3 (1992).

———. *Games Real Actors Play: Actor-Centered Institutionalism in Policy Research*. Boulder, Colo.: Westview Press, 1997.

———. "The Joint Decision Trap: Lessons from German Federalism and European Integration." *Public Administration* 66 (Autumn 1988).

———. "Legitimationsprobleme der Globalisierung: Regieren in Verhandlungssystemen." In *Regieren im 21. Jahrhundert—Zwischen Globalisierung und Regionalisierung: Festgabe für Hans-Hermann Hartwich zum 65 Geburtstag*, edited by Carl Böhret and Göttrik Wewer. Opladen, Germ.: Leske & Budrich, 1993.

———. "Negative and Positive Integration in the Political Economy of European Welfare States." In *Governance in the European Union*, edited by Gary Marks, Fritz Scharpf, Philippe Schmitter, and Wolfgang Streeck. London: Sage, 1996.

Schmalz-Bruns, Rainer. "Bürgergesellschaftliche Politik—Ein Modell der Demokratisierung der Europäischen Union." In *Projekt Europa im Übergang? Probleme, Modelle und Strategien des Regierens in der Europäischen Union*, edited by Klaus Dieter Wolf. Baden-Baden: Nomos, 1997.

———. *Reflexive Demokratie: Die demokratische Transformation moderner Politik*. Baden-Baden: Nomos, 1995.

Schmidt, G. Manfred. "Das politische Leistungsprofil der Demokratie." In *Demokratie—Eine Kultur des Westens?*, edited by Michael Th. Greven. Opladen, Germ.: Leske & Budrich, 1998.

———. *Demokratietheorien: Eine Einführung*. Opladen, Germ.: Leske & Budrich, 1995.

Schmitt, Carl. *Politische Theologie: Vier Kapitel zur Lehre von der Souveränität*. Berlin: Duncker & Humboldt, 1934.

Schmitt, Hermann. "Was war 'europäisch' am Europawahlverhalten der Deutschen? Eine Analyse der Europawahl 1989 in der Bundesrepublik." In *Wahlen und europäische Einigung*, edited by Oskar Niedermayer and Hermann Schmitt. Opladen: Westdeutscher Verlag, 1994.

Schmitter, Philippe. "Examining the Present Euro-Polity with the Help of Past Theories." In *Governance in the European Union*, edited by Gary Marx, Fritz W. Scharpf, Philippe C. Schmitter, and Wolfgang Streeck. London: Sage, 1996.

Schultze, Rainer-Olaf. "Interessenrepräsentation und Westminster-Modell: Kanada—ein abweichender Fall?" *Staatswissenschaft und Staatspraxis* 7, no. 2 (1996).

Schumpeter, Joseph. *Capitalism, Socialism and Democracy*. New York: Harper, 1943.

Shin, Doh Chull. "On the Third Wave of Democratization. A Synthesis and Evaluation of Recent Theory and Research." *World Politics* 47, no. 1 (1994).

Skowroneck, Stephen. *Building a New American State: The Expansion of National Administrative Capacities, 1877–1920*. Cambridge: Cambridge University Press, 1982.

Smith, Graham. *Federalism: The Multiethnic Challenge*. London: Longman, 1995.

Solingen, Etel. *Regional Orders at Century's Dawn*. Princeton: Princeton University Press, 1998.

Steffani, Winfried. *Pluralistische Demokratie*. Opladen, Germ.: Leske & Budrich, 1980.

Stewart, Gordon. "A Special Contiguous Country Economic Regime: America's Canadian Policy." *Diplomatic History* 6, no. 4 (Fall 1982).

Strange, Susan. *The Retreat of the State: The Diffusion of Power in the World Economy*. Cambridge: Cambridge University Press, 1996.

Streeck, Wolfgang. "Neo-Voluntarism: A New European Social Policy Regime?" In *Governance in the European Union*, edited by Gary Marks, Fritz W. Scharpf, Philippe C. Schmitter, and Wolfgang Streeck. London: Sage, 1996.

Thompson, Dennis F. "Moral Responsibility of Public Officials: The Problem of Many Hands." *American Political Science Review* 74, no. 4 (1980).

Tsebelis, George. "The Power of the European Parliament as a Conditional Agenda Setter." *American Political Science Review* 88, no. 1 (1994).

Uleri, Pier Vincenzo. "Introduction." In *The Referendum Experience in Europe*, edited by Michael Gallagher and Pier Vincenzo Uleri. Basingstoke, U.K.: Macmillan, 1996.

Vogel, David. *Trading Up: Consumer and Environmental Regulation in the Global Economy*. Cambridge: Harvard University Press, 1995.

Wagschal, Uwe. "Direct Democracy and Public Policymaking." *Journal for Public Policy* 17, no. 3 (1997).

Wallace, Helen. "The Institutions of the EU: Experience and Experiments." In *Policy-Making in the European Union*, edited by Helen Wallace and William Wallace. Oxford: Oxford University Press, 1996.

Wallace, William. "Walking Backwards Towards Unity." In *Policy-Making in the European Communities*, edited by William Wallace, Helen Wallace and Christopher Webb. London: Wiley, 1983.

Wallerstein, Immanuel. *The Age of Transition: Trajectory of the World System, 1945–2025*. London: Zed, 1996.

Walter, Gregor, Sabine Dreher and Marianne Beishem. "Globalization Processes in the OECD-World." *Institute for Intercultural and International Studies (InIIS) Working Paper Series*, no. 4-5. Bremen, Germ.: University of Bremen, 1997.

Walzer, Michael. *Spheres of Justice: A Defense of Pluralism and Equality*. New York: Basic Books, 1983.

Weber, Max. *Wirtschaft und Gesellschaft: Grundriß der verstehenden Soziologie*, 4th ed. Tübingen, Germ.: Mohr, 1956.

Weidenfeld, Werner. "Die neue demokratische Frage." In *Die Demokratie am Wendepunkt: Die demokratische Frage als Projekt des 21. Jahrhunderts,* edited by Werner Weidenfeld. Berlin: Sicoller, 1996.

Weiler, J.H.H. "Does Europe Need a Constitution? Reflections on Demos, Telos and the German Maastricht Decision." *European Law Journal* 1, no. 3 (1995).

———. "Juridification of Dispute Settlement and the Institutional Culture of the World Trade Organization." Paper presented to the University of Toronto Faculty of Law, April 1, 1998.

Weiler, J.H.H., Ulrich R. Haltern, and Franz C. Mayer. "European Democracy and Its Critique." *West European Politics* 18, no. 3 (1995).

Weiss, Linda. *The Myth of the Powerless State.* Ithaca, N.Y.: Cornell University Press, 1998.

Williams, Colin H. "A Requiem for Canada?" In *Federalism: The Multiethnic Challenge,* edited by Graham Smith. London: Longman, 1995.

Wilson, James Q., and John J. DiIulio. *American Government: Institutions and Policies,* 6th ed. Lexington, Mass.: D. C. Heath, 1995.

Wriston, Walter. *The Twilight of Sovereignty: How the Information Revolution Is Changing Our World.* New York: Scribner's, 1992.

Wuthnow, Robert. "Handeln aus Mitleid." In *Kinder der Freiheit,* edited by Ulrich Beck. Frankfurt am Main: Suhrkamp, 1997.

Zürn, Michael. "Does International Governance Meet Demand? Theories of International Institutions in the Age of Denationalization." *Institute for Intercultural and International Studies (InIIS) Working Paper Series,* no. 4-5. Bremen, Germ.: University of Bremen, 1997.

———. *Interessen und Institutionen in der internationalen Politik: Grundlegung und Anwendungen des situationsstrukturellen Ansatzes.* Opladen, Germ.: Leske and Budrich, 1992.

———. "Über den Staat und die Demokratie im europäischen Mehrebenensystem." *Politische Vierteljahresschrift* 37, no. 1 (1996).

Index

sovereignty: concept of, 47; and nation, 71, 82; rationale for ceding, 86n15, 159; violations of, 161
Soviet Union, 20, 77, 142
Spain, 83
Sports Illustrated, 160
St. Lawrence Seaway, 140
state: definition of, 47; internal relationship with nation, 63–69. *See also* nation
Strange, Susan, 15
Strasbourg, 51
Streeck, Wolfgang, 77
subsidiarity, principle of, 22, 73
subsidy code, 148, 159. *See also* Canada-United States Free Trade Agreement; North American Free Trade Agreement; World Trade Organization
supranationalism, concept of, 70–71; preferences for, 89n42
Sweden, 48, 93
Switzerland, 47, 52, 120, 123, 131–132
system theory, 39

tariffication, 159
technology, effects of, 23, 33n28
telecracy, 102, 105
television, political role of, 22, 44
10 Downing Street, 20
"tequila effect," 151
Texas, 156
Thatcher, Margaret, 15, 20
Thompson, Dennis, 126
Tiananmen Square, 20
Tocqueville, Alexis de, 128, 145
Toronto, 145
trade agreements. *See* Canada-United States Free Trade Agreement; Mercosur; North American Free Trade Agreement
trade blocs, 139–161 *passim*
Trading with the Enemy Act (U.S.), 140
transnational business, 18, 31n12, 148
transparency, problem of, 104, 127
trust, sense of, 67.
Turkey, 40–41

United Nations, 27
United States, 11, 18, 21, 28; Congress, 22–23, 33n26; as compound Republic, 128; extraterritorial application of laws, 160–161; as hegemonic power in North America, 139–161 *passim*; and Mexican immigration, 156; as model for Europe, 38, 128; in nineteenth century, 21; role of customs officials, 151; states within, 131. *See also* Washington, D.C.
"United States of Europe," 28, 38
Uruguay Round. *See* General Agreement on Tariffs and Trade

Verbändestaat, 103
volonté de tous, 41
voluntarism, 70, 72
voluntary associations, 21
voting rights, 42

Wallerstein, Immanuel, 34n40
Warsaw Pact, 80
Washington, D.C., 147, 152; as virtual capital of North America, 156
Weber, Max, 40, 47, 56n4, 64
welfare state: and democracy, 99; and European single market, 74; moral basis of, 67–69; neo-liberal attacks on, 66
Wir-Gefühl (sense of togetherness), 8, 37, 43, 56n4, 64, 96. *See also* nation; *demos*
women, rights of, 42, 145, 168
World Trade Organization (WTO), 91, 157–160
World War I, 3
World War II, 4, 5, 117
Wriston, Walter, 30
WTO. *See* World Trade Organization
Wuthnow, Robert, 110

Yugoslavia, 80

zoon politikon, 40

About the Editors and Contributors

Stephen Clarkson is professor in the department of political science at the University of Toronto.

Edgar Grande is professor in the Institut für Sozialwissenschaft, Lehrstuhl für Politische Wissenschaft in Munich.

Michael Th. Greven is professor in the Institut für Politische Wissenschaft, Universität Hamburg; in 1997–98, he held the DAAD Distinguished Visiting Professorship in German and European Studies at the University of Toronto.

Stephen Newman is associate professor of political science and department chair, York University, Ontario.

Claus Offe is professor in the Institut für Sozialwissenschaften, Humboldt Universität, Berlin.

Louis W. Pauly is professor of political science and director of the Centre for International Studies, University of Toronto.

Michael Zürn is professor in the Institut für Interkulturelle and Internationale Studien, Universität Bremen.